# EU LIABILITY AND INTERNATIONAL ECONOMIC LAW

The book provides both a legal and economic assessment of an increasingly important issue for the EU: the question of whether individuals can hold the European Union liable for damages they suffer due to its infringement of international economic law. However, liability regimes vary depending on the issue concerned. In international trade law the individual holds a weak position, being deprived of both legal remedies to seek annulment and damages. This is due to the constant refusal of the direct effect of WTO law. By contrast, international investment law has been designed in an 'individualistic' manner from the outset—states agree reciprocally to grant certain procedural and substantial individual rights, which they invoke to claim damages before international tribunals rather than domestic courts. The divergent role of the individual in the respective area of international economic law leads to a different set of research questions related to liability. In international trade law, the doctrinal exercise of de-coupling the notion of direct effect from liability is at the core of establishing liability. In international investment law, liability is connected to a number of issues emerging from the recent transfer of competence pertaining to investment issues from Member States to the EU and the nature of investment agreements as mixed agreements. Against this backdrop, exploring liability issues in the area of international economic law reveals a heterogeneous set of questions depending on the area of law concerned, thus offering different perspectives for studying liability issues.

**Volume 74 in the Series Modern Studies in European Law**

**Modern Studies in European Law**
**Recent titles in this series:**

The Impact of Union Citizenship on the EU's Market Freedoms
*Alina Tryfonidou*

Equal Citizenship and Its Limits in EU Law
*Päivi Johanna Neuvonen*

European Law on Unfair Commercial Practices and Contract Law
*Mateja Durovic*

The European Union's External Action in Times of Crisis
*Edited by Piet Eeckhout and Manual Lopez-Escudero*

The Legitimacy of Family Rights in Strasbourg Case Law: Living Instrument or Extinguished Sovereignty?
*Carmen Draghici*

Strengthening the Rule of Law in Europe: From a Common Concept to Mechanisms of Implementation
*Edited by Werner Schroeder*

The Pluralist Character of the European Economic Constitution
*Clemens Kaupa*

Exceptions from EU Free Movement Law
*Edited by Panos Koutrakos, Niamh Nic Shuibhne and Phil Syrpis*

Reconceptualising European Equality Law: A Comparative Institutional Analysis
*Johanna Croon-Gestefeld*

Marketing and Advertising Law in a Process of Harmonization
*Edited by Ulf Bernitz and Caroline Heide-Jörgensen*

The Fundamental Right to Data Protection: Normative Value in the Context of Counter-Terrorism Surveillance
*Maria Tzanou*

Republican Europe
*Anna Kocharov*

Family Reunification in the EU
*Chiara Berneri*

EU Liability and International Economic Law
*Armin Steinbach*

**For the complete list of titles in this series, see**
**'Modern Studies in European Law' link at**
**www.bloomsburyprofessional.com/uk/series/modern-studies-in-european-law**

# EU Liability and International Economic Law

Armin Steinbach

·HART·
PUBLISHING
OXFORD AND PORTLAND, OREGON
2017

**Hart Publishing**
An imprint of Bloomsbury Publishing Plc

Hart Publishing Ltd
Kemp House
Chawley Park
Cumnor Hill
Oxford OX2 9PH
UK

Bloomsbury Publishing Plc
50 Bedford Square
London
WC1B 3DP
UK

**www.hartpub.co.uk**
**www.bloomsbury.com**

Published in North America (US and Canada) by
Hart Publishing
c/o International Specialized Book Services
920 NE 58th Avenue, Suite 300
Portland, OR 97213-3786
USA

**www.isbs.com**



First published 2017



**British Library Cataloguing-in-Publication Data**
A catalogue record for this book is available from the British Library.

ISBN: HB: 978-1-50990-159-3
ePDF: 978-1-50990-160-9
ePub: 978-1-50990-161-6

**Library of Congress Cataloging-in-Publication Data**

Names: Steinbach, Armin, author.

Title: EU liability and international economic law / Armin Steinbach.

Description: Oxford ; Portland, Oregon : Hart Publishing, an imprint of Bloomsbury Publishing Plc, 2017. | Series: Modern studies in European law ; volume 74 | Includes bibliographical references and index. | "The original research for the book was, to a large extent, conducted during my PhD studies at the University of Munich and has previously been published in German with Duncker & Humblot."—ECIP Preface.

Identifiers: LCCN 2017002143 (print) | LCCN 2017003152 (ebook) | ISBN 9781509901593 (hardback : alk. paper) | ISBN 9781509901616 (Epub)

Subjects: LCSH: European Union—Claims. | Government liability—European Union countries. | Foreign trade regulation. | Government liability (International law) | Tort liability of international agencies | World Trade Organization—Rules and practice.

Classification: LCC KJE5059 .S74 2017 (print) | LCC KJE5059 (ebook) | DDC 343.2407/23—dc23

LC record available at https://lccn.loc.gov/2017002143

Typeset by Compuscript Ltd, Shannon
Printed and bound in Great Britain by TJ International Ltd, Padstow, Cornwall

To find out more about our authors and books visit www.hartpublishing.co.uk. Here you will find extracts, author information, details of forthcoming events and the option to sign up for our newsletters.

# *Preface*

Can individuals hold the EU liable for damages they suffer due to the EU's violation of international economic law? In light of growing global trade and increasing cross-border transactions, the EU frequently sees itself as a respondent in WTO litigations or as a defendant under investor-state disputes. However, liability regimes and the corresponding opportunities of individuals to seek redress follow different logics, mainly due to a distinct position of the individual in the issue areas concerned. Traditionally, under international trade law, the individual holds a weak position in the EU—it cannot invoke WTO rules against EU institutions preventing it from successfully seeking annulment and damages. This is due to the established jurisprudential stance of the Court of Justice of the European Union to deny the direct effect of WTO law. By contrast, international investment law has been designed in favour of individuals by explicitly according enforceable rights to individuals under state-to-state international treaties, under which states allow individuals to invoke specific rights before international tribunals.

The heterogeneity of liability regimes under international economic law provokes different sets of research challenges. In international trade law, the doctrinal exercise of decoupling the notion of direct effect from liability is at the core of establishing liability. Is there legal ground to argue that liability of the EU for its infringements of WTO should be recognised? And, if so, are there sound economic grounds to plead for liability, and to what magnitude damages should be paid? While these questions shall be addressed in Part One and Part Two of this study, liability issues occurring in relation to investment law are different. In this area, the new system of competences set up under the Lisbon Treaty grants the EU extended competences related to investment issues. Unlike in the past, the EU will take over the Member States' role in concluding investment treaties. Given that future investment treaties (or free trade agreements incorporating investment rules) are likely to be classified as mixed agreements encompassing both EU and Member State competences, a number of questions pertaining to the relationship between the EU and its Member States are at the core of the analysis and have been (at least partially) addressed by recent EU legislation.

Against this backdrop, exploring liability issues in the area of international economic law reveals a heterogeneous set of questions depending on the area of law concerned, thus offering different perspectives for studying liability issues. The original research for the book was, to a large extent, conducted during my PhD studies at the University of Munich and has previously been published in German with Duncker & Humblot. However, certain legal issues have remained unresolved over time, new legal challenges have arisen and numerous discussions have encouraged me to bring these issues to the discourse of international legal scholarship. I am most grateful for the astute comments and criticisms of the anonymous reviewers at Hart Publishing and special thanks are reserved to those who showed dedicated interest in my work both in academia as well as in the civil service of the German government. Mostly, however, I wish to thank Pamela for her generosity in support and spirit.

# *Table of Contents*

# Introduction

THE COURT OF Justice of the European Union (CJEU) has interpreted the European Union (EU) as a legal community that ensures comprehensive legal protection. This has led to the overall perception of the EU as legal order that guarantees a satisfactorily high level of protection for individual interests. In the area of international economic law, this view, however, cannot be entirely upheld, as there is virtually no legal domain in which the level of legal protection varies so widely depending on the issue in question. This disuniformity in the level of protection in legal redress between international trade and international investment law can largely be explained by trends with a view to the standing of the individual in the broader system of international economic law over the past decades.[1]

In the area of international investment law, the individual has been recognised as a holder of enforceable individual rights ever since the 1960s, when bilateral investment treaties (BITs) emerged as legal instrument of economic policy. BITs were initially implemented in order to secure investment activities in developing countries carried out by companies originating from industrialised countries.[2] Subsequently, BITs also gained popularity in governing the relationship between industrialised countries. Over the last decades, industrialised countries have increasingly been the subject of individual claims brought under investor–state proceedings.[3] As a result, the overall position of the individual in international economic law was rapidly strengthened. This is a notable development, for in the aftermath of the Second World War, the protection of the individual under human rights treaties progressed at a much slower pace. Nevertheless, this recognition of the individual as a rights holder and enforcer in the area of international investment law is limited to claims for monetary compensation, and does not encompass the right to annul policies adopted by a state. Under EU law, the

[1] On the historical links between trade and investment law dating back to the attempt to establish an International Trade Organisation (ITO), see PJ Kuijper, 'Study on Investment Protection Agreements as Instruments of International Economic Law' in European Parliament (ed), *Investor–State Dispute Settlement (ISDS) Provisions in the EU's International Investment Agreements, vol* 2 (Brussels, European Parliament, 2014) 28f.

[2] On the historical development see G van Herten, *Investment Treaty Arbitration and Public Law* (Oxford, Oxford University Press 2007) 25–34; R Dolzer and M Stevens, *Bilateral Investment Treaties* (The Hague, Kluwer Law International, 1995) 126; KJ Vandevelde, *Bilateral Investment Treaties* (Oxford, Oxford University Press, 2010); JW Salacuse, *The Law of Investment Treaties*, 2nd edn (Oxford, Oxford University Press, 2015) especially 100ff; SP Subedi, *International Investment Law* (Oxford, Hart Publishing, 2008) 7ff.

[3] M Sattorova, 'Return to the Local Remedies Rule in European BITs? Power (Inequalities), Dispute Settlement, and Change in Investment Treaty Law' (2012) 39 *LIEI* 223, 230.

governance of international investment treaties has rather recently undergone a significant change. Prior to the adoption of the Lisbon Treaty, EU Member States were empowered to conclude BITs. This competence has now been passed on to the EU. The EU Commission has announced it will pursue a comprehensive common international investment policy.[4] More recently, the EU enacted Regulation No 912/2014, which lays down a framework for managing investor–state disputes between the EU and third countries.[5] Investment agreements at the EU level are still in their nascency. As mixed agreements that provide for a sharing of competences between the EU and Member States, they raise a number of unanswered liability issues.

By contrast, with regard to the role of the individual, international trade law diverges considerably from international investment law.[6] There are clear deficiencies in the ability of the international trade law regime to provide individual legal protection. These deficiencies are visible not only in the limited role of the individual in proceedings before the WTO adjudicative bodies, but also in the CJEU's refusal to grant individuals the right to annul EU measures which are found by the WTO Disputes Settlement Body (DSB) to be incompatible with WTO rules. Furthermore, the right to seek compensation for damages suffered by individuals due to violations of WTO rules has consistently been denied. From a doctrinal perspective, it is the lack of direct effect granted to WTO rules in the EU legal order which has led the CJEU to extend its well-established jurisprudence in relation to primary legal redress to the sphere of secondary legal redress, notably to the right to claim damages. According to the CJEU, there are no legal grounds for individual companies to file claims for losses they suffered due to protectionist EU trade regimes or due to retaliatory measures adopted by the US as a consequence of WTO-incompatible EU measures. As regards the impossibility of individuals to seek the annulment of policies enacted by the state, international investment law and international trade law are similar. Under both regimes, individuals do not enjoy wide-reaching rights to annul state measures. However, the limitations under international trade law are greater when it comes to the possibility for claiming damages, as the CJEU refuses such rights for individuals in the domain of WTO law. One purpose of this work is to question the consistency of the linking between the effect of the WTO rules in the EU legal order, on the one hand, and the right to claim damages, on the other. Is the CJEU right in

[4] European Commission, 'Towards a comprehensive European international investment policy' (Communication) COM (2010) 343 final, 5ff.

[5] Council Regulation (EU) No 912/2014 of the European Parliament and of the Council of 23 July 2014 establishing a framework for managing financial responsibility linked to investor-to-state dispute settlement tribunals established by international agreements to which the European Union is party [2014] OJ L 257/121.

[6] On the limited role of the individual in international trade law see E-U Petersmann, 'Application of GATT by the Court of Justice of the European Communities' (1983) 20 *CML Rev* 397, 424ff; H Ruiz Fabri, 'Is There a Case—Legally and Politically—for Direct Effect of WTO Obligations?' (2014) 25 *EJIL* 151, 151.

extending its restrictive stance vis-à-vis the legality review in annulment proceedings to the level of compensation? Or are there sound reasons to distinguish the right to annulment from the right to compensation that would justify distinct treatment for these two remedies under EU law? In other words, there may be scope to argue that whilst individuals cannot attack the validity of an EU legal act based on its incompatibility with WTO law, there may be good reasons to at least hold the EU liable for the damages that result from its WTO incompatible conduct.

Therefore, regarding EU liability in the international trade domain, the fact that WTO law lacks direct effect in the EU legal order is of decisive relevance. The pivotal question is whether liability claims are valid despite such lack of direct effect. The most prominent cases decided by the CJEU are rooted in the transatlantic relationship between the EU and the US. The banana and hormone-treated beef disputes are two cases with a particular long-standing history in the WTO dispute settlement system, and they can be characterised as a tenacious back-and-forth between protectionist impulses and the effort to uphold WTO standards.[7] Not surprisingly, the adoption of retaliatory measures by the US as response to persistent WTO-incompatible conduct by the EU has caused significant economic damages to private-sector actors, encouraging numerous companies to file suits seeking compensation with the CJEU.[8] The consistent refusal to grant compensation is of interest not only from a legal perspective. The issue can also be examined through an economic lens: Does it make sense from the perspective of allocative efficiency to exclude companies from claiming damages? Which incentives

[7] On the vast literature on the banana dispute see M Salas and JH Mauricio, 'Procedural Overview of the WTO EC—Banana Dispute' (2000) 3 *JIEL* 145; JP Trachtman, 'Decisions of the Appellate Body of the World Trade Organization' (1999) 10 *EJIL* 655, 671; JH Jackson and P Grane, 'The Saga Continues: An Update on the Banana Dispute and Its Procedural Offspring' (2001) 4 *JIEL* 581; S Peers, 'Banana Split: WTO Law and Preferential Agreements in the EC Legal Order' (1999) 4 *EFA Rev* 195; A Reinisch, 'Entschädigung für die Opfer des Hormon—und Bananenstreites nach Art 288 II EG?' [2000] *EuZW* 42; H-J Rabe, 'Ausgerechnet Bananen' [1996] *NJW* 1320; C Schmid, 'Immer wieder Bananen: Der Status des GATT/WTO-Systems im Gemeinschaftsrecht' [1998] *NJW* 190; N Lavranos, 'Die Rechtswirkung von WTO Panel Reports im Europäischen Gemeinschaftsrecht und Deutschen Verfassungsrecht' [1999] *EuR* 289; on the hormone dispute see D Wüger, 'The Never Ending Story: The Implementation Phase in the Disputes between the EC and the United States on Hormone-Treated Beef' (2002) 33 *L & Policy Intl Bus* 777; B Eggers, 'Die Entscheidung des WTO Appellate Body im Hormonfall' [1998] *EuZW* 147; C Godt, 'Der Bericht des Appellate Body der WTO zum EG-Einfuhrverbot von Hormonfleisch: Risikoregulierung im Weltmarkt' [1998] *EWS* 202, 202ff.

[8] Case T-19/01 *Chiquita v Commission* [2005] ECR II-315; Case T-18/99 *Cordis Obst v Commission* [2001] ECR II-913; Case T-30/99 *Bocchi Food Trade International v Commission* [2001] ECR II-943; Case T-52/99 *T Port GmbH & Co v Commission* [2001] ECR II-981; Case C-93/02 P *Biret International v Council* [2003] ECR I-10497; Case C-104/97 P *Atlanta AG v European Community* [1999] ECR I-6983; Case T-151/00 *Le Laboratoire du Bain v Council and Commission* [2005] ECR II-23; Case T-301/00 *Groupe Fremaux SA and Palais Royal Inc v Council and Commission* [2005] ECR II-25; Case T-320/00 *CD Cartondruck AG v Council and Commission* [2005] ECR II-27; Case T-383/00 *Beamglow Ltd v European Parliament, Council and Commission* [2005] ECR II-5459; Case T-69/00 *FIAMM and FIAMM Technologies v Council and Commission* [2005] ECR II-5393; Joined Cases C-120/06 P and C-121/06 P *FIAMM and FIAMM Technologies v Council and Commission* [2008] ECR I-6513.

result for EU policy-maker and legislator from such a refusal? Furthermore, what level of compensation should be granted from an economic perspective for WTO-incompatible measures?

A different set of question emerges in the area of international investment law. The lack of direct effect is not the crucial issue, as the individuals are explicitly endowed with enforceable rights under BITs. Indeed, BITs aim to grant individuals whose rights have been violated the right to file compensation claims against states hosting foreign investment. Unlike under WTO law, most BITs define precise and clear rights and obligations for the signatories. Under the BITs, the individual investor can take recourse to the investor–state tribunal and seek compensation. Accordingly, there is no preferential status for a (political) negotiated solution, as is the case under WTO rules. However, a number of questions concerning liability under investment law have not been sufficiently explored, as they are the product of rather recent developments. The EU has only recently begun to make use of its new competence under the Lisbon Treaty in relation to investments. By adopting Regulation No 912/2014, the EU has taken a first step toward regulating liability issues pertaining to investor-to-state disputes by setting rules for financial responsibility. Liability questions arise due to the nature of investment treaties as so-called mixed agreements—that is, agreements that concern both EU and Member States competencies, and are thus concluded at both levels with a third country. If a claim is brought by an investor under such a mixed agreement, the question arises as to whether the EU, the Member State or both can be held liable vis-à-vis the investor. The answer to this question depends decisively on who has liability under the decision handed down by the investor–state tribunal. It thus has to be clarified whether the EU or the Member States assume responsibility under international law and can thus be subject to a compensation claim brought by the investor. The question of external responsibility must be distinguished from the question of internal liability within the EU legal order. Clarifying the latter—that is, whether the EU or the Member State can internally be held liable—also allows us to answer the question of who should be the respondent in an investor–state tribunal. This leads to the question of whether the EU or a Member State, if one of them has been judged responsible by the tribunal, can internally hold the other liable for the losses suffered due to the tribunal's decision.

Against this backdrop, exploring liability issues in the area of international economic law reveals a heterogeneous set of questions depending on the area of law concerned, thus offering different perspectives for studying liability issues. First, one distinguishing features is the role of the individual accorded in the specific issue area—in this sense, the liability regime offer a system of legal protection to varying degree. From a doctrinal perspective, the question then is whether the limitations on the rights accorded to individuals through international treaties could not be mitigated through a system of liability as a format of legal redress being less intrusive into states' margin of manoeuvre than rights to annulment would be. Second, another perspective on EU liability in the international context is determined by the unique features of the EU as multilevel governance construct.

Both EU and Member States may be the origin of unlawful conduct vis-à-vis individuals giving rise to questions as to the internal allocation of (financial) responsibilities and external representation. Third, EU liability pertaining to investment law is at the beginning of an evolutionary process in which the EU only recently gained additional competences and has launched a new system of treaty-based international cooperation replacing the previous Member States' regime of cooperation. And fourth, liability issues always have an economic core, not only because they typically concern individual companies operating their business and seeking to claim compensation for damages they suffered carrying out economic activities. Yet, from an economic perspective, liability issues have significant effects on those whose conduct may give rise to liability—whether and to what extent a right to compensation is recognised has significant repercussions on the EU legislator as the wrongdoer. The economic analysis of civil liability has produced insight which can (to considerable extent) be applied in exploring an optimal design of liability in the context of international economic law. In this regard, efficiency concerns as well as the incentive scheme set by certain liability regimes must be addressed. As such, an optimal liability regime should always take account of the impact that a legal interpretation of specific rules may have on the economic actors operating within the legal framework. This study explores the various aspects of liability issues across international economic law. It seeks to contribute an analytical framework for an area that is both of great significance for economic actors and evolving rapidly due to new policy initiatives and recent and prospective legislative activities.

# Part One

# EU Liability and Violations of WTO law

# 1

# *Analytical Preliminaries*

## I. TERMINOLOGICAL ISSUES—THE TERM 'DIRECT EFFECT'

LIABILITY FOR WTO-INCOMPATIBLE measures has been intrinsically linked by the Court to the notion of *direct effect*. The term 'direct effect' needs to be clarified, given a diversity of related terms such as direct applicability, direct effect and bindingness.[1] For the purposes of this analysis, the terms effect and applicability are used interchangeably. The terminological identity has also been shared in literature and jurisprudence where 'direct effect', 'direct applicability' and 'invocability' are often synonymous.[2] Applicability and effect are thus 'in the Court's language equivalent'.[3] A distinction must be drawn, however, to the binding character of a norm, as the bindingness must be seen as a prerequisite for (but less than) the direct effect or applicability. Direct effect requires a norm to be binding. Because of their binding nature, agreements become an integral part of the European legal order and they acquire the rank of EU law in Member States' legal orders.[4] By contrast, direct effect ensures the operability of the norm, which allows application of the norm to the facts and to derive legal consequences. In order for a provision to gain direct effect, it must be sufficiently clear and precise to the extent that it allows enforceability vis-à-vis the individual invoking the norm without further implementation through legal acts.[5] Under these conditions, a provision of public international law permits the individual to invoke the rights discernible from this norm before the courts of the EU.[6]

[1] See, inter alia, KJ Kuilwijk, *The European Court of Justice and the GATT Dilemma* (Beuningen, Nexed Editions, 1996) 36; JA Winter, 'Direct Applicability and Direct Effect: Two Distinct and Different Concepts in European Community Law' (1972) 9 *CML Rev* 425, 425.

[2] Case C-18/90 *Office national de l'emploi v Kziber* [1991] ECR I-221, para 15; Case 17/81 *Pabst & Richarz KG v Hauptzollamt Oldenburg* [1982] ECR 1331, 1350, para 27; Case 83/78 *Pigs Marketing Board v Raymond Redmond* [1987] ECR 2374, 66ff.

[3] P Pescatore, 'The Doctrine of 'Direct Effect': An Infant Disease of Community Law' (1983) 8 *EL Rev* 155, 155.

[4] As stated by the ECJ, see Case 181/73 *R & V Haegeman v Belgian State* [1974] ECR 449, and for customary international law Case C-162/96 *A Racke GmbH & Co v Hauptzollamt Mainz* [1998] ECR I-3655.

[5] Joined Cases C-300/98 and C-392/98 *Dior* [2000] ECR I-11344, para 42; Case C-432/92 *The Queen v Anastasiou (Pissouri) Ltd and Others* [1994] ECR I-3116, para 23; *A Racke GmbH & Co v Hauptzollamt Mainz* (n 4) para 31.

[6] Case 266/81 *SIOT v Ministero delle Finanze* [1983] ECR 731, 780, para 28; Case C-280/93 *Germany v Council* [1994] ECR I-5039, I-5073, para 109f.

## II. THE LINE OF ARGUMENT

The purpose of this chapter of the study is to trace the doctrinal ground for a claim of damages by individuals against the EU for violations of WTO law. To be clear from the outset, the focus will not be on direct effect as such—whether or not WTO is directly effective in the EU legal order has been the subject of numerous studies.[7] Rather, I argue that direct effect should not be treated as a prerequisite for a claim of damages. The focus thus lies on whether other conditions than direct effect must be fulfilled for a claim of damages. More precisely, the analysis will focus on violations of EU law (rather than WTO law) as doctrinal connection points for EU liability. At the core, the *Francovich* doctrine will be used in order to decouple the notion of direct effect from the claim for damages. Invoking the Court's ruling in *Francovich* requires transposition of the three pillars this doctrine rests on—namely the principle of *effet utile*, the notion of legal protection as well as the obligations enshrined in Article 4 para 3 TEU—into the context of EU liability for WTO-incompatible measures. By doing so, the link between direct effect and liability can be overcome.

While the legal part of the analysis focuses on delinking direct effect and liability, the results should be assessed from an economic perspective. This analysis combines the insight from both the political economy and welfare analysis in order to identify the efficiency concerns that may arise from compensation of financial losses in the context of international trade. To that end, the liability question requires, first, to apply the tools of institutional economics (in particular the concepts pertaining to public choice, principal agent and incomplete information) to the specific context of EU legislation breaching WTO rules. Second, the welfare effects resulting from WTO violations and the respective retaliatory measures must be taken into account—this requires a study of the financial losses incurred by the various injured parties in the international trade context and to discuss

[7] Ruiz Fabri, 'Direct Effect of WTO Obligations?' (Introduction, fn 6) 151; F Martines, 'Direct Effect of International Agreements of the European Union' (2014) 25 *EJIL* 129, 129; P Eeckhout, 'Remedies and Compliance' in DL Bethlehem and others (eds), *The Oxford Handbook of International Trade Law* (Oxford, Oxford University Press, 2009); T Cottier, 'A Theory of Direct Effect in Global Law' in AV Bogdandy, PC Mavroidis and Y Mény (eds), *European Integration and International Coordination: Studies in Transnational Economic Law in Honour of Claus-Dieter Ehlermann* (The Hague, Kluwer Law International, 2002); N Komuro, 'The EC Banana Regime and Judicial Control' (2000) 34 *JWT* 1; P Eeckhout, 'The Domestic Legal Status of the WTO Agreement: Interconnecting Legal Systems' (1997) 34 *CML Rev* 11; M Hilf, 'The Role of National Courts in International Trade Relations' [1997] *MJIL* 321; A Desmedt, 'European Court of Justice on the Effect of WTO Agreements in the EC Legal Order' (2000) 27 *LIEI* 93; U Everling, 'Will Europe Slip on Bananas? The Bananas Judgement of the Court of Justice and National Courts' (1996) 33 *CML Rev* 401; P Lee and B Kennedy, 'Potential Direct Effect of GATT 1994 in European Community Law' (1996) 30 *JWT* 67; F Castillo de la Torre, 'The Status of GATT in EC Law, Revisited' (1995) 29 *JWT* 53; GA Zonnekeyn, 'The Status of WTO Law in the EC Legal Order—The Final Curtain?' (2000) 34 *JWT* 111; more broadly on the function of direct effect for the legal order AV Bogdandy, 'Pluralism, Direct Effect, and the Ultimate Say: On the Relationship between International and Domestic Constitutional Law' (2008) 6 *Int'l J Const L* 397, 397; M Mendez, *The Legal Effects of EU Agreements*, 1st edn (Oxford, Oxford University Press, 2013) 174ff; on the indirect effect of WTO law in the EU legal order see J-P Hix, 'Indirect Effect of International Agreements' [2013] *Jean Monnet Working Paper* 03/13.

their congruency with the overall welfare effect. Account must also be taken of the way how WTO arbitrators assess the size of retaliation permissible as a response to a WTO violation, as this determines the damages of companies hit by retaliation. On that basis, conclusions can be drawn as to whether or not liability is desirable from an economic perspective and the damages that should be compensable under an efficient liability regime.

## III. RELEVANT DAMAGE SITUATIONS

The suits for damages hitherto brought by individual companies on cases of EU violation of WTO rules allow a certain systematic classification reflecting the nature of the damage suffered by the concerned companies. We will identify case groups for analytical purposes: first, as the need for legal redress differs by the way companies are affected by WTO-incompatible EU measures, the claim for damages should be made available only to those companies that are unable to seek legal protection otherwise.[8] Second, the classification in case groups facilitates the determinability of the 'norm intended to confer rights', which—as we will see—has been a crucial condition for suits claiming damages. In this regard, it is straightforward to see that the quality of the legal positions vary between those suffering from import restrictions and those that have been the target of WTO-approved retaliatory measures by the EU. This particularly applies to the determinability of the group of companies that should be entitled to a damage claim, given that the victims of targeted with retaliatory actions are much easier to delineate than those companies suffering disadvantages of any WTO-incompatible regime by the EU. Also, from an economic perspective, determining case groups allows to identify a certain divergence between the private damages suffered by individual companies and the overall negative welfare effects accruing to society as a whole—this distinction is relevant for a general judgment on the desirability of certain liability regimes based on efficiency considerations.

### A. Case group A

We will assign those companies to case group A that have their place of business in a state *outside* the EU and that claim damages, which by their nature have been suffered through operation of their import activities under the WTO-incompatible import regime by the EU. In *Chiquita*,[9] the General Court (GC) had to decide a legal dispute in which a US company claimed compensation for damages it suffered resulting from an EU violation of WTO law. More specifically, *Chiquita* was affected

[8] The following determination of case groups has been based on B Schoißwohl, 'Haftung der Gemeinschaft für WTO-Rechtsverletzungen ihrer Organe: Doktrin der 'Nichtverantwortung'?' [2001] *ZEuS* 689, 692ff.

[9] *Chiquita v Commission* (Introduction, fn 8) II-315.

by the EU banana regime in conducting its business operations, to the extent that it suffered a loss of market share. A basis for legal recourse for such companies could not only be seen in the EU rules allowing damage claims, but also in WTO rules. In fact, the WTO dispute settlement system could offer sufficient protection for these companies, rendering an additional legal recourse through EU damage claims dispensable. Although individual companies do not have a standing as a party under the WTO dispute settlement proceedings, the companies' interests are taken care of by the rights and actions its home countries enjoy under the dispute settlement system. Typically, companies can launch proceedings under national rules that—if the claim is well founded—induce their home country to initiate a WTO dispute against the country whose import regime caused harm to the company.

## B. Case group B

Case group B covers incidents in which EU companies seek compensation for damages they suffer due to an EU import restriction. These cases can be exemplified by the EU legal regime governing the import of bananas and hormone-treated beef. Group B typically encompasses companies having their seat of business operations *inside* the EU and that were trading with 'dollar bananas' (ie, bananas, whose trade was hampered by the EU regime). These companies were then forced to modify their business model and instead trade less profitable EU or ACP bananas. These kinds of commercial losses were raised in the damage suits in *Cordis Obst*, *Bocchi Food* and *T. Port*.[10] A similar situation was faced by companies importing hormone-treated beef, as did *Biret International SA*, which suffered losses due to the ban on imports of hormone-treated beef.[11] On other occasions, the Court dealt with cases in which economic losses were incurred not only by importing companies but rather indirectly by companies involved in remote trading activities. For example, *Atlanta AG* suffered damages because a US trading partner was forced to cancel its shipping charter order.[12] Typically, companies suffering damages due to restricted import opportunities are not just confined to those traders whose trading activities were directly affected but also extend to companies indirectly affected through their business relationship.

## C. Case group C

A third group of affected companies encompasses the traders exporting from the EU and which suffered damages due to the retaliatory measures adopted following

[10] *Cordis Obst v Commission* (Introduction, fn 8); *Bocchi Food Trade International v Commission* (Introduction, fn 8); *T Port GmbH & Co v Commission* (Introduction, fn 8).

[11] *Biret International v Council* (Introduction, fn 8).

[12] *P Atlanta AG v European Community* (Introduction, fn 8).

a decision of the DSB.[13] This group is distinct from case groups A and B, which are affected by the trade-restrictive EU regulations. By contrast, the companies hit by retaliation typically operate their business in entirely different business sectors than the one in which the EU initially infringed WTO rules. For example, case group C encompasses companies which were targeted by penalty duties imposed following the consistent refusal of the EU to comply with the DSB rulings in the hormones and banana disputes. These victims of retaliatory measures are operating their businesses in many sectors: Italian producers of batteries, producers of cosmetic products or traders of cotton blankets. The way these companies are concerned raises the question of attributability, that is whether the damages suffered can be regarded as an immediate consequence of the WTO-incompatible conduct of the EU. Attributability needs to be discussed in the context of causality as a prerequisite for a suit for damages. In other words, can the monetary damages by victims of US retaliation be considered a direct consequence of EU legislative acts?

## IV. GENERAL PRINCIPLES COMMON TO THE LAWS OF THE MEMBER STATES

The requirements establishing liability as laid down in 340 para 2 TFEU are incomplete—the provision only refers to the general principles common to the laws of the Member States. This turns out to be problematic, because national liability regimes have little in common,[14] particularly in the area of liability for legislative EU acts.[15] As a result of this legal heterogeneity across Member States, the EU liability regime has largely been developed through jurisprudence underscoring the important role the CJEU has assumed in this process.[16] In the past, for that purpose the CJEU has relied on legal comparative exercises on a very limited scale only. Rather, it drew on the idiosyncrasies of the EU legal system with a view to shaping a liability regime concurrent with EU law.[17] This process of 'legal creativity' on the part of the CJEU has been deemed admissible, to the extent that the

[13] *Le Laboratoire du Bain v Council and Commission* (Introduction, fn 8); *Groupe Fremaux SA and Palais Royal Inc v Council and Commission* (Introduction, fn 8); *CD Cartondruck AG v Council and Commission* (Introduction, fn 8); *Beamglow Ltd v European Parliament, Council and Commission* (Introduction, fn 8); *FIAMM and FIAMM Technologies v Council and Commission* (Introduction, fn 8).

[14] R Streinz, 'Primär- und Sekundärrechtsschutz im Öffentlichen Recht' (2002) 61 *VVDStRL* 300, 330; F Schockweiler, G Wivenes and JM Godart, 'Le règime de la responsabilité extra-contractuelle du fait d´actes juridiques dans la Communauté européenne' [1990] *RTDeur* 27, 29ff.

[15] I Pernice, 'L'accès á la justice dans l'Union Européenne: Le recours en indemnité' [1995] *CDE*, 650f; for a comparative study on liability for normative acts see A Czaja, *Die außervertragliche Haftung der EG für ihre Organe*, 1st edn (Baden-Baden, Nomos 1996), 73ff.

[16] TC Hartley, *The Foundations of European Union Law*, 8th edn (Oxford, Oxford University Press, 2014), 464; F Dumon, 'La responsabilité extracontractuelle des Communautés Européennes et de leurs agents' [1969] *CDE* 3, 42.

[17] See also the sporadic references by the Court to the national legal orders in Case 256/81 *Pauls Agriculture v Commission and Council* [1982] ECR 1707, 1721; Case C-152/88 *Sofrimport v Commission* [1990] ECR I-2477, I-2512; Joined Cases C-104/89 and C-37/90 *Mulder and Others and Heinemann v Council and Commission* [1992] ECR I-3061, I-3136.

solutions developed by the CJEU would be compatible (or at least not evidently incompatible) with national liability regimes.[18]

Reference to the general principles common to the laws of the Member States, as stipulated in Article 340 para 2 TFEU, requires an assessment of whether and to what extent national legal orders foresee liability for the violation of international treaties (or even for infringements of WTO agreements). It also raises the question of which conditions must apply for an individual to be able to invoke an international treaty. First, this pertains to the question of whether international agreements are recognized by the national legal order to serve as the standard of legality for national legal acts. Second, the issue of invocability relates to the subsequent question of an individual seeking to derive rights from this agreement, and specifies the precise requirements for a liability claim. This work does not aim at undertaking a comprehensive comparative legal study of the liability regime of the 28 Member States. I have examined a number of national liability regimes elsewhere.[19] Not surprisingly, a comparative study shows heterogeneity across legal orders in dealing with damages based on violations of international treaties. This implies that it cannot be proven that liability for WTO infringements would be recognised in each Member State. However, there seems to be a certain degree of consistency in that liability for damages resulting from violations of international agreements is generally possible (even if the precise conditions may vary across Member States). By contrast, there is no general exclusion of individuals invoking international agreements as a ground for liability in national legal orders, provided that the agreement has become an integral part of the national legal order (which again may differ as to the conditions under which national legal orders import international agreements into their system). Under these circumstances, international agreements can generally become the legal standard in actions for damages. However, a comparative study also shows that in a number of legal orders, limitations to the ability to invoke international agreements as a legal standard result from the exclusion of parliamentary laws to be reviewed on the basis of international treaties.

Heterogeneity persists across national legal orders as to the precise conditions the agreement has to meet in terms of granting individual rights, in order to serve as a basis for damage claims. Requirements differ as some national legal orders require the agreement to be directly effective, while in other legal orders the standard in terms of invocability is less strict. The comparative analysis reveals that in a majority of national legal systems, there is some kind of subjective right necessary for the invocability of an international agreement.[20] However, this does not allow one to conclude that this requirement necessarily also applies for EU liability. In line with general jurisprudence on the development of EU liability,

[18] R Streinz, *Europarecht*, 10th edn (Heidelberg, CF Müller 2016), para 689.

[19] A Steinbach, *Die Haftung der EG und ihrer Mitgliedsstaaten für WTO-Rechtsverletzungen aus rechtswissenschaftlicher und ökonomischer Perspektive* (Berlin, Duncker & Humblot, 2009) 33ff.

[20] ibid.

the particularities of EU law must be taken into account when determining the requirements for liability. This means that the CJEU does not rely on a minimum standard of what exists in the national legal order, but rather chooses (and develops) liability principles that appear suitable in light of the general particularities of EU law (even if they would not be identical with the requirements set under Member States' laws).[21] National liability regimes are thus only a point of reference, but do not have determinative power. Against this background, in the past the Court has already developed the principles of Member States' liability for legislative acts incompatible with EU law, even though liability for a legislative act could certainly not be inferred from the majority of Member States' legal orders.[22]

For the purpose of this work, the foregoing has the following implications: assessing liability for WTO-incompatible acts is not necessarily precluded, given that liability for the violation of international agreements is recognised under most national laws. Moreover, pertaining to the requirement of direct effect as a prerequisite of liability, this analysis will explore the ways under which the idiosyncrasies of EU law allow for considering the direct effect of WTO law as dispensable for liability.

## V. THE STANDARD OF UNLAWFULNESS

Both the development and the relevance of EU liability in the system of legal redress have to been seen in light of the high hurdle that EU law poses for legal protection aimed at annulment of EU secondary law.[23] In that sense, liability for unlawful legislative conduct fulfils a compensatory function for the limited possibilities of individuals to annul legislative acts.[24] Liability for legislative acts has been developed by the Court in *Schöppenstedt*.[25] As a general feature in jurisprudence, high liability thresholds shield the scope for manoeuvre of legislative organs. In the domain of economic policy, the CJEU has established the requirement of a 'sufficiently serious breach of a superior rule of law for the

[21] G Isaac and M Blanquet, *Droit communautaire général*, 10th edn (Paris, Armand Colin, 2012), 600.

[22] For legal comparisons see R Fetzer, *Die Haftung des Staates für legislatives Unrecht* (Berlin, Duncker & Humblot, 1994), 189ff; M Herdegen, *Die Haftung der Europäischen Wirtschaftsgemeinschaft für fehlerhafte Rechtsetzungsakte* (Berlin, Duncker & Humblot, 1983), 53ff.

[23] F Ossenbühl and M Cornils, *Staatshaftungsrecht*, 6th edn (München, CH Beck, 2013), 596ff; J Schwarze, 'Rechtsschutz Privater gegenüber normativen Rechtsakten im Recht der EWG' in I von Münch (ed), *Staatsrecht—Völkerrecht—Europarecht: Festschrift für Hans-Jürgen Schlochauer zum 75. Geburtstag am 28. März 1981* (Berlin, De Gruyter 1981) 937; AV Bogdandy, 'Europa 1992—Die außervertragliche Haftung der Europäischen Gemeinschaften' [1990] *JuS* 872, 873.

[24] RM Winkler and T Trölitzsch, 'Wende in der EuGH-Rechtsprechung zur Haftung der EG für fehlerhafte EG-Rechtsetzungsakte und prozessuale Bewältigung der Prozeßflut' [1992] *EuZW* 663, 664; G Nicolaysen, 'Der Gerichtshof—Funktion und Bewährung der Judikative' [1972] *EuR* 375.

[25] Case 5/71 *Schöppenstedt v Council* [1971] ECR 975, 975ff.

protection of the individual'.[26] In the Court's view, this restriction is justified by the wide discretion, which the legislative organs must enjoy and which is necessary in order not to impede the decision-making process.[27] Otherwise, the scope of discretion by the legislator would be exposed to liability claims.[28]

In light of the foregoing, the question arises: how does the Court set the standard of legality when reviewing EU secondary law lying at the intersection of EU internal market policy and external trade policy? Past jurisprudence shows that actions pertaining to external policies are not generally dismissed for reasons of inadmissibility. In *Fediol* I,[29] the Court had to rule on an inadmissibility claim raised by the Commission concerning an action brought by Brazil against an anti-dumping investigation. In contrast to what the Commission had argued regarding the non-reviewability of the issue, due to its political character, the Court referred to Article 164 EEC requiring the Court to ensure that the law is observed and thus considered the case to be admissible.[30] The Court took a similar stance in *Faust*, concerning an action for damages by a German importer of Chinese mushrooms from Taiwan challenging the quota limitation of his imports. The arguments made by the claimant regarding the violation of legitimate interests were reviewed by the Court in substance, without considering the potential inadmissibility of the claim.[31] The Court further consolidated this line of jurisprudence, in relation to the admissibility of actions against EU acts having external policy links in *Adams*[32] and *Clemessy*[33]—from all these judgments, it can be inferred that action for damages being related to external trade policy would not necessarily be considered inadmissible.[34]

Despite this generous stance on admissibility issues, a general restraint of the Court can be observed in reviewing EU acts concerned in substance and thus

[26] ibid para 11, confirmed in *Mulder and Others and Heinemann v Council and Commission* (n 17) I-3061; Case T-267/94 *Oleifici Italiani v Commission* [1997] ECR II-1239, II-1239; regarding safeguarding measures against imports Case 52/81 *Faust v Commission* [1982] ECR 3745, 3745; concerning WTO violations see *T Port GmbH & Co v Commission* (Introduction, fn 8) 1000, para 45; see also Ossenbühl and Cornils, *Staatshaftungsrecht* (2013) (n 23) 607f.

[27] Case 83 and 94/76, 4, 15 and 40/77 *HNL and Others v Council and Commission* [1978] ECR 1209, para 5; Case T-571/93 *Lefebvre v Commission* [1995] ECR II-2379, para 38; M Ruffert in C Calliess and M Ruffert (eds), *EUV/AEUV*, 5th edn (München, CH Beck, 2016) Art 340 TFEU, para 16; Ossenbühl and Cornils, *Staatshaftungsrecht* (2013) (n 23) 608; Reinisch, 'Opfer des Hormon- und Bananenstreites' (Introduction, fn 7) 49.

[28] Case 9 and 11/71 *Compagnie d'approvisionnement v Commission* [1972] ECR 391, 408; Case 74/74 *CNTA v Commission* [1975] ECR 533, 547; Ossenbühl and Cornils, *Staatshaftungsrecht* (2013) (n 23) 608, 610ff.

[29] Case 191/82 *Fediol v Commission* [1983] ECR 2913, 2913.

[30] ibid 2935, para 29f.

[31] Case C-241/87 *Maclaine Watson v Council and Commission* [1990] ECR I-1797, Opinion of AG Darmon, I-1807, para 62.

[32] Case 53/84 *Stanley Adams v Commission* [1985] ECR 3595, 3595.

[33] Case 267/82 *Développement SA and Clemessy v Commission* [1986] ECR 1907, 1907.

[34] *Maclaine Watson v Council and Commission* (n 31) Opinion of AG Darmon, I-1807, para 55ff; A Ott, 'Der EuGH und das WTO-Recht: Die Entdeckung der politischen Gegenseitigkeit—altes Phänomen oder neuer Ansatz?' [2003] *EuR* 504, 515f.

granting a wide margin of discretion of EU institutions.[35] In *Faust*, the Court dismissed an action for damages, by reference to the wide discretion held by the Commission when choosing the policy instruments it considers suitable for the pursuit of its policy goals. Also, the Court argued that it would be inevitable that a change of trade policies would have an effect on the business of market operators in the relevant field, thereby shifting the risk of legislative changes into the sphere of market operators.[36] On other occasions in relation to the EU external trade policy, the European Courts connect the requirement of a 'sufficiently serious breach' to the wide margin of EU legislative organs.[37] In this vein, in *Lefebvre*, where an action for damages was based on the refusal to grant import licenses for bananas, the Court dealt with the particularities of agricultural policy and found that in this area legislative activities would be characterised by the wider margin of discretion going beyond the typically already wide margin in economic policy domains. The Court referred to an evident and significant breach of competences as a condition for liability.[38] Similar considerations were made by the Court in *Nölle*.[39]

This line of jurisprudence has also been followed by the Court in the action for damages due to EU violations of WTO law. In the three damage suits brought by *Port*, *Bocchi* und *Cordis Obst*, in which compensation was sought for losses due to the EU banana regime, the Court referred to its case law, according to which the 'Community institutions enjoy a margin of discretion in the choice of the means needed to implement their policy, operators cannot claim to have a legitimate expectation that an existing situation which is capable of being altered by decisions taken by those institutions within the limits of their discretionary power will be maintained'.[40] This wording was used by the Court in the action for damages in *Atlanta* (again concerning the banana regime) as well and referred to the common agricultural policy, the purpose of which would be to allow a permanent adaptation of the legal regime to the economic situation.[41] Consequently, a review of the policy discretion would only be made in cases of obvious errors or a clear violation of discretion.[42] In the cases concerning isoglucose, the Court further specified the scope of discretion to the extent that the conduct of the EU legislator 'was verging

[35] GA Zonnekeyn, 'EC Liability for non-implementation of Adopted WTO Panel and Appellate Body Reports' in V Kronenberger (ed), *The European Union and the International Legal Order: Discord or Harmony?* (The Hague, Kluwer Law International, 2001) 261.

[36] *Faust v Commission* (n 26) 3761, para 23.

[37] For the trade policy see Case T-167/94 *Nölle v Council and Commission* [1995] ECR II-2589, para 85; for the common agricultural policy see Joined Cases 56-60/74 *Kampffmeyer v Council and Commission* [1976] ECR 711, 744; *Lefebvre v Commission* (n 27) para 32.

[38] *Lefebvre v Commission* (n 27) para 32.

[39] *Nölle v Council and Commission* (n 37) para 85.

[40] *T Port GmbH & Co v Commission* (Introduction, fn 8) II-983, para 99.

[41] *P Atlanta AG v European Community* (Introduction, fn 8) I-6983; *Germany v Council* (n 6) I-4973; Case C-350/88 *Delacre and others v Commission* [1990] ECR I-395, I-395; Case 43/72 *Merkur v Commission* [1973] ECR 1055, 1055; see Ott, 'EuGH und WTO-Recht' (n 34) 514.

[42] Joined Cases T-33/98 and T-34/98 *Petrotub and Republica v Council* [1999] ECR II-3837, II-3840; Case 55/75 *Balkan-Import Export GmbH v Hauptzollamt Berlin-Packhof* [1976] ECR 19, 19; *Faust v Commission* (n 26) 3758, para 9.

on the arbitrary'.[43] In other words, economic policy decisions can be considered tantamount to granting wide discretion to the EU legislator.[44]

This line of jurisprudence is further reflected in the claim for damages brought in relation to the EU's association agreements. *Lubella* concerned compensation payments the Commission charged to *Lubella* for the import of cherries from Poland, Hungary and the Czech Republic. Even though the rights enshrined in the association agreement are widely recognised to enjoy direct effect,[45] the Court justified the safeguarding measures by the wide scope of discretion enjoyed by the EU institutions, which led the Court to state that the operators cannot rely on the continuity of the current legal situation that can be altered by the EU institutions within the margin of their discretion at any time.[46]

Which requirements does the Court set as the threshold of unlawfulness of an EU act? Article 340 para 2 TFEU is silent on unlawfulness, but it is well established that liability requires a violation of a superior legal norm.[47] More precisely, unlawfulness as such is not sufficient but the rule infringed must also be 'intended to safeguard the interest' of the individual claiming liability.[48] While the establishment of such a requirement corresponds to the line of jurisprudence discussed above shielding the EU legislators from the risk of liability, the Court seems to

[43] Joined Cases 116 and 124/77 *Amylum v Council and Commission* [1979] ECR 3497, 3561, para 19; Case 143/77 *Koninklijke Scholten-Honig v Council and Commission* [1979] ECR 3583, 3626, para 14.

[44] C Friese, Kompensation von Embargoschäden bei Embargomassnahmen der Europäischen Union (Köln, Heymanns, 2000) 126; SA Haack, Die ausservertragliche Haftung der Europäischen Gemeinschaften für rechtmässiges Verhalten ihrer Organe (Frankfurt am Main, P Lang, 1995) 42f.

[45] See only Case C-113/97 *Babahenini v Belgian State* [1998] ECR I-183, para 17; Case C-179/98 *Belgian State v Mesbah* [1999] ECR I-7955, para 23; Case C-416/96 *Eddline El-Yassini v Secretary of State for Home Department* [1999] ECR I-1209, para 27; on recent developments in excluding direct effect in free trade agreements A Semertzi, 'The Preclusion of Direct Effect in the Recently Concluded EU Free Trade Agreements' (2014) 51 *CML Rev* 1125, 1125ff.

[46] Case C-64/95 *Lubella v Hauptzollamt Cottbus* [1996] ECR I-5105, I-5138, para 31; see also Ott, 'EuGH und WTO-Recht' (n 34) 517 criticising the CJEU for not sufficiently discussing the citizens' rights enshrined in the interim agreements. However, there is strong indication for the lawfulness of the measure on the basis of the interim agreement, see Art 14 of the agreement. In this vein, Case 245/81 *Edeka v Germany* [1982] ECR 2745, para 27; *Faust v Commission* (n 26) para 27.

[47] See only *Biret International v Council* (Introduction, fn 8) para 55; established case law since Case 4/69 *Lütticke v Commission* [1971] ECR 325, 325; A Arnull, 'Liability for Legislative Acts under Article 215(2) EC' in T Heukels and A McDonnell (eds), *The Action For Damages In Community Law* (The Hague, Kluwer Law International, 1997) 136; Streinz, Europarecht (2016) (n 18) para 692; W Berg in J Schwarze (ed), *EU-Kommentar*, 3rd edn (Baden-Baden, Nomos, 2012) Art 340 TFEU, para 35; Reinisch, 'Opfer des Hormon- und Bananenstreites' (Introduction, fn 7) 45; Ossenbühl and Cornils, Staatshaftungsrecht (2013) (n 23) 607. However, on other occasions, the Court indicated that liability for lawful conduct would also be possible, see *FIAMM and FIAMM Technologies v Council and Commission* (Introduction, fn 8) 155ff.

[48] For the first time in Case 9 and 12/60 *Vloeberghs v High Authority* [1961] ECR 219, 469; see in literature H-W Rengeling, A Middeke and M Gellermann, *Rechtsschutz in der Europäischen Union. Durchsetzung von Gemeinschaftsrecht vor europäischen und deutschen Gerichten* (München, CH Beck, 1994), para 266; R Geiger in R Geiger, D-E Khan and M Kotzur (eds), *EUV/AEUV*, 6th edn (München, CH Beck, 2016) Art 340 TFEU, para 41; M Gellermann in R Streinz (ed), *EUV/AEUV*, 2nd edn (München, CH Beck, 2012) Art 340 TFEU, para 19.

interpret this criterion rather widely. The Court already accepts an intention of the norm to safeguard individual rights, if such norm primarily aims at common affairs and only secondarily (as a 'reflex') also serves individual interests.[49] It is thus not the violation of a fully-fledged subjective right which necessarily has to be protected by the violated norm, but a legally protected interest suffices.[50]

In sum, one can connect the various strands of jurisprudence to conclude that the *political question doctrine* implying a general exclusion of reviewability of EU acts pertaining to external (trade) affairs in general and regarding EU liability in particular has not been applied throughout the Court's jurisprudence.[51] Legal actions linked to external affairs are not as such inadmissible, even though there is a wide margin for EU institutions to manoeuvre in pursuing their policy goals. It seems accurate to characterise the respect of such wide discretion as a weak form of judicial restraint. The *Schöppenstedt*-formula has been applied as a mechanism to allow a reduced legal review where suits of damages are concerned. It serves as a filter, without generally excluding acts pertaining to economic or external policies from reviewability.[52] By using thresholds such as 'evident errors', 'manifest violation' or—in the case of damage suits—'sufficiently serious breaches', the Court accounts for the need of EU legislators to maintain its scope of manoeuvring without having to fear a high risk of liability claims.

[49] Case 5, 7 and 13-24/66 *Kampffmeyer and Others v Commission [1967]* ECR 317, 354; *CNTA v Commission* (n 28) 549; in the literature see Ossenbühl and Cornils, Staatshaftungsrecht (2013) (n 23) 607; Gellermann (n 48) Art 340 TFEU, para 20; Ruffert (n 27) Art 340 TFEU, para 13.

[50] H-J Prieß, 'Die Haftung der EG-Mitglieder bei Verstößen gegen das Gemeinschaftsrecht' [1993] NVwZ 118, 122; C Henrichs, Haftung der EG-Mitgliedstaaten für Verletzung von Gemeinschaftsrecht, 1st edn (Baden-Baden, Nomos, 1995) 28; Reinisch, 'Opfer des Hormon- und Bananenstreites' (Introduction, fn 7) 45; Friese, Kompensation (2000) (n 44) 123; for a different view see Herdegen, Haftung (1983) (n 22) 113, who identifies the risk of EU liability being overly expanded.

[51] Similarly *Maclaine Watson v Council and Commission* (n 31) Opinion of AG Darmon, I-1806ff; Ott, 'EuGH und WTO-Recht' (n 34) 517.

[52] E Grabitz, 'Zur Haftung der Europäischen Gemeinschaften für normatives Unrecht' in WG Grewe, H Rupp and H Schneider (eds), *Europäische Gerichtsbarkeit und nationale Verfassungsgerichtsbarkeit: Festschrift zum* 70. Geburtstag von Hans Kutscher (Baden-Baden, Nomos, 1981) 227; Herdegen, Haftung (1983) (n 22) 110; E-W Fuß, 'Zur Rechtsprechung des Europäischen Gerichtshofs über die Gemeinschaftshaftung für rechtswidrige Verordnungen' in H Kipp, F Mayer and A Steinkamm (eds), *Um Recht und Freiheit: Festschrift für von der Heydte* (Berlin, Duncker & Humblot, 1977) 178.

# 2

# *The Lack of Direct Effect of DSB Rulings*

IN PRINCIPLE, INTERNATIONAL law can serve as the basis for an EU liability claim if the relevant norm has become an integral part of the EU legal order.[1] It is also undisputed that directly effective provisions grant subjective rights to individuals and as such meet the threshold of a 'norm intended to confer rights upon individuals'. According to the European Courts, claimants bringing an action for damages based on WTO law have been denied 'as the WTO rules are not in principle intended to confer rights on individuals' and 'the Community cannot incur non-contractual liability as a result of infringement of them'.[2] The Court's reasoning relates to the lack of direct effect, which it not only denies for the WTO agreements but also for the rulings rendered by the DSB (Dispute Settlement Body).[3] Whereas in *Biret* the Court did not rule unambiguously on whether the DSB decision could have a direct effect once the losing party failed to comply with it, in *Léon van Parys* the Court subsequently made it clear that it would not make a distinction between the effect of the WTO agreements and individual DSB decisions.[4]

In literature, there has been a long-standing discussion about the direct effect of WTO law.[5] One core argument could be that there are good reasons to distinguish

[1] Zonnekeyn, 'EC Liability' (ch 1, fn 35) 265.

[2] *Bocchi Food Trade International v Commission* (Introduction, fn 8) para 56; *Cordis Obst v Commission* (Introduction, fn 8) para 50; *T Port GmbH & Co v Commission* (Introduction, fn 8) para 50; a similar wording is used in *Chiquita v Commission* (Introduction, fn 8) para 114; Case C-377/02 *Léon Van Parys v BIRB* [2005] ECR I-1465, para 39.

[3] *Léon Van Parys v BIRB* (n 2) para 54; see also A Steinbach, 'Zur Rechtswirkung von WTO-Streitbeilegungsentscheidungen in der Gemeinschaftsrechtsordnung' [2005] *EuZW* 331, 331ff.

[4] See below ch 2 C.

[5] See the studies by Ruiz Fabri, 'Direct Effect of WTO Obligations?' (Introduction, fn 6); J Errico, 'The WTO in the EU: Unwinding the Knot' (2011) 44 *Cornell Int'l L J* 179; A Ott, *GATT und WTO im Gemeinschaftsrecht* (Köln, Heymanns, 1997); T Becker, *Das WTO-Subventionsübereinkommen* (Frankfurt am Main, P Lang, 2001); HA Hinderer, *Rechtsschutz von Unternehmen in der WTO*, 1st edn (Berlin, Berliner Wissenschafts-Verlag, 2004); CA Flemisch, *Umfang der Berechtigungen und Verpflichtungen aus völkerrechtlichen Verträgen* (Frankfurt am Main, P Lang, 2002); A Wünschmann, *Geltung und gerichtliche Geltendmachung völkerrechtlicher Verträge im Europäischen Gemeinschaftsrecht* (Berlin, Duncker & Humblot, 2003); A Oehmichen, *Die unmittelbare Anwendbarkeit der völkerrechtlichen Verträge der EG* (Frankfurt am Main, P Lang, 1992); K Höher, *Die Haftung der Europäischen Gemeinschaft für Verstöße gegen das WTO-Recht*, 1st edn (Baden-Baden, Nomos, 2006); S Görgens, *Die außervertragliche Haftung der Europäischen Gemeinschaft für Verletzungen des WTO-Rechts durch ihre Organe*, 1st edn (Berlin, Duncker & Humblot, 2006).

between the WTO agreements in general and the DSB decisions in particular.[6] In general, the decisive issue for a DSB decision to be accepted as having a direct effect is that 'in regard to its wording and the purpose and nature of the agreement itself, the provision contains a clear and precise obligation that is not subject, in its implementation or effects, to the adoption of any subsequent measure'.[7]

## I. DIRECT EFFECT OF DSB DECISIONS IN THE COURT'S JURISPRUDENCE

### A. Atlanta

In *Atlanta*,[8] for the first time the Court had the opportunity to rule on the direct effect of DSB decisions. In this case, the claimants requested compensation for damages suffered as a result of the EU banana market rules. For procedural reasons, however, the Court managed to escape a clear answer. At the first instance of proceedings, the Court had dismissed the claim based on WTO violations by reference to its judgments in *Germany v Council* and the lack of the direct effect stipulated in that ruling.[9] The claimants had challenged the judgment of the General Court before the Court of Justice. According to the procedural rules of the Court of Justice, the claimant is obliged to state all his arguments in the initial brief of appeal. However, the claimants failed to argue in favour of the direct effect of the DSB decision only in a subsequent rebuttal of the proceedings. The Court of Justice found this to be 'too late' and it thus remained unaddressed.

### B. Biret

It its *Biret* decision, the Court had the opportunity to rule on the effect of the DSB decision of 13 February 1998, in which the EU import regime governing the

[6] Zonnekeyn, 'WTO Law in the EC Legal Order' (ch 1, fn 7) 111ff; A Thies, 'Biret and beyond: The status of WTO rulings in EC law' (2004) 41 CML Rev 1661, 1681f; Eeckhout, 'Domestic Legal Status' (ch 1, fn 7) 48; Lavranos, 'WTO Panel Reports' (Introduction, fn 7) 289; N Lavranos, 'Die EG darf WTO-Recht weiter ignorieren' [2004] EWS 293, 296; C Cascante, Rechtsschutz von Privatrechtssubjekten gegen WTO-widrige Maßnahmen in den USA und in der EG (Berlin, Duncker & Humblot, 2003), 296; H-D Kuschel, 'Wie geht es weiter mit der Bananenmarktordnung?' [1996] EuZW 645, 650; JM Beneyto, 'The EU and WTO: Direct Effect of the New Dispute Settlement System' [1996] EuZW 295, 299; Biret International v Council (Introduction, fn 8) Opinion of AG Alber, para 74ff; A Weber and F Moos, 'Rechtswirkungen von WTO-Streitbeilegungsentscheidungen im Gemeinschaftsrecht' [1999] EuZW 229, 234; W Meng, 'Verfahrensrechtliche Rechtsstellung der Individuen in Bezug auf das WTO-Recht' in H-W Arndt and others (eds), Völkerrecht und deutsches Recht: Festschrift für Walter Rudolf zum 70. Geburtstag (München, CH Beck 2001) 85.

[7] On the conditions for direct effect of decisions rendered under association agreements, Case C-192/89 *Sevince v Staatssecretaris van Justitie* [1990] ECR I-3461, para 15; Case 104/81 *Hauptzollamt Mainz v Kupferberg* [1982] ECR 3641, para 23.

[8] *P Atlanta AG v European Community* (Introduction, fn 8) I-6983.

[9] ibid II-1723, para 77 with reference to *Germany v Council* (ch 1, fn 6) I-5071, para 103ff.

import of hormone-treated beef was found to be incompatible with WTO law.[10] The General Court had stated that there is 'an inescapable and direct link between the [DSB] decision and the plea alleging infringement of the SPS Agreement, and the decision could therefore only be taken into consideration if the Court had found that Agreement to have direct effect in the context of a plea alleging the invalidity of the directives in question'.[11] On the appeal stage of that proceeding, the Court of Justice took recourse to its well-established jurisprudence that 'the WTO agreements are not in principle among the rules in the light of which the Court is to review the legality of measures adopted by the Community institutions',[12] unless 'the Community has intended to implement a particular obligation assumed in the context of the WTO, or where the Community measure refers expressly to the precise provisions of the WTO agreements, that it is for the Court to review the legality of the Community measure in question in the light of the WTO rules'.[13] Subsequently, the Court of Justice rejected the arguments made by the General Court as insufficient[14] by stating that the General Court failed 'to address the argument that the legal effects of the DSB decision of 13 February 1998 vis-à-vis the European Community called into question the Court's finding that the WTO rules did not have direct effect and provided grounds for a review by the Community Courts of the legality [...] in the light of those rules in the action for damages brought by the then applicant effects of the DSB decision of 13 February 1998'.[15] The Court seems to have abandoned its previous case law by clearly making a distinction between the WTO agreements in general and the individual DSB decision. However, while the distinction is methodologically an innovation, a distinct question is whether the Court would also uphold the distinction regarding its assessment of the direct effect.[16] In literature, there is some controversy on how this ruling could be interpreted: some scholars have read the ruling to the effect that the Court would give the individual the possibility to invoke the DSB decision, if the period set to comply with the DSB decision has expired.[17] Other parts of literature have been less optimistic about the *Biret* ruling, and have stressed that the only conclusion to be drawn from the judgment would be that there is no compelling link between the WTO agreements and the DSB decision

[10] On the *Biret* judgment see Thies, 'Biret and beyond' (n 6) 1661ff.

[11] *Biret International v Council* (Introduction, fn 8) para 67.

[12] ibid para 52.

[13] ibid para 53.

[14] ibid para 59.

[15] ibid para 57.

[16] In this vein, S Bartelt, 'Die Haftung der Gemeinschaft bei Nichtumsetzung von Entscheidungen des WTO-Streitbeilegungsgremiums' [2003] *EuR* 1077, 1080; more reserved GA Zonnekeyn, 'EC Liability for Non-implementation of WTO Dispute Settlement Decisions—are the Dice Cast?' (2004) 7 *JIEL* 483, 483; for an opposing view see C Pitschas, 'EuGH: Kein Schadensersatz wegen Importverbots für Hormonfleisch' [2003] *EuZW* 758, 761.

[17] Bartelt, 'Haftung' (n 16) 1082; Zonnekeyn, 'EC Liability' (n 16) 488; Thies, 'Biret and beyond' (n 6) 1681; similarly, Lavranos, 'WTO-Recht' (n 6) 296.

which, however, would require the DSB decision to meet the regular standard criteria for a provision to have direct effect.[18]

## C. Léon van Parys

Those views in literature expressing scepticism regarding the Court's willingness to accept the direct effect of DSB rulings were confirmed by the Court's ruling in *Léon van Parys*. In that case, a Belgian importer of bananas sought to enforce the import licenses he had obtained under the application of the banana regulation No 1637/98[19] and the respective implementing regulation No 2362/98.[20] These regulations had been adopted by the EU legislator following a ruling of the DSB dating 25 September 1997,[21] in which the initial regulation No 404/93[22] governing the market organisation for bananas had been found incompatible with the GATT rules. That DSB decision set a compliance period, according to which the EU would have to implement the ruling by 1 January 1999 by way of modifying its banana import regime. Indeed, the regulations No 1637/98 and No 2362/98 entered into force by 1 January 1999, within the time period set by the DSB. However, only a few months later Ecuador requested the establishment of a WTO panel under Article 21 para 5 DSU, putting forward that the new regulation would have insufficiently complied with the DSB ruling and would thus continue to be in violation of WTO rules—a view that was confirmed by the panel[23] whose report was approved by the DSB on 6 May 1999. *Léon van Parys* had brought the claim of incompatibility of the EU regulations with WTO law before a Belgian court, which referred the case in a preliminary request to the CJEU. The question to be answered by the CJEU was whether the regulations could be 'held to be unlawful from the point of view of Community law in a case where a DSB decision found that a previous Community regime for the import of bananas was inconsistent with the WTO rules'.[24]

[18] Pitschas, 'Hormonfleisch' (n 16) 762. For an interpretation of *Biret* as granting direct effect to DSB decisions W Berg, 'Opfer von Handelsstreitigkeiten können auf Ersatz hoffen Unternehmen können sich leichter auf WTO-Vorschriften berufen' (15 October 2003) *Frankfurter Allgemeine Zeitung* 23.

[19] Council Regulation (EC) No 1637/98 of 20 July 1998 amending Regulation (EEC) No 404/93 on the common organisation of the market in bananas [1998] OJ L210/28.

[20] Commission Regulation (EC) No 2362/98 of 28 October 1998 laying down detailed rules for the implementation of Council Regulation (EEC) No 404/93 regarding imports of bananas into the Community (Text with EEA relevance) [1998] OJ L293/32.

[21] WTO: *European Communities—Regime for the Importation, Sale and Distribution of Bananas—Report of the Appellate Body* (9 September 1997) WT/DS27/AB/R.

[22] Council Regulation (EEC) No 404/93 of 13 February 1993 on the common organization of the market in bananas [1993] OJ L47/1.

[23] WTO: *European Communities—Regime for the Importation, Sale and Distribution of Bananas—Report of the Panel* (12 April 1999) WT/DS27/RW/ECU; see G Meier, 'Bananas IV: Der Bericht des WTO-Panels vom 12.4.1999' [1999] *EuZW* 428, 428.

[24] *Léon Van Parys v BIRB* (n 2) Opinion of AG Tizzano, para 35.

In its judgment, the Court relies on its apodictic and well-established formula that 'given their nature and structure, the WTO agreements are not in principle among the rules in the light of which the Court is to review the legality of measures adopted by the Community institutions'.[25] The Court's main argument refers to the interpretation of the DSU in general and the practical implementation of the DSB ruling in the banana dispute in particular. The Court recognises that measures others than the removal of the WTO-incompatible measures could prevail on a temporary basis only. However, the Court interprets the DSU rules in a way that, even after expiry of the period of implementation of the DSB rulings, parties would continue to enjoy the scope to manoeuvre for certain solutions, such as the negotiation of monetary compensation and the adoption of retaliatory measures (Article 22 para 2 DSU), as well as the possibility laid down in Article 22 para 8 DSU to come to a 'mutually satisfactory solution'.[26] The Court not only refers to the parties' scope to find temporary alternatives to comply with the DSB ruling, but also underscores to what extent the EU had availed of this scope to manoeuvre during the banana dispute. The fact that the EU had concluded agreements with the US and Ecuador highlighted, in the Court's view, the EU's effort to bring its import regime into compliance with the DSB ruling by way of negotiations. This led the Court to conclude that the opportunity of negotiation between the parties would be 'compromised if the Community Courts were entitled to judicially review the lawfulness of the Community measures in question in light of the WTO rules upon the expiry of the time-limit'.[27] In this vein, the Court also ruled in the following judgment in *FIAMM and Fedon*. By way of reference, it reiterated its previous stance in *Biret* that special considerations apply to DSB rulings following their implementation period and stressed the hindering effect of DSB rulings as standard of review on the exercise of the powers of the legislator.[28]

## II. 'WHETHER' TO COMPLY WITH THE DSB RULING

Although the Court rightly points at one of the sensitive spots of the DSU, by stressing the scope for negotiation even *after* the expiry of the time limit, a careful analysis of the obligation to comply with the DSB ruling should distinguish between 'whether' to comply on the one hand, and 'how' or 'when' to comply on the other hand. An argument frequently raised to highlight the lack of compelling compliance pressure exerted by the DSU is to refer to Article 22 para 2 DSU, according to which besides compliance with the DSB ruling the WTO Member States retain the

[25] ibid para 39.
[26] ibid para 45f.
[27] ibid para 50.
[28] *FIAMM and FIAMM Technologies v Council and Commission* (Introduction, fn 8) I-6513, paras 120–122, 128. On the criticism of this judgment see BM Hoekman and PC Mavroidis, 'Bite the Bullet: Trade Retaliation, EU Jurisprudence and the Law and Economics of "Taking One for the Team" (2014) 20 *European Law Journal* 317, 317.

opportunity to maintain the measure in violation of WTO agreements by granting monetary compensation in return. Consequently, the party would not be obliged to comply with the DSB ruling.[29] This argument, however, does not account for the fact that Article 22 para 1 DSU only offers the temporary possibility to agree on compensation payment and that such a solution is not seen as equivalent to the removal of the WTO-inconsistent measure.[30] More specifically, the possibility to compensate is not an equivalent, but only a secondary and temporary option to react to a DSB ruling.[31] The primary obligation of the losing party is to modify or remove the non-compliant measure.[32] Article 22 para 2 DSU gives scope for negotiation for a mutually agreeable compensation, only if the losing party is unable to comply with the ruling within an appropriate time period pursuant to Article 22 para 3 DSU. This can be seen as 'compensation of delay' for being in default in bringing the measures into conformity with WTO law.[33] According to Article 22 para 8 DSU, suspension of concessions only applies until the WTO-inconsistent measure is removed. This results from Article 3 para 7 DSU, which states that 'the first objective of the dispute settlement mechanism is usually to secure the withdrawal of the measures'. This is further supported by a contextual interpretation of Article 22 DSU and Article XVI para 4 of the WTO agreements, which lays down the general obligation that each WTO Member ensures the conformity of its laws, regulations and administrative procedures with its obligations under the WTO

[29] Some scholars view the payment of compensation as alternative to the removal of WTO-incompatible measures, see *P Atlanta AG v European Community* (Introduction, fn 8) Opinion of AG Mischo, para 29; JH Bello, 'The WTO Dispute Settlement Understanding: Less is More' (1996) 90 *AJIL* 416, 417; J Berkey, 'The European Court of Justice and Direct Effect of GATT. A Question worth Revisiting' (1998) 9 *EJIL* 626, 642; T Reiff and M Florestal, 'Revenge of the Push-me, Pull-You: The Implementation Process under the WTO Dispute Settlement Understanding' (1998) 32 *International Lawyer* 755, 763; A Sykes, 'The Remedy for Breach of Obligations under the WTO Dispute Settlement Understanding: Damages or Specific Performance' in M Bronckers and R Quick (eds), *New Directions in International Economic Law: Essays in Honour of John H. Jackson* (The Hague, Kluwer Law International, 2000) 349; J Sack, 'Von der Geschlossenheit und den Spannungsfeldern in einer Weltordnung des Rechts' [1997] *EuZW* 650, 650.

[30] JH Jackson, 'The WTO Dispute Settlement Understanding—Misunderstandings on the Nature of Legal Obligations' (1997) 91 *AJIL* 60, 60; GA Zonnekeyn, 'The Bed Linen Case and its Aftermath—Some Comments on EC's "WTO Enabling Regulation"' (2002) 36 *JWT* 993, 998; PX Pierros and M Maciejewski, 'Specific Performance or Compensation and Countermeasures: Are These Alternative Means of Compliance under the WTO Dispute Settlement System' (2001) 6 *ITLR* 167, 168; S Griller, 'Enforcement and Implementation of WTO Law in the European Union' in F Breuss, S Griller and E Vranes (eds), *The Banana Dispute: An Economic and Legal Analysis* (New York, Springer, 2003) 274ff; G Berrisch and HG Kamann, 'WTO Recht im Gemeinschaftsrecht—(k)eine Kehrtwende des EuGH' [2000] *EWS* 89, 93; Wünschmann, *Gemeinschaftsrecht* (2003) (n 5) 205; Weber and Moos, 'WTO-Streitbeilegungsentscheidungen' (n 6) 235; Kuschel, 'Bananenmarktordnung' (n 6) 647; M Krajewski, *Verfassungsperspektiven und Legitimation des Rechts der Welthandelsorganisation (WTO)* (Berlin, Duncker & Humblot. 2001), 62f.

[31] Krajewski, *Verfassungsperspektiven* (2001) (n 30) 62.

[32] Jackson, 'WTO Dispute Settlement' (n 30) 63.

[33] Berrisch and Kamann, 'Gemeinschaftsrecht' (n 30) 93; Wünschmann, *Gemeinschaftsrecht* (2003) (n 5) 206; similarly Krajewski, *Verfassungsperspektiven* (2001) (n 30) 62.

agreements.[34] Compensation and suspension of concessions are by no means alternatives to compliance with WTO rules, but are considered to be a remedy of international law to sanction the breach of WTO rules.[35] The opportunity to compensate is, thus, by no means an equivalent to 'whether' to comply with the DSB ruling.[36]

## III. NO UNCONDITIONALITY REGARDING THE 'HOW' OF A COMPLIANCE OBLIGATION

Yet, even if the DSU has an unconditional character as to the 'whether' of removal of the WTO-inconsistent measure, the provisions of the DSU lack compelling force regarding 'how' the state of WTO-conformity can be reached.[37] First, the possibility of compensation granted under Article 22 DSU gives the parties to the dispute the opportunity to temporarily not to comply with the DSB ruling. Even if Article 22 DSU does not exempt the parties on 'whether' to comply with the ruling, there is scope to manoeuvre on when to comply.[38] This temporary scope to manoeuvre would be compromised, if the parties would be forced to comply with the DSB ruling based on a national court ruling applying the DSB ruling in order to override national acts.[39] In other words, the recognition of the direct effect of

[34] Wünschmann, *Gemeinschaftsrecht* (2003) (n 5) 206; for a critical view see Krajewski, *Verfassungsperspektiven* (2001) (n 30) 58; PT Stoll, 'Freihandel und Verfassung. Einzelstaatliche Gewährleistung und die konstitutionelle Funktion der Welthandelsordnung' (1997) 57 *ZaöRV* 83-14, 128 considers this obligation to reflect the parties' intention to make the provision directly effective.

[35] Berkey, 'Direct Effect of GATT' (n 29) 644; Schmid, 'Status des GATT/WTO' (Introduction, fn 7) 196; Eeckhout, 'Domestic Legal Status' (ch 1, n 7) 54; E-U Petersmann, 'GATT/WTO-Recht: Dublik' [1997] *EuZW* 651, 653.

[36] Similarly JH Jackson, 'Designing and Implementing Effective Dispute Settlement Procedures: WTO Dispute Settlement, Appraisal and Prospects' in A Krueger (ed), *The WTO as an International Organization* (Chicago, University of Chicago Press, 1998) 169; Jackson, 'WTO Dispute Settlement' (n 30) 60ff; Zonnekeyn, 'WTO Law in the EC Legal Order' (ch 1, fn 7) 123; S Griller, 'Judicial Enforceability of WTO Law in the European Union. Annotation to Case C-149/96, Portugal vs. Council' (2000) 3 *JIEL* 441, 452; W Schroeder and P Schonard, 'Die Effektivität des WTO-Streitbeilegungssystems' [2001] *RIW* 658, 660; T Oppermann, 'Die Europäische Gemeinschaft und Union in der Welthandelsorganisation (WTO)' [1995] *RIW* 919, 924; A Becker-Celik, 'Ist die Ablehnung der unmittelbaren Anwendbarkeit der GATT-Vorschriften durch den EuGH heute noch gerechtfertigt?' [1997] *EWS* 12, 14.

[37] Similarly, but with different arguments, P Koutrakos, *EU International Relations Law*, 2nd edn (Oxford, Hart Publishing, 2015), 297; P Royla, 'WTO-Recht—EG-Recht: Kollision, Justiziabilität, Implementation' [2001] *EuR* 495, 511; S Hörmann and G Göttsche, 'Die Haftung der EG für WTO-Rechtsverletzungen—Neue Tendenzen in der EuGH-Rechtsprechung?' [2003] *RIW* 689, 693; Thies, 'Biret and beyond' (n 6) 1669; Meng, 'Rechtsstellung der Individuen' (n 6) 85; Wünschmann, *Gemeinschaftsrecht* (2003) (n 5) 205; Krajewski, *Verfassungsperspektiven* (2001) (n 30) 66ff; Ott, *GATT und WTO* (1997) (n 5) 179; A Rosas, 'Case C-149/96, Portugal v. Council. Judgment of the Full Court of 23 November 1999, nyr' (2000) 37 *CML Rev* 797, 808ff.

[38] See Art 21 para 3 DSU and Trachtman, 'World Trade Organization' (Introduction, fn 7) 668f.

[39] T Cottier, 'Dispute Settlement in the World Trade Organization: Characteristics and Structural Implications for the European Union' (1998) 35 *CML Rev* 325, 373f; A Davies, 'Bananas, Private Challenges, the Courts and the Legislature' (2002) 21 *YEL* 299, 317; Weber and Moos, 'WTO-Streitbeilegungsentscheidungen' (n 6) 235; Wünschmann, *Gemeinschaftsrecht* (2003) (n 5) 207; similarly Krajewski, *Verfassungsperspektiven* (2001) (n 30) 67.

DSB decisions would undermine the opportunities granted under international law, because the direct effect would enable national courts to apply the DSB ruling.[40] But even for the period following the expiry of the time limit, a systematic interpretation of the DSU does not determine an unconditional point in time when compliance with the DSB ruling must have been reached. Article 22 para 2 sent 2 DSU stipulates that after the expiry of the implementation period, the party may request authorisation from the DSB to suspend the application to the Member concerned of concessions. However, Article 22 para 8 sent 1 DSU provides that even after the authorisation of suspension of concessions by the DSB, the losing party may 'provide a solution to the nullification or impairment of benefits' or to achieve an otherwise 'mutually satisfactory solution'.[41] Article 22 para 8 DSU is silent on the possible content of such a solution. A systematic interpretation of sentences 1 and 2 of Article 22 para 8 DSU shows that this cannot refer to monetary compensation.

Different considerations could apply, if one follows the reasoning developed by the Advocate General, Tizzano, in *Léon van Parys*. According to him, the DSB changes the dispute 'by limiting the parties' freedom to seek alternative negotiated solutions', because the 'solutions too must remain with the framework of the WTO rules and, consequently within the DSB decision'.[42] In that vein, he invokes the order of Article 3 para 5 DSU, which prescribes that all solutions must be compatible with the WTO provisions.[43] Thus, the content of the DSB ruling stating the violation of the WTO provisions is decisive. After expiry of the implementation period, there would no longer be any negotiation position that could be compromised, because the parties are not allowed to agree on continuation of the WTO violation. Based on these considerations, the Advocate General concludes that it is impossible that 'in a 'Community governed by law', DSB decisions must be considered as a criterion of the legality of Community measures'.[44]

One can follow the Advocate General's reasoning in one regard: if the negotiated solution is not allowed to substantially deviate from the DSB ruling, this would be an argument for a direct effect of the decision, since it has the unconditional and precise character and the room for negotiation would factually be precluded. However, the alleged restriction of the parties' freedom to seek alternative solutions can only exist, if the DSB decision contains a sufficiently precise normative order as to what the WTO compatible solution is—and only if it is clear that no alternative to negotiations exists. Yet, this is not the case in practice: the Panel and Appellate Body typically undertake a judicial review leading to a

[40] Cottier, 'Dispute Settlement' (n 39) 372ff; Trachtman, 'World Trade Organization' (Introduction, fn 7) 669; Wünschmann, *Gemeinschaftsrecht* (2003) (n 5) 207.

[41] See also W Weiß, 'Das Streitbeilegungsverfahren' in C Herrmann, W Weiß and C Ohler (eds), *Welthandelsrecht*, 2nd edn (München, CH Beck, 2007) § 10, 140, para 327.

[42] *Léon Van Parys v BIRB* (n 2) Opinion of AG Tizzano, para 57; for the following see Steinbach, 'WTO-Streitbeilegungsentscheidungen' (n 3) 332ff.

[43] *Léon Van Parys v BIRB* (n 2) Opinion of AG Tizzano, para 55, fn 37.

[44] ibid Opinion of AG Tizzano, para 73.

finding on the violation or impairment of certain obligations, which the losing party is obliged to remove according to Article 19 DSU. Importantly, the DSB usually confines itself to stating the violation, without giving clear instructions as to *how* compliance should be reached.[45] This self-restriction of the DSB corresponds to the two-tier structure of the *pacta sunt servanda* principle, according to which international treaty law must be implemented in national law in terms of its objective ('obligation of objectives'), but states retain the freedom of choice regarding the means to implement the objective ('freedom of means').[46] As an expression of the 'freedom of means', the losing party can exercise its discretion as to the precise means it considers appropriate to reach a WTO-compliant situation.[47] Yet, if the DSB lacks precision as to which measures are considered WTO compliant, the decision can hardly limit the parties' freedom to seek alternative negotiated solutions—the 'how' to reach WTO compliance is not determined by the ruling and thus cannot compromise the parties' freedom to negotiate potential solutions. The arguments put forward by the Advocate General, Tizzano, are ultimately not convincing, because they impede the scope for negotiated solutions following expiry of the implementation period.

Thus, even if there is unconditionality regarding 'whether' to comply, it remains a general principle of the dispute settlement mechanism to promote—provisionally and temporarily—a mutually satisfactory solution, even after expiry of the implementation period set by the DSB.[48] There is no unconditionality regarding the 'when' and 'how' of implementation.[49] The only condition attached to such solution is, as can be taken from Article 3 para 5, that it is compatible with the DSB ruling. However, there is no precise time period following the expiry of which the parties could no longer deviate from the obligation to comply. If one were to accord the direct effect to the DSB decision at the moment of expiry of the implementation period, the legislative institutions of the EU would be deprived of their

[45] T Cottier, 'Das Streitschlichtungsverfahren in der Welthandelsorganisation: Wesenszüge und Herausforderungen' in P-C Müller-Graff (ed), *Die Europäische Gemeinschaft in der Welthandelsorganisation: Globalisierung und Weltmarktrecht als Herausforderung für Europa*, 1st edn (Baden-Baden, Nomos, 1999/2000) 186; Hinderer, *Rechtsschutz* (2004) (n 5) 442f; T Gabler, *Das Streitbeilegungssystem der WTO und seine Auswirkungen auf das Antidumping-Recht der Europäischen Gemeinschaft* (Frankfurt am Main, P Lang, 1997), 143; different view Weber and Moos, 'WTO-Streitbeilegungsentscheidungen' (n 6) 234f.

[46] Wünschmann, *Gemeinschaftsrecht* (2003) (n 5) 55; Winter, 'Direct Applicability' (ch 1, fn 1) 426; similarly already *Hauptzollamt Mainz v Kupferberg* (n 7) para 18; also, the European Court of Human Rights typically exercises judicial restraint in merely declaring a violation of the Convention, even though there are judgments in which the European Court of Human Rights is more specific as to what measures are necessary for compliance, see E Lambert Abdelgawad, 'The Execution of the Judgments of the European Court of Human Rights: Towards a Non-coercive and Participatory Model of Accountability' (2009) 69 *ZaöRV* 471.

[47] Gabler, *Streitbeilegungssystem der WTO* (1997) (n 45) 84.

[48] See Art 3 para 7 sent 3 DSU.

[49] See for the identical result but with different arguments Pitschas, 'Hormonfleisch' (n 16) 762; Royla, 'WTO-Recht' (n 37) 511; Hörmann and Göttsche, 'Haftung' (n 37) 693; Meng, 'Rechtsstellung der Individuen' (n 6) 85; Krajewski, *Verfassungsperspektiven* (2001) (n 30) 66ff; Rosas, 'Case C-149/96' (n 37) 808ff.

leeway to find other solutions within the meaning of Article 22 para 8 DSU.[50] In light of the flexibility on the implementation of the DSB ruling, there can be no direct effect of this decision within the national legal order. This finding is in line with the jurisprudence of the CJEU, the roots of which can be traced to the Court's reasoning in *Portugal v Council* on the lack of a binding and unconditional character of the dispute settlement mechanism.[51]

If the DSB lacks a direct effect even after expiry of the implementation period, an explicit EU measure intended to implement the DSB decision remains possible as grounds for a liability claim.[52] In line with its established case law, there may be an exception to the general rule of WTO law not having any direct effect.[53] Indeed, the Court recognises WTO law as the legality standard for EU secondary law, if the secondary act is explicitly 'intended to comply with its international obligations' (*Nakajima*)[54] or if the respective EU act refers to specific WTO provisions (*Fediol III*).[55] The EU act then serves as a transforming act for WTO law to become the standard of legal review, and thereby indirectly applicable.[56] In the context of the repeated attempts by the EU to modify its banana market regulation in light of DSB rulings, there has been a debate on whether the Court failed to apply the Nakajima doctrine accurately.[57] This relates to the difficulty in assessing the intention of the EU policymaker to implement WTO law, and the criteria used to identify the policymaker's intent encompassing both objective and subjective factors.[58] Similarly problematic is the question of which criteria need to be met in order to

[50] This argument had already been put forward by the Court in order to highlight the parties' freedom to choose between compensation and compliance in Case C-149/96 *Portugal v Council* [1999] ECR I-8395, para 46; Cottier, 'Direct Effect' (ch 1, fn 7) 111; W Weiß, 'Zur Haftung der EG für die Verletzung des WTO-Rechts' [2005] *EuR* 277, 285; for a different view see Schroeder and Schonard, 'WTO-Streitbeilegungssystem' (n 36) 662, who seem not to take into account that the lack of alternatives to WTO conformity does not, as such, deprive the parties of any scope of manoeuvre regarding how to reach the WTO-compliant state.

[51] *Portugal v Council* (n 50) para 40; confirmed in *Léon Van Parys v BIRB* (n 2) para 42.

[52] GA Zonnekeyn, 'The Latest On Indirect Effect of WTO Law In The EC Legal Order. The Nakajima Case Law Misjudged?' (2001) 4 *JIEL* 597, 600ff; Zonnekeyn, 'EC Liability' (n 16) 489f; Hörmann and Göttsche, 'Haftung' (n 37) 695ff; Royla, 'WTO-Recht' (n 37) 506f.

[53] Wünschmann, *Gemeinschaftsrecht* (2003) (n 5) 205.

[54] On the GATT 1947 for the first time in Case C-69/89 *Nakajima v Council* [1991] ECR I-2069, para 2; confirmed later for the WTO agreements in *Portugal v Council* (n 50) I-8425, para 49.

[55] On the GATT 1947 for the first time in Case 70/87 *Fediol v Commission* [1989] ECR 1781, 1830f, confirmed later for the WTO agreements in *Portugal v Council* (n 50) I-8425, para 49.

[56] See also Weiß, 'Verletzung des WTO-Rechts' (n 50) 288.

[57] See, for example, Steinbach, 'WTO-Streitbeilegungsentscheidungen' (n 3) 331ff; W Berg and J Beck, 'Zur jüngsten Rechtsprechung der Gemeinschaftsgerichte zur unmittelbaren Anwendung von WTO-Recht im Gemeinschaftsrecht' [2005] *RIW* 401, 401ff; S Peers, 'WTO Dispute Settlement and Community Law' (2001) 26 *EL Rev* 605, 611; Davies, 'Bananas' (n 39) 312; Hörmann and Göttsche, 'Haftung' (n 37) 695; Zonnekeyn, 'EC Liability' (ch 1, fn 35) 261; *Léon Van Parys v BIRB* (n 2) Opinion of AG Tizzano, para 99ff.

[58] Similarly F Snyder, 'The Gatekeepers: The European Courts and WTO Law' (2003) 40 *CML Rev* 313, 347: 'it emphasizes subjective rather than objective factors'; CJ Hermes, *TRIPS im Gemeinschaftsrecht* (Berlin, Duncker & Humblot, 2002), 172f; on the criticism that the criteria would be too subjective M Montanà I Mora, 'Equilibrium: A Rediscovered Basis for the Court of Justice of the European Communities to Refuse Direct Effect to the Uruguay Round Agreements?' (1996) 30 *JWT* 43, 47.

prove *Nakajima*, that is to show that 'the Community intended to implement a particular obligation assumed in the context of the WTO'.[59]

In sum, an interpretation of the DSU in light of the distinction between 'whether' and 'how' DSB rulings have to be complied with, we conclude that there remains a certain degree of flexibility. Even though the DSU rules are unconditional, in the sense that DSB rulings must eventually be complied with, there remains a certain leeway as to how and when compliance must be achieved. In that vein, Article 22 para 1 DSU only allows for temporary agreement on compensation rather than compliance, without compensation being an equivalent to compliance with the DSB ruling. However, Article 22 DSU offers leeway as to *when* the national legislation must be brought into conformity with the DSB ruling and this flexibility goes beyond the expiry of the time limit set by the DSB. The EU legislative organs would be significantly compromised in their leeway to find alternative temporary solutions within the meaning of Article 22 para 8 DSU, if the DSB ruling would be accorded a direct effect after the expiry of the implementation period.

[59] *Portugal v Council* (n 50) I-8425, para 49.

# 3

# *Dispensability of Direct Effect for EU Liability*

## I. INTRODUCTION

THE FOREGOING ANALYSIS has shown that we cannot rely on directly effective DSB decisions as grounds for liability. This leads to the question whether the notion of direct effect is dispensable as an element of liability, and that it is rather the violation of EU law which forms the basis of an action for damages. This part of the study will focus on using the established principles of the *Francovich* doctrine, in order to assess whether a liability for WTO violations can be founded without requiring any direct effect. To that end, the genuine differences between an action for annulment and an action for damages will be shown, in order to support the decoupling of direct effect and liability. However, before exploring the parallelism between *Francovich* and EU liability for WTO violation, we need to study the alleged strong link between direct effect and WTO violations, which both jurisprudence and parts of the literature have supported in the past.

### A. The direct effect of WTO law as a liability prerequisite

On several occasions, the CJEU has underlined its stance to view direct effect as an unsurmountable hurdle for liability claims. Conceptually, the reason for doing so lies in the general requirement for an action for damage (as described above)[1] that a 'norm intended to confer rights upon individuals'[2] must have been violated. The Court ties this requirement to the concept of direct effect, as it made clear in *Atlanta*:[3]

> There is in this regard an inescapable and direct link between the WTO decision and the plea of breach of the provisions of GATT, raised by the appellant before the Court of First Instance and not repeated by it in its pleas on appeal. Such a decision could only be taken into consideration if the Court of Justice had found GATT to have direct effect in the context of a plea alleging the invalidity of the common organisation of the market.

[1] See above Ch 1 V.
[2] Case C-352/98 P *Bergaderm and Goupil v Commission* [2000] ECR I-5291, para 42.
[3] *P Atlanta AG v European Community* (Introduction, fn 8) paras 19–20.

Similarly, the indispensability of a directly effective DSB decision, as a requirement for conferring rights upon individuals, has been put forward in *Cordis Obst*, *T Port* and *Bocchi*, where German importers of bananas sued for damages they suffered due to the WTO inconsistency of the banana market regulations. The General Court stated in all three judgments (using identical wording):

> It is clear from that judgment that as the WTO rules are not in principle intended to confer rights on individuals, the Community cannot incur non-contractual liability as a result of infringement of them.[4]

Also, in *Chiquita* the General Court found the WTO not to be suitable for serving as a legality standard for the decisions by EU institutions and could thus not be the grounds for liability.[5] Finally, the strong link between the conferral of individual rights and the direct effect was also at the core of the Court's reasoning in *Biret*. The General Court had referred to well-established jurisprudence, according to which:

> individuals cannot rely on them before the courts and that any infringement of them will not give rise to non-contractual liability on the part of the Community.[6]

In its appeal decision, the Court did not contradict this finding. Rather, its critical comments vis-à-vis the General Court's ruling were limited to the necessity of assessing the direct effect of DSB rulings independently from the direct effect of the underlying WTO agreements.[7]

To conclude from this line of jurisprudence, there is a strong link between the general requirement of damage claims of having a norm 'intended to confer rights' and the direct effect of WTO rules or the DSB decision. The generous stance the CJEU takes on other occasions when applying the term 'intended to confer rights' to the end that individual interests would need to be protected only indirectly,[8] is not the one the Court takes when considering liability of WTO violations. Rather, the Court equates a 'norm intended to confer rights upon individuals' within the meaning of the *Schöppenstedt*-formula, with the direct effect of an international treaty. This equation will be one main point of criticism to be developed throughout this chapter: from a doctrinal perspective, the notion of direct effect must be distinguished from the question of whether and the prerequisites under which a norm intends to confer rights upon individuals.[9] The scope of norms serving individual interests (directly or indirectly) goes beyond the protection of individual rights enshrined in direct effect norms.

[4] *Cordis Obst v Commission* (Introduction, fn 8) para 51; *Bocchi Food Trade International v Commission* (Introduction, fn 8) para 56; *T Port GmbH & Co v Commission* (Introduction, fn 8) para 51.

[5] *Chiquita v Commission* (Introduction, fn 8) para 114.

[6] Case T-174/00 *Biret International v Council* [2002] ECR II-17, para 71.

[7] *Biret International v Council* (Introduction, fn 8) para 60.

[8] *Kampffmeyer and Others v Commission* (ch 1, fn 49) 354; *CNTA v Commission* (ch 1, fn 28) 549; Ossenbühl and Cornils, *Staatshaftungsrecht* (2013) (ch 1, fn 23) 607; Gellermann (ch 1, fn 48) Art 340 TFEU, para 20; Ruffert (ch 1, fn 27) Art 340 TFEU, para 13.

[9] See also Ruffert (ch 1, fn 27) Art 340 TFEU, para 16ff.

Astonishingly, the Court's abandoning of the previous *Schöppenstedt*-line of jurisprudence regarding the criterion of conferral of individual rights has provoked comparatively little criticism in literature.[10] Many scholars in literature follow the restrictive position of the Court and do not raise doubts vis-à-vis the transfer of direct effect from the context of an annulment proceeding to a suit for damages. More specifically, it has been argued that individuals can derive individual rights from international agreements under very limited conditions only, and that the notion of direct effect would be the only conceptual approach available—this would also apply on the level of secondary legal redress (ie, for liability claims).[11] In his opinion rendered in *Biret*, Advocate General Alber found that direct effect would also be decisive in a liability claim, because the individual would invoke an infringement of a specific provision.[12] Likewise, some commentators apply the general concept of direct effect to liability proceedings and since the WTO rules lack direct effect, there would be no grounds for them to accept liability. A similar understanding is reflected in the opinion of Advocate General Mayras in *Stimming*, who raised doubts as to the individual being able to invoke GATT provisions and thus precludes liability of the EU.[13]

There are two reasons why strictly transferring the requirement of direct effect into the context of damage claims appears questionable. First, there is virtually no argument made as to why a liability suit, which does not alter the validity of a certain EU act (unlike under the annulment proceedings that are aimed at removing that specific measure), would have to rely on the concept of direct effect.[14] Indeed, the legal implications of direct effect are strongest if they result in an annulment of a certain measure, while compensation does not have such wide-reaching

[10] An exception is Schoißwohl, 'Haftung' (ch 1, fn 8) 697ff; Hinderer, *Rechtsschutz* (2004) (ch 2, fn 5) 450ff; other supporters of a liability of the EU for WTO breaches rather argue in favor of direct effect of DSB decisions or the application of the Nakajima-doctrine, see Reinisch, 'Opfer des Hormon- und Bananenstreites' (Introduction, fn 7) 48; Peers, 'WTO Dispute Settlement' (ch 2, fn 57) 614f; Lavranos, 'WTO-Recht' (ch 2, fn 6) 296; Görgens, *Außervertragliche Haftung* (2006) (ch 2, fn 5) 117; Zonnekeyn, 'EC Liability' (ch 2, fn 16) 483ff; *Biret International v Council* (Introduction, fn 8) Opinion of AG Alber, para 103; Davies, 'Bananas' (ch 2, fn 39) 326.

[11] H-J Prieß and G Berrisch, *WTO-Handbuch* (München, CH Beck, 2003), 764, para 28; Wünschmann, *Gemeinschaftsrecht* (2003) (ch 2, fn 5) 231; similarly AV Bogdandy, 'Legal Effects of World Trade Organization Decisions Within European Union Law: A Contribution to the Theory of the Legal Acts of International Organizations and the Action for Damages Under Article 288(2) EC' (2005) 39 *JWT* 45, 58; Davies, 'Bananas' (ch 2, fn 39) 325f; Höher, *Haftung* (2006) (ch 2, fn 5) 329ff.

[12] *Biret International v Council* (Introduction, fn 8) Opinion of AG Alber, para 49, who argues in favor of a direct effect of DSB decisions; by contrast, other commentators provide no explanation at all for transferring direct effect into the liability context, see Hermes, *TRIPS* (2002) (ch 2, fn 58) 163; Meng, 'Rechtsstellung der Individuen' (ch 2, fn 6) 92f.

[13] Case 90/77 *Stimming v Commission* [1978] ECR 995, Opinion of AG Mayras, 1016.

[14] Similarly the criticism raised by J Wiers, 'One Day, You are Gonna Pay: The European Court of Justice in Biret' (2004) 31 *LIEI* 143, 147f; Reinisch, 'Opfer des Hormon- und Bananenstreites' (Introduction, fn 7) 47; Schoißwohl, 'Haftung' (ch 1, fn 8) 697; M Herdegen, *Europarecht*, 17th edn (München, CH Beck 2015), 485f; Weiß, 'Verletzung des WTO-Rechts' (ch 2, fn 50) 297, taking this aspect into account but still requiring direct effect as precondition for a liability claim as well as Bogdandy, 'Legal Effects' (n 11) 58.

consequences. Actions for annulment and damages have fundamentally different goals: the action of annulment pursuant to Article 263 TFEU aims at removing the EU act, while the action for damages based on Article 288 TFEU only regulates financial effects accruing from the unlawfulness of a certain measure, while preserving the validity of the measure concerned. Put differently, functions and goals of these two proceedings are fundamentally different and this lays the ground for discussing the dispensability of direct effect in a liability proceeding.

Second, by invoking the *Francovich*-doctrine, one may question whether the requirement of direct effect for compensation claims is in line with the Court's well-established jurisprudence on Member States' liability for breaches of EU law.[15] There is no direct effect requirement in the context of Member States' liability. We thus have to explore whether the doctrinal foundations underlying the EU liability regime can support a delinking of direct effect from liability claims in the context of WTO violations.

## B. Francovich and delinking direct effect from liability

In *Francovich*, the Court ruled that, notwithstanding the lack of direct effect of the insolvency directive, Italy would be obliged to compensate those damages that accrued to individuals due to its failure to implement the directive in a timely manner, precluding the individuals from seizing the rights enshrined in the directive.[16] According to the Court, individuals being able to invoke directly effective provisions of the EU treaties only provides a minimum guarantee, but does not suffice in comprehensively applying the EU treaties.[17] If the individual rights foreseen in the directive lack direct effect and cannot, for precisely this reason, offer primary legal redress by way of a proceeding for annulment, *Francovich* laid the grounds to seek at least compensation. Granting compensation bridges the gap between the Member States' obligation to implement the directive and the lacking right of the individual to effectively claim the implementation.[18] *Francovich* thus decouples individual rights from the notion of direct effect.[19] The pivotal issue

[15] In this vein, some approaches are offered by Hinderer, *Rechtsschutz* (2004) (ch 2, n 5) 453ff; Schoißwohl, 'Haftung' (ch 1, fn 8) 700ff; Peers, 'WTO Dispute Settlement' (ch 2, fn 57) 612; P Gasparon, 'The Transposition of the Principle of Member States Liability into the Context of External Relations' (1999) 10 *EJIL* 605, 619ff.

[16] Joined Cases C-6/90 and C-9/90 *Francovich v Italy* [1991] ECR I-5357, I-5407, para 10ff.

[17] Case 168/85 *Commission v Italy* [1986] ECR 2945, para 11; Case C-120/88 *Commission v Italy* [1991] ECR I-621, para 10; Case C-119/89 *Commission v Spain* [1991] ECR I-641, para 9; M Deckert, 'Zur Haftung des Mitgliedstaates bei Verstößen seiner Organe gegen europäisches Gemeinschaftsrecht' [1997] *EuR* 203, 216.

[18] Henrichs, *Haftung* (1995) (ch 1, fn 50) 56.

[19] D Curtin, 'State Liability under Community Law: A New Remedy for Private Parties' (1992) 21 *ILJ* 74, 78f; H-G Fischer, 'Staatshaftung nach Gemeinschaftsrecht' [1992] *EuZW* 41, 43; U Diehr, *Der Staatshaftungsanspruch des Bürgers wegen Verletzung des Gemeinschaftsrechts durch die deutsche öffentliche Gewalt* (Frankfurt am Main, P Lang, 1997), 95; M Ross, 'Beyond Francovich' (1993) 56 *MLR* 55, 57;

for granting compensation in *Francovich* has been the directive's aim to accord certain rights to individuals—this term has to be distinguished from direct effect: Even if the latter does not exist, it still remains possible that a legal provision grants rights to individuals.[20] In other words, the directive does not necessarily need to grant a 'full right' to the individuals, in the sense that the individual would be able to directly invoke this right before a court. For a liability claim to be successful, it suffices that the directive seeks to confer certain (not directly applicable) rights to individuals.[21] In this vein, it could be sufficient that a certain identifiable interest exists, which may even be only a 'not-yet-right' or prospective right.[22]

The crucial question for the purpose of this analysis is, therefore: can the doctrinal move performed by the Court in *Francovich* by decoupling liability and direct effect be contextualised in a way that it can also be applied to the issue of liability of noncompliance with WTO DSB rulings? If the answer were in the affirmative, it would further need to be examined whether the DSB decision confers individual rights, in the sense that a certain identifiable right or individual interest can be derived from that decision. More specifically, transferring *Francovich* into the WTO context requires a parallel application of the three fundamental pillars bearing the *Francovich* approach, notably the principle of *effet utile*, the notion of legal redress accruing from the rule of law and the loyalty principles laid down in Article 4 para 3 TEU.

## II. EFFET UTILE AND ARTICLE 216 PARA 2 TFEU

Exploring *Francovich* and the basis for delinking direct effect and action for damages dictates the approach for examination as follows: the three pillars of *Francovich* (*effet utile*, legal redress, loyalty principle) are going to be assessed in view of their transferability into the context of liability claims for WTO breaches.

The first layer of *Francovich* was the notion of *effet utile*, according to which the 'right to reparation is the necessary corollary of the direct effect of the Community provision whose breach caused the damage sustained'.[23] The argument

G Betlem and E Rood, 'Francovich-aansprakelijkheid' [1992] *NJB* 250, 252; G Bebr, 'Joined Cases C-6/90 and 9/90, Francovich v. Italy, Bonifaci v. Italy Judgment of the Court of Justice of 19 November 1991' (1992) 29 *CML Rev* 557, 576.

[20] *Francovich v Italy* (n 16) Opinion of AG Mischo, para 60; Diehr, *Staatshaftungsanspruch* (1997) (n 19) 95; F Russo Spena, 'La Corte di giustizia ridefinisce la responsabilità degli Stati membri per violazione del diritto comunitario' [1992] *RIDPC* 163, 166; J Geiger, 'Die Entwicklung eines europäischen Staatshaftungsanspruchsrechts' [1993] *DVBl* 465, 468.

[21] Diehr, *Staatshaftungsanspruch* (1997) (n 19) 95.

[22] S Kopp, 'Staatshaftung wegen Verletzung von Gemeinschaftsrecht' [1994] *DÖV* 201, 204; M Cornils, *Der gemeinschaftsrechtliche Staatshaftungsanspruch*, 1st edn (Baden-Baden, Nomos, 1995), 232; *Francovich v Italy* (n 16) Opinion of AG Mischo, I-5391, para 60.

[23] Joined Cases C-46/93 and C-48/93 *Brasserie du Pêcheur v Germany and Rv Secretary of State for Transport, ex parte Factortame III* [1996] ECR I-1029, para 22.

of practical effectiveness[24] is closely tied to the conferral of individual rights as accorded by EU law[25] and which ultimately seeks to ensure both legal protection and the safeguarding of substantial EU law provisions.[26] However, the term 'practical effectiveness' has a meaning beyond the aim of legal protection. Practical effectiveness is more comprehensive and aims at full realisation of EU law in all aspects.[27] In respect of the violation of WTO rules by non-implementation of DSB rulings, the question arises whether in this context EU law must be brought into practical effectiveness to the extent that a liability claim should be recognised, notwithstanding a lack of direct effect of the DSB ruling. Article 216 para 2 TFEU would be the legal basis to which the principle of *effet utile* is applied. According to this norm, agreements concluded by the Union are binding upon its institutions and Member States. Comparison with *Francovich* highlights that *effet utile* is not applied to the individual rights and interests protected by the DSB ruling, but rather to the obligation of the EU to comply with an international agreement (in this case: implementation of the DSB ruling) laid down in Article 216 para 2 TFEU. This is underlined by the analogy with *Francovich*: in that case, Article 189 para 3 EEC (now Article 288 TFEU) was the relevant norm to which the principle of practical effectiveness was applied, because if a:

> Member State fails to fulfil its obligation under the third paragraph of Article 189 of the Treaty to take all the measures necessary to achieve the result prescribed by a directive, the full effectiveness of that rule of Community law requires that there should be a right to reparation provided that three conditions are fulfilled.[28]

Consequently, it is the provision of EU primary law, which has to be interpreted in light of the *effet utile* principle, while the DSB ruling—as was the content of the directive in *Francovich*—will be considered only when the question of individual rights and interests is at stake.

In literature, criticism has been repeatedly voiced according to which the EU would ignore the normative command of Article 216 para 2 TFEU when breaching WTO rules and, in particular, not bringing EU secondary law into conformity

[24] On the interchangeable use of terms such as 'useful effect', 'practical effectiveness' or 'spirit and purpose' see R Streinz, '"Der effet utile" in der Rechtsprechung des Gerichtshofs der Europäischen Gemeinschafts' in O Due, M Lutter and J Schwarze (eds), *Festschrift für Ulrich Everling*, 1st edn (Baden-Baden, Nomos, 1995) 1495; see also HD Jarass, 'Voraussetzungen der innerstaatlichen Wirkung von EG-Richtlinien' [1990] *NJW* 2420, 2422.

[25] Since *van Gend & Loos* and *Costa/ENEL*, the CJEU has been stressing the task of the Court to ensure the full effectiveness of EU law and to protect individuals' rights. In this vein, the Court decided in *Simmenthal* that national courts were obliged to apply EU law within the scope of their competence and to protect individuals' rights by not applying national rules incompatible with EU law, see Streinz, 'Effet Utile' (n 24) 1498f; Geiger, 'Staatshaftungsanspruchsrechts' (n 20) 468.

[26] F Snyder, 'The Effectiveness of European Community Law: Institutions, Processes, Tools and Techniques' (1993) 56 *MLR* 19, 46; Henrichs, *Haftung* (1995) (ch 1, fn 50) 62.

[27] Ross, 'Francovich' (n 19) 61.

[28] *Francovich v Italy* (n 16) I-5415, para 39 of the judgment, while the Court refers in para 33 to the 'full effectivenes of Community rules' without specifying to which rules the Court refers.

with DSB rulings.[29] Less frequently, this criticism is articulated in a way to hint at the tension between this continuous practice of non-compliance with DSB rulings and the principle of practical effectiveness.[30] Given the widespread criticism on the disrespect of Article 216 para 2 TFEU, it is surprising that hitherto there appears to be no doctrinal analysis of this tension.[31] The few studies examining this issue came to the conclusion that *effet utile* cannot be invoked for the purpose of liability for WTO breaches, because this would exert pressure on EU institutions to comply with international treaty law, which would be tantamount to limiting the institutions' discretion.[32] This argument (which resembles the argument referred to above on why DSB rulings cannot be considered directly effective, given the flexibility granted under the DSU) would appear less persuasive, if an interpretation of Article 216 para 2 TFEU would require the EU to implement DSB decisions.

## A. The duty to implement DSB rulings

Does Article 216 para 2 TFEU command an obligation to bring EU secondary law into compliance with international agreements similar to the command of Article 288 TFEU requiring Member States to implement directives as put forward by the Court in *Francovich*? Given that in *Francovich* liability was linked to an omission (ie, non-implementation of the directive), one has to identify a legal obligation to act in a specific way.[33] If this were the case, in a following step, one has to examine whether the EU principle of *effet utile* can be applied to Article 216 para 2 TFEU, to the end that liability would be the legal consequence of an omission of the obligation to act.

### i. *Article 216 TFEU and international law treaties*

Assessing whether Article 216 para 2 TFEU imposes an obligation on EU institutions to implement DSB rulings requires scrutiny of the general relationship of this provision in relation to international agreements. Again, the foregoing distinction between bindingness and direct effect must be recalled.[34] While bindingness

[29] E-U Petersmann, 'Grundfragen der Beteiligung der Europäischen Gemeinschaft an der Welthandelsorganisation' in P-C Müller-Graff (ed), *Die Europäische Gemeinschaft in der Welthandelsorganisation: Globalisierung und Weltmarktrecht als Herausforderung für Europa*, 1st edn (Baden-Baden, Nomos, 1999/2000) 85f; M Hilf, 'Grundfragen der Beteiligung der EG an der WTO' in P-C Müller-Graff (ed), *Die Europäische Gemeinschaft in der Welthandelsorganisation: Globalisierung und Weltmarktrecht als Herausforderung für Europa*, 1st edn (Baden-Baden, Nomos, 1999/2000) 93f; Cascante, *Rechtsschutz* (2003) (ch 2, fn 6) 295f.

[30] Lavranos, 'WTO-Recht' (ch 2, fn 6) 293; Schoißwohl, 'Haftung' (ch 1, fn 8) 707.

[31] One approach in this regard is provided by Hinderer, *Rechtsschutz* (2004) (ch 2, fn 5) 460ff.

[32] Schoißwohl, 'Haftung' (ch 1, fn 8) 703; Görgens, *Außervertragliche Haftung* (2006) (ch 2, fn 5) 91f.

[33] Lavranos, 'WTO-Recht' (ch 2, fn 6) 295.

[34] See above ch 1 I.

within the meaning of Article 216 para 2 TFEU characterises the status of the agreement in the EU legal order and its consequences, direct effect implies the invocability of individuals of the agreement, which then serves as a standard of legality review.[35] It is widely acknowledged that Article 216 para 2 TFEU does not regulate the direct effect of an international agreement in the EU legal order, but is limited to stipulate the validity and bindingness of the agreement.[36]

More generally, Article 216 para 2 TFEU cannot be interpreted as 'unionising' international treaties—rather these agreements maintain the public international law character, also after being incorporated into the EU legal order.[37] This does not mean that Article 216 para 2 TFEU is merely declaratory and only repeats the principle of 'pacta sunt servanda',[38] given that the EU is bound by this principle of public international law even without the command of Article 216 TFEU.[39] The normative force of Article 216 para 2 TFEU lies in that it extends the order of bindingness from the interstate sphere of international law to address also EU institutions and Member States, and thus makes the bindingness an order of EU law going beyond the international law obligation.[40] Hence, EU institutions and Member States have to observe international agreements as they do EU law,[41] because the agreements have become part of the EU legal order.[42]

[35] Similarly A Bleckmann, *Begriff und Kriterien der innerstaatlichen Anwendbarkeit völkerrechtlicher Verträge* (Berlin, Duncker & Humblot, 1970), 57ff; Krajewski, *Verfassungsperspektiven* (2001) (ch 2, fn 30) 54; A Koller, *Die unmittelbare Anwendbarkeit völkerrechtlicher Verträge und des EWG-Vertrages im innerstaatlichen Bereich* (Bern, Stämpfli, 1971), 119ff; T Öhlinger, *Der völkerrechtliche Vertrag im staatlichen Recht* (Wien, Springer, 1973), 112.

[36] Cascante, *Rechtsschutz* (2003) (ch 2, fn 6) 296; Weiß, 'Verletzung des WTO-Rechts' (ch 2, fn 50) 296; W Fikentscher, 'Was bedeutet "self executing "?' in JF Baur, KJ Hopt and KP Mailänder (eds), *Festschrift für Ernst Steindorff* (Berlin, De Gruyter, 1990) 1186; Griller, 'Enforcement' (ch 2, fn 30) 293; by contrast, more far-reaching P Pescatore, 'Die Rechtsprechung des Europäischen Gerichtshofs zur innergemeinschaftlichen Wirkung völkerrechtlicher Abkommen' in R Bernard and others (eds), *Völkerrecht als Rechtsordnung Internationale Gerichtsbarkeit Menschenrechte: Festschrift für Hermann Mosler* (Berlin, Springer, 1983) 671, arguing that the qualification as integrated part of the legal order indicates the Court's inclination to accept direct effect.

[37] *Biret International v Council* (Introduction, fn 8) para 35; A Epiney, 'Zur Stellung des Völkerrechts in der EU' [1999] *EuZW* 5, 6; C Weber, 'Wirtschaftsabkommen im System der Europäischen Gemeinschaft: Die Rechtsprechung des Europäischen Gerichtshofs' (1997) 35 *AVR* 295, 313.

[38] Weiß, 'Verletzung des WTO-Rechts' (ch 2, fn 50) 279f referring to K Schmalenbach in C Calliess and M Ruffert (eds), *EUV/AEUV*, 5th edn (München, CH Beck, 2016) Art 300 EGV, para 48; Griller, 'Enforcement' (ch 2, fn 30) 291; A Bleckmann, 'Die Position des Völkerrechts im inneren Rechtsraum der EG—Monismus oder Dualismus der Rechtsordnungen?' (1975) 18 *JIR* 300, 306f; by contrast, the representative of the Council argued in *Germany v Council* rather in favor of a purely declaratory effect of Article 216 para 2 TFEU, see Case C-122/95 *Germany v Council* [1998] ECR I-973, para 41.

[39] The binding effect already follows from the universal character of this principle G Dahm, J Delbrück and R Wolfrum, *Völkerrecht*, vol I/1, 2nd edn (Berlin, De Gruyter, 1989), 31; Bleckmann, 'Monismus oder Dualismus' (n 38) 301ff; on the application of international customary law in the EU see *A Racke GmbH & Co v Hauptzollamt Mainz* (ch 1, fn 4) para 49.

[40] Weiß, 'Verletzung des WTO-Rechts' (ch 2, fn 50) 279f.

[41] Kuilwijk, *GATT Dilemma* (1996) (ch 1, fn 1) 84; Bleckmann, 'Monismus oder Dualismus' (n 38) 302.

[42] R Arnold and E Meindl, 'Außenhandelsrecht—Grundregeln' in MA Dauses (ed), *Handbuch des EU-Wirtschaftsrechts*, 38th edn (München, CH Beck, 2015) K. para 14.

For the purpose of this analysis, we can summarise that Article 216 para 2 TFEU stipulates the bindingness of international agreements for EU secondary law by virtue of an EU law command—this must, however, be distinguished from direct effect and the invocability of the agreement that follows from a different set of criteria, notably whether the agreement is sufficiently clear, precise and unconditional. In other words, Article 216 para 2 regulates the 'objective' effect of bindingness for the EU and Member States, while direct effect describes the 'subjective' effect in terms of invocability of the agreement by individuals.[43] We draw this distinction in order to support the comparative exercise with the *Francovich* doctrine and Article 288 TFEU, which formed the legal basis to which the principle of practical effectiveness was applied in *Francovich*. Both Articles 216 and 288 TFEU lack a 'subjective' character in the sense that they only stipulate objective commands on bindingness without setting the criteria of invocability. Article 216 TFEU lays down the bindingness of international agreements for EU institutions, while Article 288 TFEU stipulates the obligation of EU Member States to implement EU directives.[44]

WTO law thus becomes binding on EU institutions and Member States through the order of bindingness, as stated by Article 216 para 2 TFEU. This implies an obligation of EU institutions to conduct their legislative and administrative practice in a way that no responsibility under international law occurs due to violations of international agreements.[45] That is, even if the international agreement lacks direct effect, the EU must *ex officio* ensure that the international agreement is observed.[46] Every measure in breach with the WTO agreements also amounts to a violation of EU law, notably of Article 216 para 2 TFEU.[47] Given that compliance with DSB ruling requires active legislation, ie, the violation of Article 216 TFEU occurs through an omission, there must be a duty to act in a specific manner. Put differently, the order of bindingness must also entail the obligation of the EU to set its laws and practices in line with the international agreement.[48] In this vein, in

[43] P Manin, 'A propos de l'accord sur les marchés publics: la question de l'invocabilité des accords internationaux conclus par la Communauté européenne' [1997] *RTDeur* 399, 405; Weiß, 'Verletzung des WTO-Rechts' (ch 2, fn 50) 280f; P Eeckhout, 'Judicial Enforcement of WTO Law in the European Union—Some further Reflections' (2002) 5 *JIEL* 91, 98; Griller, 'Enforcement' (ch 2, fn 30) 291.

[44] See below ch 3 II A ii.

[45] I MacLeod, ID Hendry and S Hyett, *The External Relations of the European Communities* (Oxford, Oxford University Press, 1996), 126; H-D Kuschel, 'Die EG-Bananenmarktordnung vor deutschen Gerichten' [1995] *EuZW* 689, 692; Cascante, *Rechtsschutz* (2003) (ch 2, fn 6) 317; V Epping, *Die Außenwirtschaftsfreiheit* (Tübingen, Mohr Siebeck, 1998), 603; W Meng, 'Gedanken zur Frage unmittelbarer Anwendung von WTO-Recht in der EG' in U Beyerlin and others (eds), *Recht zwischen Umbruch und Bewahrung: Völkerrecht Europarecht Staatsrecht, Festschrift für Rudolf Bernhardt* (Berlin, Springer, 2014) 1069.

[46] Epping, *Außenwirtschaftsfreiheit* (1998) (n 45) 622.

[47] See *Hauptzollamt Mainz v Kupferberg* (ch 2, fn 7) para 13.

[48] Meng, 'WTO-Recht in der EG' (n 45) 1069; similarly Pescatore, 'Innergemeinschaftlichen Wirkung' (n 36) 684, para 23; C Tomuschat, 'Zur Rechtswirkung der von der Europäischen Gemeinschaft abgeschlossenen Verträge in der Gemeinschaftsrechtsordnung' in G Lüke and G Ress (eds), *Rechtsvergleichung, Europarecht und Staatenintegration: Gedächtnisschrift für Léontin-Jean Constantinesco* (Köln, Heymanns, 1983) 804.

*Kupferberg* the Court recognised the EU institutions to be bound by international agreements and, in addition, the obligation to undertake all measures necessary to ensure compliance with the agreement.[49] If an EU legislator fails to observe the provision of a binding agreement or, more specifically, if she omits to adopt the necessary means to comply with a DSB ruling, the EU not only violates an international agreement but also its duties under EU law.[50] The binding character of international agreements thus corresponds to an obligation to act in conformity with international treaties and extends to the duty of actively implementing the DSB decision in the EU legal order—not only as an obligation under international law but also as a duty under EU law.

#### *ii. Structural comparability of Articles 216 para 2 TFEU and Art 288 TFEU*

Interpreting Article 216 para 2 TFEU requiring the implementation of DSB rulings is supported by a structural comparison with the nature and content of the obligation under Article 288 TFEU. There is a parallelism when comparing the effects of EU directives and DSB decisions in the EU legal order. As mentioned above, a difference exists between bindingness and direct effect. Under EU law, this distinction becomes most visible when considering the difference between regulations and directives. Regulations are directly applicable, while the directive is only binding on Member States.[51] Analogously to Article 288 TFEU, Article 216 para 2 TFEU refers to the binding force of international agreements but not to their direct effect. The effect of international agreements pursuant to Article 216 para 2 TFEU may thus be compared with the effect of an EU directive—both are binding, though lacking direct effect.[52] Also, in their specific case of application, both provisions deal with structurally similar legal acts. Both EU directives and DSB rulings are addressed to their respective Member States, not to individuals. In principle, they thus cannot entail rights and obligations for individuals.[53]

Further, Article 288 TFEU contains a mandatory order vis-à-vis the Member States as to the objective set by the directive. Member States are obliged to reach the objectives defined in the directive, but they are free to choose the form

[49] *Hauptzollamt Mainz v Kupferberg* (ch 2, fn 7) para 11f.

[50] ibid para 11.

[51] Case 43/71 *Politi v Italian Ministry of Finance* [1971] ECR 1039, 1049.

[52] Weiß, 'Verletzung des WTO-Rechts' (ch 2, fn 50) 281, arguing that liability is only possible if international agreements have direct effect without recognising that EU directives do not require direct effect in order to establish liability.

[53] See for the EU directive Case 152/84 *Marshall v Southampton Health Authority* [1986] ECR 723, para 48; Case C-355/96 *Silhouette v Hartlauer* [1998] ECR I-4799, para 36; explicitly also *Biret International v Council* (Introduction, fn 8) Opinion of AG Alber, para 109; on the difference between EU directive and DSB ruling see Thies, 'Biret and beyond' (ch 2, fn 6) 1678; the term objective is understood to be a predetermined result, W Schroeder in R Streinz (ed), *EUV/AEUV*, 2nd edn (München, CH Beck 2012) Art 288 TFEU, para 77; HP Ipsen, *Europäisches Gemeinschaftsrecht* (Tübingen, Mohr Siebeck 1972), 458.

and measures to reach the objective. This principle of mandatory objectives, in combination with the freedom in measures, is characteristic also of international agreements, in particular WTO law and the implementation of DSB decisions. Article 216 para 2 TFEU extends the international law principle 'pacta sunt servanda' to EU institutions, making it a genuine obligation under EU law. Accordingly, the structure of international agreements typically obliges parties of the agreement to implement the agreement in the respective national legal order (ie, mandatory in reaching the objectives or results), but the parties retain the freedom to choose the measures they apply to achieve the objective (freedom of measures), unless the agreement stipulates otherwise.[54] The duality of obligation and freedom is thus a common feature of EU directives and many international agreements.

The duality is particularly prevalent regarding the implementation of WTO law in the EU legal order. According to Article XVI para 4 WTO Agreement, each Member shall ensure the conformity of its laws, regulations and administrative procedures with its obligations under the WTO agreements. There are no further provisions governing how Member States are obliged to comply with their obligations.[55] Article 1 of the TRIPS Agreement even lays down explicitly that Members shall be free to determine the appropriate method of implementing the provisions of the agreement within their own legal system and practice. Thus, Member States are free to determine the implementation of their obligations into their national legal orders.[56] The obligation to comply with DSB rulings follows a similar structure. As developed above at length, the question of 'whether' to comply with the ruling is compulsory, and there is no alternative to ultimate compliance with the decision (albeit some temporary flexibility).[57] Once the Panel or Appellate Body report has been adopted by the DSB, the obligation under international law is to reach a WTO-compliant legal status, which can be reached either by modification or removal of the measures concerned.[58] Thus, there is some degree of flexibility in implementing the DSB decision, as regards the measures taken to reach the mandatory objective of compliance with WTO rules. This holds even if one considers non-compliance of the EU with the DSB ruling as a factual (rather than normative) alternative, which may trigger retaliatory measures imposed by other countries. EU institutions would also have the factual option at hand to not

[54] Wünschmann, *Gemeinschaftsrecht* (2003) (ch 2, fn 5) 55; Winter, 'Direct Applicability' (ch 1, fn 1) 426; *Hauptzollamt Mainz v Kupferberg* (ch 2, fn 7) 3663, para 18.

[55] Meng, 'WTO-Recht in der EG' (n 45) 1063.

[56] JK Butler, *Die Beteiligung von Privatpersonen am WTO-Streitbeilegungsverfahren* (Frankfurt am Main, P Lang, 2002), 64; Winter, 'Direct Applicability' (ch 1, fn 1) 426.

[57] Above ch. 2 II; Griller, 'Judicial Enforceability' (ch 2, fn 36) 450ff; Steinbach, 'WTO-Streitbeilegungsentscheidungen' (ch 2, fn 3) 333; Wünschmann, *Gemeinschaftsrecht* (2003) (ch 2, fn 5) 205f; Zonnekeyn, 'WTO Law in the EC Legal Order' (ch 1, fn 7) 122f; Desmedt, 'Effect of WTO Agreements' (ch 1, fn 7) 100; *Biret International v Council* (Introduction, fn 8) Opinion of AG Alber, para 82ff; Schroeder and Schonard, 'WTO-Streitbeilegungssystem' (ch 2, fn 36) 660.

[58] Weiß, 'Streitbeilegungsverfahren' (ch 2, fn 41) 134, para 309.

implement EU directives and expose themselves to sanctions imposed under EU law for non-implementation of the directive. However, this freedom to breach the international law treaty is not a legal option granted under the agreement, but rather the consequence of the sovereignty principle under public international law.

From the perspective of the individual, the duality of obligation in the objective and freedom by measure underlines the individual's dependency on implementation of the EU directive and the DSB ruling, respectively, because in both cases 'the full effectiveness of Community rules is subject to prior action on the part of the State and where, consequently, in the absence of such action, individuals cannot enforce before the national courts the rights conferred upon them by Community law.'[59] Both the implementation of an EU directive and a DSB ruling requires measures adopted by Members and the failure to implement curtails the effectiveness of the respective legal act. From a perspective of legal protection, the addressees of the duty to implement should not benefit from their unlawful conduct, and the individual should not be disadvantaged by such conduct.[60] The issue that should be discussed next is: whether or not the omission of a legal obligation to adopt measures towards compliance with WTO law should give raise to sanctions promoting the practical effectiveness of Article 216 para 2 TFEU by way of liability.

### *iii. Effet utile and obligations under Article 216 para 2 TFEU*

The foregoing has shown that Article 216 para 2 TFEU commands an obligation to implement DSB rulings. Recalling the context of *Francovich*, the next question would be whether practical effectiveness of this provision should give rise to liability, notwithstanding the lack of direct effect. The outstanding role of *effet utile* for the Court's development of the *Francovich* principle for the purpose of legal protection has already been touched upon above. Besides the aspect of ensuring individuals' legal redress, the principle of practical effectiveness has also been applied to counter the deficient implementation of EU law by Member States.[61] This notion is also relevant in relation to the duties by EU institutions, whose inadequate implementation can also pose risks to the coherent application of EU law. In other words, even if the principle of *effet utile* has been applied in the past to safeguard the effectiveness of EU law vis-à-vis the Member States, the fundamental principle of EU law can also be applied to the conduct of EU institutions in order to ensure comprehensive safeguarding of EU law.

[59] Regarding the implementation of EU directives, *Francovich v Italy* (n 16) para 34; on the implementation of DSB rulings see *Biret International v Council* (Introduction, fn 8) Opinion of AG Alber, para 92.

[60] On the comparison of the two incidents of non-implementation see ibid Opinion of AG Alber, para 106ff.

[61] Streinz, 'Effet Utile' (n 24) 1506.

### *iv. Effectiveness of Article 216 para 2 TFEU*

The Court has used the principle of practical effectiveness on various occasions.[62] While the wording differs,[63] it has been used for the direct effect of directives,[64] the supremacy of EU law,[65] the implementation of EU law by Member States' courts and administrative bodies[66] as well for the extension of EU competences.[67] The lack of effectiveness has been discussed, particularly in the empirical and sociological branches of literature,[68] but it also drew attention among political scientists and economists.[69] In principle, a law is considered effective if it is complied with.[70] In this regard, Article 216 para 2 TFEU could be read both as a ban to not act in contradiction to international agreements, and as an order to set legislation in line with international agreements. As such, effectiveness can empirically be assessed in terms of compliance of EU law with an international agreement.[71] Judging by the incentives of addressees to comply or not comply with the agreement, one can infer that violation will occur more often the greater the incentives to disrespect the rules. Incentives to comply are a function of the probability that non-compliance is found and to the sanctions, which the addressee is likely to be subjected to in case of non-compliance. Non-compliance is, thus, a function of the gravity of the sanction and the likelihood whether a violation will be found.[72] Building on the insight provided by public choice theory,[73] the factors determining the compliance record of international agreements under Article 216 para 2 TFEU must then be assessed in view, inter alia, of the lobbying pressure exerted by

[62] On the classification of case groups see ibid 1491ff; instructively, M Mosiek, *Effet utile und Rechtsgemeinschaft* (Münster, LIT, 2003), 6ff.

[63] On the use of synonymous terms see Streinz, 'Effet Utile' (n 24) 1495.

[64] Case 41/74 *Van Duyn v Home Office* [1974] ECR 1337, 1348, para 12; Case 48-75 *Royer* [1976] ECR 497, 517, para 69.

[65] Case 6/64 *Costa v ENEL* [1964] ECR 1259, 1269, para 8ff.

[66] Joined Cases 205 to 215/82 *Deutsche Milchkontor v Germany* [1983] ECR 2633, 2665, para 17.

[67] Case 242/87 *Commission v Council* [1989] ECR 1425, 1425ff; Case 56/88 *United Kingdom v Council* [1989] ECR 1615, 1615ff.

[68] H Ryffel, *Rechtssoziologie* (Neuwied, Luchterhand 1988), 251ff; M Rehbinder and H Schelsky, *Zur Effektivität des Rechts. Jahrbuch für Rechtssoziologie und Rechtstheorie*, vol III (Düsseldorf, Bertelsmann, 1972).

[69] P Jost, *Effektivität von Recht aus ökonomischer Sicht* (Berlin, Duncker & Humblot, 1998); H Kriesi (ed), *Vollzugsprobleme. Schweizerisches Jahrbuch für Politische Wissenschaften* (Bern, Haupt, 1993).

[70] On the various terms and synonyms dealing with effectiveness, see Deckert, 'Haftung' (n 17) 96, fn 37 with further references; J-F Perrin, 'Was versteht man unter der Effektivität einer Rechtsnorm?' in M Rehbinder (ed), *Schweizerische Beiträge zur Rechtssoziologie* (Berlin, Duncker & Humblot, 1984) 75ff; M Voß, *Symbolische Gesetzgebung* (Ebelsbach, Gremer, 1989), 54; T Öhlinger, 'Planung der Gesetzgebung und Wissenschaft' in T Öhlinger (ed), *Methodik der Gesetzgebung: Legistische Richtlinien in Theorie und Praxis* (Wien, Springer 1982) 11; P Noll, 'Die Berücksichtigung der Effektivität der Gesetze bei ihrer Schaffung' in T Öhlinger (ed), *Methodik der Gesetzgebung: Legistische Richtlinien in Theorie und Praxis* (Wien, Springer, 1982) 132; Jost, *Effektivität* (1998) (n 69) 59, 62.

[71] Generally Noll, 'Effektivität der Gesetze' (n 70) 134. Less clear is the assessment of effectiveness of organisational rules.

[72] Jost, *Effektivität* (1998) (n 69) 58; Noll, 'Effektivität der Gesetze' (n 70) 137.

[73] See below ch 8 II.

interest groups pushing for compliance or non-compliance with WTO rules. Considering the well-established phenomenon of powerful interest groups influencing the decision-making process of EU legislation, protectionist pressure may explain both the initial violation of WTO rules (through import restrictions, for instance), as well as a persistent lack of compliance even after a violation was found by a DSB decision.

From a legal perspective, sanctions for non-compliance that serve at the same time as effective counter-pressure against protectionist lobbying are insignificant, given that judicial control of EU secondary law inconsistent with WTO law virtually does not exist, especially due to the lack of the direct effect of WTO rules. Hence, legislation and jurisprudence would in principle have possibilities to increase incentives to comply, by imposing sanctions through the threat of legal review. The most obvious and strongest sanction clearly would be a recognition of the direct effect of WTO law—as discussed above;[74] however, this would undermine the flexibility granted under the DSU for Members to find negotiation solutions on a temporary basis. An alternative legal solution that would not compromise the scope to manoeuvre under the DSU would be the liability for breaches of Article 216 para 2 TFEU.[75]

At least for the long-standing trade disputes on bananas and hormones, one can infer that the objective of Article 216 para 2 TFEU, which is to induce the EU institutions to comply with the DSB ruling, has hardly been complied with effectively. Given the persistent non-compliance, despite several Panel and Appellate Body findings on the unlawfulness of the EU's import regimes, Article 216 para 2 TFEU does not ensure effectiveness of this provision in relation to WTO rulings. An interpretation of Article 216 para 2 TFEU with a view to ensuring its practical effectiveness would imply strengthening this provision's command of bindingness.[76] Giving individuals the possibility to sanction non-compliance through liability would certainly increase the effectiveness of the binding character of WTO law for EU institutions, without encroaching upon the EU's freedom to decide on the validity of secondary law.

### a. WTO and EU: Distinct character by integration?

When the Court introduced Member State liability through its *Francovich* doctrine, there was a widely shared perception that this step would also be owed to the predominant function of integration in the European legal and political order. In this vein, comments referred to the judgment as 'stimulus of integration'[77] and to the creation of a decentralised integration mechanism[78]—this raises the question

[74] See above ch 2 I.
[75] On the optimisation of incentives through liability see the economic analysis below, ch 8.
[76] F Ossenbühl, 'Der gemeinschaftsrechtliche Staatshaftungsanspruch' [1992] *DVBl* 993, 995.
[77] T von Danwitz, 'Die gemeinschaftliche Staatshaftung der Mitgliedstaaten' [1997] *DVBl* 1, 2.
[78] J Masing, *Die Mobilisierung des Bürgers für die Durchsetzung des Rechts* (Berlin, Duncker & Humblot, 1997), 48ff.

of whether the character of the EU as the integration project is unique in a way that would preclude an application of the *effet utile* to the context of WTO law.

The obligation of Article 288 TFEU differs from the obligation under Article 219 para 2 TFEU, in that the former requires the implementation of genuine Union law, while the latter concerns the order of bindingness of international agreements in the EU legal order. This implies that the difference in international law, unlike EU law, is that it does not have the inherent claim to be directly effective in another legal order. The general international law principle of *pacta sunt servanda* does not claim a direct effect for international law, nor does another international law provision exist that requires a direct effect in the national legal order.[79] Consequently, international law treaties gain effect in the national legal order only through an order under national law,[80] whereas EU law inherently claims supremacy over the legal order of its Member States. More specifically, the EU directive not only has its origin in the EU legal order and, as such, enjoys supremacy over national law, but also constitutes a central element of harmonisation of Member States' legal orders, with a view to promoting European integration and the full functioning of EU law.[81]

It appears questionable whether similar considerations pertaining to integration can be applied in the relationship between EU law and WTO law.[82] There are sound arguments pointing at the different integration purposes of EU law and WTO law: in the EU legal order, liability for breaches of EU law promotes, inter alia, the goal of deepening integration, while WTO generally promotes (but is limited to) the elimination of trade barriers, by otherwise accepting the heterogeneity of national legal orders. In that sense, EU law depends more than WTO law on a liability regime as an instrument to ensure a uniform and effective application of EU law in the Member States' legal orders.[83]

This finding would be in line with functionalist theories of integration, according to which a process of integration would require a dynamic interpretation of supranational law deepening this process.[84] In this vein, the individual

[79] Wünschmann, *Gemeinschaftsrecht* (2003) (ch 2, fn 5) 55.

[80] See, inter alia, E Jiménez de Aréchaga, 'Self-executing provisions of international law' in K Hailbronner, G Ress and T Stein (eds), *Staat und Völkerrechtsordnung: Festschrift für Karl Doehring* (Berlin, Springer, 1989) 410; Koller, *Anwendbarkeit* (1971) (n 35) 61; ELM Volker, 'The Direct Effect of International Agreements in the Community's Legal Order' (1983) 10 *LIEI* 131, 133; M Zuleeg, 'Die innerstaatliche Anwendbarkeit völkerrechtlicher Verträge am Beispiel des GATT und der Europäischen Sozialcharta' (1975) 35 *ZaöRV* 341, 345.

[81] *Costa v ENEL* (n 65) 1259; see also C Herrmann, *Richtlinienumsetzung durch die Rechtsprechung*, 1st edn (Berlin, Duncker & Humblot, 2003), 26f; A Dendrinos, *Rechtsprobleme der Direktwirkung der EWG-Richtlinien* (Frankfurt am Main, P Lang, 1989), 97; see F Emmert, *Europarecht* (München, CH Beck, 1996), § 14, 143, para 7.

[82] Critical H Krück, *Völkerrechtliche Verträge im Recht der Europäischen Gemeinschaften* (Berlin, Springer, 2011), 168; Flemisch, *Umfang* (2002) (ch 2, fn 5) 61.

[83] Hörmann and Göttsche, 'Haftung' (ch 2, fn 37) 695; AV Bogdandy, 'Rechtsgleichheit, Rechtssicherheit und Subsidiarität im transnationalen Wirtschaftsrecht' [2001] *EuZW* 357, 363; Görgens, *Außervertragliche Haftung* (2006) (ch 2, fn 5) 92.

[84] E-U Petersmann, 'Darf die EG das Völkerrecht ignorieren? Zu den verfassungs- und völkerrechtlichen Grundlagen des Europäischen Wirtschaftsrechts' in B Grossfeld (ed), *Festschrift für Wolfgang*

performs an important role with a view to effective enforcement of EU law—the individual's rights to pursue actions for annulment and to claim damages then serve as procedural safeguards driving the integration process.[85] Conversely, Article 219 para 2 TFEU could have a comparatively less important function for the integration process than Article 288 TFEU. These differences could raise doubts as to the transferability of the *effet utile* principle into the ambit of Article 219 para 2 TFEU.

However, there are three main arguments supporting the contrary. Firstly, by adopting an integration perspective, one could put forward that WTO genuinely seeks to promote economic (or more narrowly: trade-related) integration in the global economic order to which the *effet utile* can be applied. Secondly, EU law exhibits great openness towards integrating international law into the EU legal order. Also, the degree to which trade-related freedoms and principles are recognised in the EU legal order underlines its congruence with WTO principles. Thirdly, the Court has frequently applied the *effet utile* principle to EU international agreements with a view towards ensuring their practical effectiveness.

### b. The economic integration character of the WTO

From an integrationist view, States agree on a contractual basis to the establishment of a new entity enjoying some independence from the States.[86] Integration can be comprehensive or limited to certain areas. Distinctions can be made between, inter alia, political, economic and legal dimensions of the integration processes.[87] There is no doubt that the EU has achieved a more profound and qualitatively different level of integration than the WTO. In particular, political integration has been advanced by way of transferring competences from the national to the supranational level, compared to the more intergovernmental mechanism of the WTO.

The EU has passed significant milestones of legal and political integration through the recognition of supremacy of EU over national law, and the direct effect of EU law. The EU is distinguished from the level of economic integration of the WTO, through establishment of a common market enabling free trade, sidelined by the free movement of goods, services and persons.

However, even if the difference in depth of the integration level is considerable, it cannot be denied that the integrationist character of the WTO is limited to a narrow

*Fikentscher zum 70. Geburtstag* (Tübingen, Mohr Siebeck, 1998) 969; E-U Petersmann, 'Darf die EG das Völkerrecht ignorieren?' [1997] *EuZW* 325, 326; M Zuleeg, 'Die Rechtswirkung europäischer Richtlinien' [1980] *ZGR* 466, 475; Krajewski, *Verfassungsperspektiven* (2001) (ch 2, fn 30) 50.

[85] S Magiera, 'Die Durchsetzung des Gemeinschaftsrechts im europäischen Integrationsprozess' [1998] *DÖV* 173, 174; Masing, *Mobilisierung* (1997) (n 78) 50ff.

[86] Krajewski, *Verfassungsperspektiven* (2001) (ch 2, fn 30) 49; see also U Meyer-Cording, 'Fortschritte der Europapolitik nur mit wirklich integrierenden Maßnahmen möglich!' in E-J Mestmäcker, H Möller and H-P Schwarz (eds), *Eine Ordnungspolitik für Europa: Festschrift für Hans von der Groeben zu seinem 80. Geburtstag* (Baden-Baden, Nomos, 1987) 221.

[87] P Behrens, 'Integrationstheorie' (1981) 45 *RabelsZ* 8, 13.

scope of economic policy. Many definitions have been given to the term 'economic integration'. Some argue that, besides the elimination of trade barriers, there must be common policies, institutions and certain coordination mechanisms in place.[88] For others, the orientation of integration towards political unions is decisive.[89] Another view argues that integration starts where at least some barriers for free trade or service are removed entirely, rather than just being reduced.[90] Given that the WTO only aims at 'reduction' and not 'elimination' of barriers, this would underscore the WTO's character as an international cooperation rather than integration.[91] The shortcoming of these approaches lies in their static view disregarding the dynamic character of integration.[92] Rather, for the purpose of exploring economic integration, one should focus on the objective of creating welfare gains to be achieved through (sector-specific) measures.[93] In that sense, there is no qualitative difference between the WTO and the EU.[94] By pursuing the principles of free trade, the WTO agreements are the outcome of a dynamic process, fuelled by frequent rounds of negotiations aimed at further reductions in trade barriers. There is a process of trade integration, which is directed towards the ultimate elimination of trade barriers. Because of the dynamics of liberalisation, the WTO law has an economically integrating function, which advances gradually, and which has its distinguishing feature from the EU in the limitation to trade issues excluding, in particular, political integration.

It is also worthwhile recalling that even the European Community was seen for a long time as a predominantly economic project—the slow and gradual removal of customs that took until the 1970s and underscored the initially economic dimension of the integration process. Also, the EU's current level of political integration and supranationality was achieved mainly by the recognition of the supremacy of EU law and the direct effect of its provisions. It was the integration-oriented role of the CJEU that occasionally released integrationist impulses for the European integration process.[95] This should not lead, however, to requesting such a far-reaching effect in favour of the WTO law—there are good reasons to deny the direct effect to these rules, as discussed above. However, the argument presented is that one should not make a high level of economic and political integration a

[88] J Tinbergen, *International Economic Integration*, 2nd edn (Amsterdam, Elsevier Applied Science, 1965), 122; AM El-Agraa, 'What is economic integration?' in AM El-Agraa (ed), *The European Union: Economics and policies*, 9th edn (Cambridge, Cambridge University Press, 2011) 1.

[89] J Pinder, 'Problems of European Integration' in GR Denton (ed), *Economic Integration in Europe* (London, Weidenfeld & Nicolson, 1969) 143ff.

[90] B Balassa, *The Theory of Economic Integration* (Abingdon, Routledge, 2011), 2; Behrens, 'Integrationstheorie' (n 87) 26.

[91] Krajewski, *Verfassungsperspektiven* (2001) (ch 2, fn 30) 51.

[92] MN Jovanović, *The Economics of European Integration*, 2nd edn (Cheltenham, Edward Elgar Publishing, 2014), 584ff; J Dunker, *Regionale Integration im System des liberalisierten Welthandels* (Frankfurt am Main, P Lang, 2002), 41.

[93] Dunker, *Regionale Integration* (2002) (n 92) 41; F Machlup, *A History of Thought on Economic Integration* (New York, Columbia University Press, 1977), 43.

[94] J Drexl, 'Unmittelbare Anwendbarkeit des WTO-Rechts in der globalen Privatrechtsordnung' in B Grossfeld (ed), *Festschrift für Wolfgang Fikentscher zum 70. Geburtstag* (Tübingen, Mohr Siebeck, 1998) 844; Hinderer, *Rechtsschutz* (2004) (ch 2, fn 5) 390.

[95] Ipsen, *Gemeinschaftsrecht* (1972) (n 53) 66ff; Dunker, *Regionale Integration* (2002) (n 92) 87.

prerequisite for recognising the trade-limited integrationist character of the WTO, and thus allow the application of the *effet utile* to the order of Article 216 para 2 TFEU, which is to implement and abide by rulings of the DSB.[96]

c. The openness of EU law towards international law

Furthermore, the EU legal order provides various mechanisms promoting the integration of international law into the EU legal order, of which the order of Article 216 para 2 TFEU is only one example. According to the Court's well-established jurisprudence, WTO law has become an 'integral part' of the EU legal order which, in turn, has the protection of the individual as a core principle.[97] If one would disregard the principle of individual legal protection for international law treaties integrated into the EU legal order, this would lead to establishing different standards of legal protection within the same legal order—creating inherent risks to the uniform application of the legality principle and the coherence of the legal order. Frictions between integrated international treaty law and formal EU law would be inevitable.[98]

Such a tendency of disintegration appears incompatible with the EU treaties in several regards: firstly, the EU has the protection of individual rights, democracy and the rule of law as a core principle. Legal protection has proven to allow 'integration through participation'.[99] Disregarding the legality principle for integrated international agreements, and the lack of effective legal protection against WTO violations, reduces the scope of the rule of law principle and has disintegrating effects pertaining to international agreements of the EU.[100] Secondly, there is the principle of applying and interpreting EU law in compatibility with international law (agreement-consistent interpretation):[101] namely *Petersmann* has derived such a principle from the purpose and objective of Articles 300–307 ECT (today Articles 215, 220, 350, 351 TFEU).[102] These provisions enshrine the idea of

[96] Hinderer, *Rechtsschutz* (2004) (ch 2, fn 5) 390; H-W Arndt and others (eds), *Völkerrecht und deutsches Recht* (München, CH Beck, 2001), 85.

[97] See only *R & V Haegeman v Belgian State* (ch 1, fn 4) para 2ff; *Sevince v Staatssecretaris van Justitie* (ch 2, fn 7) para 8.

[98] Petersmann, 'Darf die EG das Völkerrecht ignorieren?' (n 84) 970.

[99] Petersmann, 'Darf die EG das Völkerrecht ignorieren?' (n 84) 971; Flemisch, *Umfang* (2002) (ch 2, fn 5) 136; Kuschel, 'Bananenmarktordnung' (ch 2, fn 6) 649.

[100] Petersmann, 'Beteiligung der Europäischen Gemeinschaft' (n 29) 83; Petersmann, 'Darf die EG das Völkerrecht ignorieren?' (n 84) 979.

[101] See also Hix, 'Indirect Effect' (ch 1, fn 7) 18ff; JH Jackson, 'Direct Effect of Treaties in the US and the EU, the Case of the WTO: Some Perceptions and Proposals' in A Arnull, P Eeckhout and T Tridimas (eds), *Continuity and Change in EU Law: Essays in Honour of Sir Francis Jacobs* (Oxford, Oxford University Press, 2008) 367. Cf also G Gattinara, 'Consistent Interpretation of WTO Rulings in the EU Legal Order?' in E Cannizzaro, P Palchetti and RA Wessel (eds), *International Law as Law of the European Union* (Boston, Martinus Nijhoff Publishers, 2011) 271.

[102] Flemisch, *Umfang* (2002) (ch 2, fn 5) 136; Petersmann, 'Darf die EG das Völkerrecht ignorieren?' (n 84) 974; T Cottier and K Nadakavukaren Schefer, 'The Relationship between World Trade Organization Law, National and Regional Law' (1998) 1 *JIEL* 83, 90.

seeking compatibility with international law, corresponding to the *pacta sunt servanda* principle and avoiding collisions of international treaties.[103] These norms and principles add to the overall trade-promoting character of the European treaties. This disposition of the EU treaties also resonates in Article 206 TFEU, according to which Member States contribute 'to the harmonious development of world trade, the progressive abolition of restrictions on international trade and on foreign direct investment'.[104] Also, references to the abolition of restrictions on international trade can be found in almost identical wording in both the preamble of the TFEU and the WTO agreement. In addition, the functional relationship between external and internal markets and references to the 'market economy' (Articles 3 TEU, 119, 120, 127 TFEU) underscore the importance of economic freedoms safeguarded in international law.[105] Integration of WTO agreements in the EU legal order thus serves the realisation of genuine EU objectives. The relation between European integration and the EU's disposition to seek compatibility with international economic law obligations has in the past been a pronounced element in the liberalisation and harmonisation of Member States' trade policies, in the course of which the obligations of the GATT have been an important instrument and point of reference for the EU's shaping of trade policy.[106]

On balance, the European treaties are designed in a manner underscoring the integrationist stance of the EU vis-à-vis international law in general, and international economic law obligations in particular. The WTO agreements have set in motion an integration process which, albeit limited to the area of international trade, aims at liberalising trade in line with the EU's market economy principle and economic freedoms. Both the openness of the EU treaty towards international (economic) law and the economic integrationist orientation of the WTO allow an application of the *effet utile* principle to Article 216 para 2 TFEU directed at the implementation of DSB rulings in the EU legal order. Further, from an integrationist perspective, recognising liability for WTO breaches would render the individual (once more) the driver of a trade-focused integration process (while being restricted to liability and not extended to annulment). Finally, non-uniform and divergent standards of individual legal protection between integrated international law and other EU law pose a risk to the coherence of the legal order and uniform application of the legality principle.

[103] This is also occasionally reflected in CJEU jurisprudence, see Case C-308/06 *Intertanko and Others v Secretary of State for Transport* [2008] ECR I-4057, I-4057, para 52: 'In view of the customary principle of good faith, which forms part of general international law, and of Article 10 EC, it is incumbent upon the Court to interpret those provisions [of secondary EU law] taking account of Marpol 73/78.' In the *International Dairy Agreement* case, the Court decided that secondary Union law must be interpreted in a way that is consistent with international agreements concluded by the Union, see Case C-61/94 *Commission v Germany* [1996] ECR I-3989, I-3989, para 52. Comprehensively, Hix, 'Indirect Effect' (ch 1, fn 7) 65.

[104] Kuschel, 'EG-Bananenmarktordnung' (n 45) 691.

[105] Petersmann, 'Darf die EG das Völkerrecht ignorieren?' (n 84) 980.

[106] N Lavranos in Hvd Groeben, J Schwarze and A Hatje (eds), *Europäisches Unionsrecht*, 7th edn (Baden-Baden, Nomos, 2015) Art 351 TFEU, para 3.

### d. Effet utile of international agreements in the Court's jurisprudence

*Effet utile* is not only a principle of EU law. More broadly, this principle is a special variation of the legal interpretation based on purpose and spirit,[107] which applies both in international law as well as EU law.[108] In that sense, interpreting WTO law with a view to its full effectiveness is not only an imperative accruing from its character as an 'integrated part' of EU law, but also as a matter of international law.

On a number of occasions, the Court was led by these considerations when applying the *effet utile* to EU international agreements, particularly where free-trade agreements and association agreements were concerned. In this vein, in *Tetik*,[109] the Court found that effectiveness of Decision No 1/80, which was rendered under the Community's association agreement with Turkey, required that Turkish employees would be allowed to give up their current occupation and search for a new one.[110] Similarly, in *Ertanir*, the Court found that Decision No 1/80 would be deprived of 'any practical effect' if Turkish employees would be denied certain rights.[111] Also, regarding the free-trade agreement between the Community and Austria, the Court decided in *Eurim-Pharm*, pertinent to the parallel import of medicine, that the provisions of the agreement would be deprived of 'much of their effectiveness' if they would not oppose the refusal of the health authority to allow a medical product on the German market.[112] That is, the Court typically interprets EU international law to ensure its practical effectiveness. There is no indication why WTO agreements should not be interpreted to the same effect.

## III. THE NEED FOR LEGAL REDRESS

Besides the principle of effectiveness, the notion of ensuring effective legal redress was the second pillar on which *Francovich* was built and which led to delinking of the notion of direct effect and the liability claim. The idea of legal protection is inspired by the self-image of the EU as an autonomous legal order in which not only Member States are the subject of rights and obligations, but in which the individual also hold enforceable rights.[113] Against this background, the individual's right to obtain an effective remedy not only constituted the basis for the *Francovich* doctrine, but has more generally been considered as a 'general

[107] Flemisch, *Umfang* (2002) (ch 2, fn 5) 74, fn 257.

[108] A Verdross and B Simma, *Universelles Völkerrecht* (Berlin, Duncker & Humblot, 2010), 492, § 776.

[109] Case C-171/95 *Recep Tetik v Land Berlin* [1997] ECR I-329, para 31.

[110] G Hirsch, 'Die Rechtsprechung des Europäischen Gerichtshofs zu Assoziierungsabkommen' [1997] *BayVBl* 449, 452.

[111] Case C-98/96 *Ertanir v Land Hessen* [1997] ECR I-5179, para 32.

[112] Case C-207/91 *Eurim-Pharm* [1993] ECR I-3748.

[113] For the first time in Case 26/62 *Van Gend en Loos v Netherlands Inland Revenue Administration* [1963] ECR 1, 25.

principle of law which underlies the constitutional traditions common to the Member States'.[114]

## A. Individual rights and WTO violations

As a minimum requirement for individual legal protection, there must be an identifiable individual right for which an effective remedy could be claimed. Liability can only incur, if such individual right exists. However, determination of an individual right is not only a requirement to substantiate a liability claim, but also of relevance as a prerequisite to justify the dispensability of the direct effect of a DSB ruling. This raises further the question of the legal act or provision from which such individual right has to originate. There are three possibilities: first, one could identify an individual right (or legitimate individual interests) in the DSB ruling as such; or, second, it could be traced in Article 216 para 2 TFEU, which would then require to be intended for protecting (at least indirectly) individual interests; or, third, a combination of the obligation to implement the DSB decision as foreseen by Article 216 para 2 TFEU and the DSB ruling intended to protect individual interests. Thus, the issue here is to localise the individual right—by contrast, the question of how such a right must be substantiated (ie, how 'strong' the individual right must be) has to be addressed in a subsequent step.

Article 216 para 2 TFEU does not have any direct effect. This provision only generally requires EU institutions to be bound by international agreements, but does not allow discernment of individual rights.[115] The issue is less clear concerning the DSB ruling. It has been argued that one could recognise two levels of direct effect: if a norm could not be granted any direct effect for the purpose of annulment procedures, one could at least grant the DSB ruling a direct effect for liability purposes.[116] Such differentiation of the concept of direct effect creates obvious frictions—the conditions for direct effect are typically tied to the clarity, precision and unconditionality of a norm, whereby the purpose of invoking the provision for annulment or compensation does not play a role.

If one ties the existence of individual rights to the notion of direct effect intrinsically, neither the DSB ruling nor Article 216 para 2 TFEU would then offer an identifiable individual right.[117] However, one could consider a combined evaluation

[114] Case 222/84 *Marguerite Johnston v Chief Constable of the Royal Ulster Constabulary* [1986] ECR 1651, 1682, para 18f; Case 222/86 *UNECTEF v Heylens* [1987] ECR 4097, 4117, para 14; see also Petersmann, 'Darf die EG das Völkerrecht ignorieren?' (n 84) 971; E Schmidt-Aßmann, 'Empfiehlt es sich, das System des Rechtsschutzes und der Gerichtsbarkeit in der Europäischen Gemeinschaft weiterzuentwickeln?' [1994] *JZ* 832, 832; Cornils, *Staatshaftungsanspruch* (1995) (n 22) 181.

[115] Similarly Weiß, 'Verletzung des WTO-Rechts' (ch 2, fn 50) 279f.

[116] *Biret International v Council* (Introduction, fn 50) Opinion of AG Alber, para 93f; agreeing Lavranos, 'WTO-Recht' (ch 2, fn 6) 296; for a critical view Bogdandy, 'Legal Effects' (n 11) 57; Hörmann and Göttsche, 'Haftung' (ch 2, fn 37) 694.

[117] Cornils, *Staatshaftungsanspruch* (1995) (n 22) 231.

of the DSB ruling and Article 216 para 2 TFEU with a view to assessing an individual right. A combined view would be consistent from a doctrinal perspective, given the Court's approach in *Francovich*. In that case, the Court based its finding of liability, despite the lack of any direct effect, precisely on the obligations under Article 288 TFEU (ie, implementation of a directive), in combination with the EU directive protecting individual interests. The individuals' position to claim rights was thus derived from both the general duty to implement under Article 288 TFEU and the directive.[118] On an abstract level, this implies that in combining a primary law provision (eg, Article 216 para 2 TFEU) with a secondary law act (eg, the DSB ruling), it suffices that the primary law norm is limited to the command of bindingness, while individual protection can be discerned from the secondary law act.[119]

Combining a primary law obligation with a secondary legal act is thus the doctrinal approach set out in *Francovich* and which can be pursued for our purposes: Article 216 para 2 TFEU only stipulates bindingness of international agreements and requires the EU institution to transpose DSB rulings into EU secondary law without creating a position of individual rights. As complementary to the primary law obligation, the DSB ruling constitutes a secondary legal act under the WTO agreements, and as such may provide the individual right that gains force and becomes the basis for a liability claim through the primary law obligation. Having thus demonstrated how the *Francovich* approach of combining two legal acts serves as the basis for delinking liability from direct effect, the follow-up question is whether the DSB does indeed contain individual rights. We will need to discuss what the requirements are for an individual right to be discernible from the DSB decision.

## B. Case groups and the need for legal relief

The notion of ensuring effective legal redress as a second pillar for the doctrinal delinking of liability and direct effect can offer useful instruments to distinguish

[118] Prieß, 'Haftung' (ch 1, fn 50) 122; S Detterbeck, 'Staatshaftung für die Mißachtung von EG-Recht' (1994) 85 *VerwArch* 159, 179; Henrichs, *Haftung* (1995) (ch 1, fn 50) 26.

[119] This represents the main view in literature, see A Musil, 'Richtliniensetzung und Normerlassanspruch' [1998] *EuR* 705, 711f; SU Pieper, 'Mitgliedstaatliche Haftung für die Nichtbeachtung von Gemeinschaftsrecht' [1992] *NJW* 2454, 2454ff; Diehr, *Staatshaftungsanspruch* (1997) (n 19) 97; C Albers, *Die Haftung der Bundesrepublik Deutschland für die Nichtumsetzung von EG-Richtlinien* (Baden-Baden, Nomos, 1995), 97ff; S Seltenreich, *Die Francovich-Entscheidung des EuGH und ihre Auswirkungen auf das deutsche Staatshaftungsrecht* (Konstanz, Hartung-Gorre, 1997), 63; T Eilmansberger, *Rechtsfolgen und subjektives Recht im Gemeinschaftsrecht*, 1st edn (Baden-Baden, Nomos, 1997), 225; K Hailbronner, 'Staatshaftung bei säumiger Umsetzung von EG-Richtlinien' [1992] *JZ* 284, 285; K Bahlmann, 'Haftung der Mitgliedstaaten bei fehlerhafter Umsetzung von EG-Richtlinien' [1992] *DWiR* 61, 63f; Mosiek, *Effet utile* (2003) (n 62) 44; for a critical view Ossenbühl, 'Staatshaftungsanspruch' (n 76) 995; Cornils, *Staatshaftungsanspruch* (1995) (n 22) 230.

between the case groups identified above, regarding their need for legal relief.[120] The lack of effective legal remedies has often been lamented, given the episodes of the banana and hormone disputes.[121] The need for legal redress may, however, vary according to the remedies available to respective members of the case groups. In other words, the need for legal redress must be demonstrated in order to support the construction of a liability claim resting fundamentally on the notion of legal protection.

More specifically, the need for effective legal redress might be particularly imminent for members of case groups B (EU companies affected by unlawful EU import regime) and C (victims of retaliation following EU's noncompliance with the DSB ruling). These companies with their seat of operation in an EU Member State have hardly any remedy at hand against the WTO-incompatible acts of the EU institutions: they have no standing before the WTO panels, nor are they entitled to initiate panel proceedings. Actions for annulment, pursuant to Article 263 TFEU tackling WTO-inconsistent secondary law, fail because of the direct effect lacking in WTO law. Moreover, the remedies provided under the *Trade Barrier Regulation*[122] are at one's disposal only to challenge WTO breaches of states other than the EU. If one considers the individual as a subject of the EU legal order holding rights and obligations, as the Court does,[123] there are good reasons to compensate the lack of legal remedies for individuals to claim their rights, at least in cases where damages result from unlawful EU conduct. This argument cannot easily be dismissed by arguing that WTO matters of a purely interstate nature are at stake. First, the doctrinal basis for the liability claim is not (only) WTO law but rather (as in *Francovich*) a failure to comply with an obligation to act under primary EU law (Article 216 para 2 TFEU). Second, effective legal protection is only possible, if an individual is able to avail oneself of the rights and opportunities enshrined in the DSB decision, which the EU is under obligation to comply with. If the lawful implementation of the DSB had accorded rights to the individual, the need for legal protection is particularly strong where incurring damages cannot be avoided, because no annulment claim exists due to the lack of direct effect in WTO law. In this regard, the function of a claim for damages in the system of legal protection

[120] Above ch 1 III.

[121] Petersmann, 'Darf die EG das Völkerrecht ignorieren?' (n 84) 973, 979, referring to a judicial restraint in favor of the executive branch of the Union; S Oeter, 'Gibt es ein Rechtsschutzdefizit im WTO-Streitbeilegungsverfahren' in C Nowak and W Cremer (eds), *Individualrechtsschutz in der EG und der WTO: Der zentrale und dezentrale Rechtsschutz natürlicher und juristischer Personen in der Europäischen Gemeinschaft und der Welthandelsorganisation*, 1st edn (Baden-Baden, Nomos, 2002) 222; Reinisch, 'Opfer des Hormon- und Bananenstreites' (Introduction, fn 7) 43; Schoißwohl, 'Haftung' (ch 1, fn 8) 706.

[122] Council Regulation (EC) No 3286/94 of 22 December 1994 laying down Community procedures in the field of the common commercial policy in order to ensure the exercise of the Community's rights under international trade rules, in particular those established under the auspices of the World Trade Organization [1994] OJ L349/71; for an overview see Becker, *WTO-Subventionsübereinkommen* (2001) (ch 1, fn 5) 64ff.

[123] *Francovich v Italy* (n 16) para 31.

becomes particularly important. Liability closes the gap of legal protection where primary legal redress is impossible. This role of liability has already been contemplated when EU liability for unlawful legislative acts has initially been developed by the Court. In *Schöppenstedt*, AG *Roemer*[124] stressed the need for effective legal protection, given the high barriers for individuals to submit a claim for annulment of EU secondary acts.[125] In *Francovich*, the Court stated that obtaining redress is 'particularly indispensable' in cases where full effectiveness of the individual's rights depends on prior action on the part of the state[126]—this reasoning also applies to the faith of companies, in case groups B and C, who incurred damages due to an omission of action on the part of the EU in bringing its secondary law into compliance with the DSB ruling.

By contrast, the need for legal protection could be significantly less urgent for members of case group A (foreign companies suffering damages due to the unlawful EU import regime), so that the absence of an opportunity to claim damages would imply less adverse effects than for case groups B and C. Members of case group A have their seat of business outside the EU and their interests could be safeguarded through the WTO dispute settlement system or domestic trade policy mechanisms.[127] Foreign companies suffering damages due to EU import restrictions may benefit from the opportunities of their home countries to initiate proceedings against the EU before the WTO. Even if an individual company has no standing in such proceedings, there are domestic procedures typically available for individual companies to influence the country's conduct in dispute settlement proceedings.[128] Moreover, under the DSU, Members can be allowed to take retaliatory measures and negotiate compensation, if the losing country does not comply with the DSB decision. The financial means generated through retaliation or compensation can be redistributed to companies suffering damages due to the EU import restrictions, thereby offering financial relief to these companies. Thus, the DSU offers a system of legal redress to home countries of companies adversely affected by EU trade measures—both on the level of seeking the removal of the WTO-inconsistent measure as well as regarding the possibility to obtain financial compensation through their home countries. Against that background, companies of group A typically have more remedies at their disposal to seek legal protection than market operators of groups B and C. Thus, it could well be argued that the notion of legal protection does not offer a compelling reason to establish a liability regime for companies of group A, given their opportunities to otherwise seek legal redress. On the other hand, the mere possibility of obtaining financial compensation through their home countries does not necessarily mean that such

[124] *Schöppenstedt v Council* (ch 1, fn 25) Opinion of AG Roemer, 989ff.
[125] See Schoißwohl, 'Haftung' (ch 1, fn 8) 704.
[126] *Francovich v Italy* (n 16) I-5414, para 34.
[127] Schoißwohl, 'Haftung' (ch 1, fn 8) 706.
[128] See, for example, the US legal instruments provided in Section 301 of the Trade Act of 1974, Cascante, *Rechtsschutz* (2003) (ch 2, fn 6) 41ff.

compensation actually takes place, let alone in an amount corresponding to actual losses. In *Chiquita*,[129] the Court dealt with an action for damages brought by a US company seeking compensation for damages it suffered due to a breach of EU law. However, the Court did not elaborate to deal with considerations regarding the need for legal protection, as it confined itself to discuss the application of the *Nakajima* principles. Yet, it seems that *Chiquita* did not receive any payments from the US government as compensation for continued losses due to the unlawful EU banana import regime—in these incidents of legal action brought by companies of case group A, the need for legal protection would thus have to be discussed on an individual basis in light of the company's options to have its interests represented by the US before the WTO adjudicative bodies and the possibilities to obtain compensation through its home country.

At this stage, we conclude that for the purpose of assessing an individual right for liability, we draw from two legal sources: the 'objective' duty to comply with DSB rulings as derived from Article 216 para 2 TFEU, and the 'subjective' rights enshrined in the DSB ruling. Further, considerations related to the need for legal protection vary depending on the possibilities the companies concerned have at their disposal and must be assessed on a case-by-case basis—the above classification between case groups permits a differentiation in regard to the urgency of legal protection.

## IV. THE PRINCIPLE OF COOPERATION UNDER ARTICLE 4 PARA 3 TEU

The third legal basis in *Francovich* was the principle of cooperation pursuant to Article 4 para 3 TEU. According to Article 4 para 3 TEU, 'the Union and the Member States shall, in full mutual respect, assist each other in carrying out tasks which flow from the Treaties'. More specifically, Member States are obliged to take all measures necessary to comply with their obligations under EU law and, vice versa, to refrain from measures posing a risk to the accomplishment of the objectives of the EU Treaties. The issue at stake is whether Article 4 para 3 TEU can be invoked, in order to justify a liability of the EU for WTO breaches. By its mere wording, Article 4 para 3(2) and (3) TEU addresses Member States only. There is unanimity, however, in that the obligations stipulated under this provision apply to EU institutions alike.[130] This norm of mutual assistance and sincere cooperation, based on the

[129] *Chiquita v Commission* (Introduction, fn 8) II-315.

[130] R Streinz in R Streinz (ed), *EUV/AEUV*, 2nd edn (München, CH Beck, 2012) Art 4 para 3 TEU, para 4; HD Jarass, 'Die Kompetenzverteilung zwischen der Europäischen Gemeinschaft und den Mitgliedstaaten' (1996) 121 *AöR* 173, 196; A Epiney, 'Gemeinschaftsrecht und Föderalismus: "Landes-Blindheit" und Pflicht zur Berücksichtigung innerstaatlicher Verfassungsstrukturen' [1994] *EuR* 301, 309ff; H-W Rengeling, 'Deutsches und europäisches Verwaltungsrecht—wechselseitige Einwirkungen' (1994) 53 *VVDStRL* 202, 233; M Zuleeg, 'Deutsches und europäisches Verwaltungsrecht—wechselseitige Einwirkungen' (1994) 53 *VVDStRL* 154, 179; J Wuermeling, 'Die Gemeinschaftstreue und die Rechtsakte der Gesamtheit der Mitgliedstaaten der EG' [1987] *EuR* 237, 242; S Lehr, *Einstweiliger*

notion of loyalty, has been applied by the Court on various occasions and can be interpreted as a general rule that has to be applied on a case-by-case basis, in order to balance possibly conflicting interests between the EU and Member States.[131]

Before exploring the obligations accruing from Article 4 para 3 TEU in relation to liability for WTO-incompatible measures, the relevance of this provision for the *Francovich* approach of delinking liability and direct effect has to be considered. In *Francovich*, the Court explicitly stated that a 'further basis for the obligation of Member States to make good such loss and damage is to be found in Article 5 of the Treaty, under which the Member States are required to take all appropriate measures, whether general or particular, to ensure fulfilment of their obligations under Community law. Among these is the obligation to nullify the unlawful consequences of a breach of Community law'.[132] However, the wording used by the Court suggests that recourse to Article 4 para 3 TEU (ex Article 5 EEC) rather served to strengthen other arguments put forward to justify liability, without this norm serving as an independent source of normative force. Accordingly, the principle of cooperation was seen to be rather of an auxiliary, complementary nature for the liability finding.[133] This view is supported by a contextual reading of the judgment. Reference to the cooperation principle of Article 4 para 3 TEU was made only after the Court stated that a 'principle, whereby a State must be liable for loss and damage' would exist.[134] Hence, this provision, which can be read as requiring Member States to fulfil their obligations under primary and secondary EU law, supports rather than establishes the liability regime.[135]

## A. The relation between Article 4 para 3 TEU and Article 216 para 2 TFEU

The relevance of the principle of cooperation also depends on whether this norm is able to provide legal positions invocable by individuals, or if the main function of this principle lies in strengthening existing legal obligations, without having the effect of offering invocable legal positions.[136] In this context, one might consider applying Article 4 para 3 TEU to safeguard the principle of effective legal

*Rechtsschutz und Europäische Union* (Berlin, Springer, 2012), 291ff; F Schoch, 'Die Europäisierung des Allgemeinen Verwaltungsrechts' [1995] *JZ* 109, 120.

[131] Established jurisprudence: Case 230/81 *Luxembourg v European Parliament* [1983] ECR 255, 287; Case 94/87 *Commission v Germany* [1998] ECR 175, 192; Case C-2/88 *Zwartveld and Others* [1990] ECR I-3365, I-3367; Joined Cases C-36/97 and C-37/97 *Kellinghusen and Ketelsen* [1998] ECR I-6337, I-6361f; see also Schoißwohl, 'Haftung' (ch 1, fn 8) 709; AV Bogdandy and S Schill in E Grabitz, M Hilf and M Nettesheim (eds), *Das Recht der Europäischen Union*, 58th edn (München, CH Beck, 2016) Art 4 TEU, para 56.

[132] *Francovich v Italy* (n 16) I-5414, para 36.

[133] Eilmansberger, *Gemeinschaftsrecht* (1997) (n 119) 42f; Hailbronner, 'Staatshaftung' (n 119) 286; Geiger, 'Staatshaftungsanspruchsrechts' (n 20) 469; Cornils, *Staatshaftungsanspruch* (1995) (n 22) 243f.

[134] *Francovich v* Italy (n 16) I-5414, para 35.

[135] Mosiek, *Effet utile* (2003) (n 62) 15ff.

[136] More generally Streinz (n 130) Art 4 para 3 TEU, para 27f.

protection, by establishing the direct effect of WTO law. In general, Article 4 para 3 TEU is not directly applicable in the sense that an individual could discern an identifiable right from this provision to be claimed before a court,[137] even if it is acknowledged that Article 4 para 3 TEU can be an autonomous basis for legal obligations.[138] It has been submitted that for some cases a specific obligation should gain direct effect by virtue of Article 4 para 3 TEU, if legal redress cannot be obtained otherwise.[139] As a precondition, there must be no special provision dealing with the issues, and there must be no discretion as to the choice of the appropriate measure.[140]

There is, however, a significant problem with applying this provision as a means to address the lack of legal redress by individuals in case of WTO violations—it would undermine the legal text of the WTO as a source of public international law, as the flexibility explicitly granted (and discussed above) under the DSU would be compromised. Further, this would be at odds with the above finding that Article 216 para 2 TFEU constitutes the primary source of obligation to comply, to which the principle of practical relevance is applied, albeit not to the extent that DSB rulings would gain any direct effect.

Against this background, from a doctrinal perspective Article 4 para 3 TEU does not offer autonomous and identifiable legal obligation in this case, but is limited to its function to support an otherwise established obligation—in this case, the supportive function would lie in confirming the above developed liability regime based on Article 216 para 2 TFEU. The principle of loyalty enshrined in Article 4 para 3 TEU would thus support the EU's obligation to comply with the DSB ruling. This way of interpretation corresponds to the function the Court had given to this provision in *Francovich*, where it did not deliver an autonomous meaning. Thus, there is no doctrinal barrier to refer to Article 4 para 3 TEU in order to support the duties under Article 216 para 2 TFEU. In a subsequent step, it needs to be shown why the principle of cooperation would entail a duty of the EU vis-à-vis the Member States to accept a liability for WTO-inconsistent measures. Unlike under Article 288 TFEU as referred to in *Francovich*, Article 216 para 2 TFEU concerns the reverse relationship in obligation—a duty the EU has to meet vis-à-vis the Member States.

[137] D Triantafyllou, 'Haftung der Mitgliedstaaten für Nichtumsetzung von EG-Recht' [1992] *DÖV* 564, 568; D Curtin, 'Directives: The Effectiveness of Judicial Protection of Individual Rights' (1990) 27 *CML Rev* 709, 734.

[138] Streinz (n 130) Art 4 para 3 TEU, para 27; Epiney, 'Gemeinschaftsrecht' (n 130) 310; W Kahl in C Calliess and M Ruffert (eds), *EUV/AEUV*, 5th edn (München, CH Beck, 2016) Art 4 TEU, para 43; further references in case-law are provided by M Lück, *Die Gemeinschaftstreue als allgemeines Rechtsprinzip im Recht der Europäischen Gemeinschaft*, 1st edn (Baden-Baden, Nomos, 1992), 79f; critical Eilmansberger, *Gemeinschaftsrecht* (1997) (n 119) 43.

[139] Streinz (n 130) Art 4, para 27; Albers, *Haftung* (1995) (n 119) 174.

[140] Kahl (n 138) Art 4 TEU, para 43.

## B. Obligations resulting from Article 4 para 3 TEU

Past jurisprudence on Member States' obligations vis-à-vis the EU has shown that Article 4 para 3 TEU can establish duties not explicitly foreseen in the EU Treaties.[141] Obligations arising out of Article 4 para 3 TEU must meet three conditions.[142] First, the obligation must serve the functioning of the EU within the scope of the European Treaties. Second, the obligation must be sufficiently discernible in the specific case. Third, the obligation must remain within the distribution of competences set by the EU Treaties.

A duty arising out of Article 4 para 3 TEU must serve the functioning of the EU.[143] In that sense, Article 4 para 3 also aims at ensuring the practical effectiveness of EU law.[144] The loyalty principle has, therefore, been interpreted as a treaty-based provision of the *effet utile* principle,[145] even though the loyalty principle and *effet utile* can also produce opposing interpretations on the same issue. This appears particularly possible in cases of conflicts of interests, where Member States' concerns have to be balanced with the exercise of EU powers, that is when Member States may be adversely affected in cases where the EU exercises its EU Treaty-based competences.[146] Regarding liability for WTO breaches, such conflicts are unlikely to occur. Establishing a liability for WTO infringements creates incentives for EU institutions to act in conformity with WTO law, and thus supports the compliance command of Article 216 para 2 TFEU for the EU to act in line with its obligations under international agreement, without creating tensions in interests among Member States and the EU.

Moreover, for several reasons Article 4 para 3 TEU can be the ground for sustaining EU liability for WTO breaches, with a view to ensuring the functioning of the EU. First, such an obligation would be in line with the bindingness of DSB rulings, as it arises under Article 216 TFEU promoting the effectiveness of this norm.[147] Second, liability would ensure a uniform regime of individual legal protection. In turn, a refusal to recognise individual legal protection for violation of international agreements not only generally questions uniform application of the

[141] Bogdandy and Schill (n 131) Art 4 TEU, para 52; Kahl (n 138) Art 4 para 3 TEU, para 15; Mosiek, *Effet utile* (2003) (n 62) 162f.

[142] AV Bogdandy in E Grabitz and M Hilf (eds), *Das Recht der Europäischen Union* (München, CH Beck, 2005) Art 10 ECT, para12.

[143] Bogdandy and Schill (n 138) Art 4 TEU, para 108; Kahl (n 138) Art 4 TEU, para 35; Streinz (n 130) Art 4 TEU, para 25; *Vloeberghs v High Authority* (ch 1, fn 48); A Hatje, *Loyalität als Rechtsprinzip in der Europäischen Union* (Baden-Baden, Nomos, 2001), 60.

[144] M Zuleeg, 'Die föderativen Grundsätze der Europäischen Union' [2000] *NJW* 2846, 2847; Mosiek, *Effet utile* (2003) (n 62) 15f; E Schmidt-Aßmann, 'Deutsches und Europäisches Verwaltungsrecht—wechselseitige Einwirkungen' [1993] *DVBl* 924, 931.

[145] Mosiek, *Effet utile* (2003) (n 62) 15.

[146] ibid 177.

[147] Likewise Schoißwohl, 'Haftung' (ch 1, fn 8) 710.

legality principle for all matters of EU law, but also poses a risk to the uniformity of the legal order. Third, Article 4 para 3 requires that the obligation must be clearly identifiable in the specific case, in order to meet the principle of legal security.[148] As regards liability for WTO violations, this requirement would be met because liability follows the conditions developed under Article 340 TFEU. And finally, obligations arising from Article 4 para 3 TEU must not compromise the EU's internal allocation of competences.[149] In this vein, the principle of loyalty must balance both Member States' and EU's interests in the context of a liability for WTO infringements. Denial of liability, as a result of the CJEU's jurisprudence, affects Member States' interests considerably. The EU institutions failing to comply with DSB decisions ultimately force Member States' authorities to implement EU law in violation of international law. This is particularly problematic, as both the EU and Member States are bound under Article 216 para 2 TFEU to the WTO agreements as so-called mixed agreements. These agreements were concluded by both EU and Member States, because they concern issues which fall into the shared competences.[150] Under these circumstances, both the EU and Member States are bound under international law and, thus, assume common liability for the acts of the other part.[151]

Thus, the shared international responsibility under mixed agreements has significant adverse effects on Member States. The EU's persistent refusal to bring its regulations into compliance with the DSB rulings leads to Member States' responsibility under international law.[152] Given that the acts of EU institutions, their WTO-inconsistent practice in particular, is attributed to Member States, the EU inflicts international responsibility on Member States. Hence, this creates a conflict with the loyalty principle pursuant to Article 4 para 3 TEU, because the EU is under the obligation to avoid measures inducing international responsibility of Member States, especially in contexts without involvement of the Member States.[153]

[148] Bogdandy (n 142) Art 10 ECT, para15.

[149] Bogdandy and Schill (n 131) Art 4 TEU, para 100.

[150] Vgl dazu Flemisch, *Umfang* (2002) (ch 2, fn 5) 28ff; Epiney, 'Völkerrechts in der EU' (n 37) 7.

[151] G Gaja, 'The European Community's Rights and Obligations under Mixed Agreements' in D O'Keeffe and HG Schermers (eds), *Mixed Agreements* (Deventer, Kluwer Law and Taxation Publishers, 2009) 137; Everling, 'Will Europe Slip on Bananas?' (ch 1, fn 7) 423; A Bleckmann, 'Der gemischte Vertrag im Europarecht' [1976] *EuR* 301, 311; M Footer, 'The EU and the WTO Global Trading System' in P-H Laurent and M Maresceau (eds), *The State of the European Union: Deepening and Widening* (Boulder, Lynne Rienner Publishers, 1998) 320; E Staebe, *Europarecht*, 1st edn (Baden-Baden, Nomos, 1998), 218; R Kovar, 'La participation des Communautés Européennes aux conventions multilatérales' [1975] *AFDI* 903, 915; Flemisch, *Umfang* (2002) (ch 2, fn 5) 137; M Cremona, 'The Doctrine of Exclusivity and the Position of Mixed Agreements in the External Relations of the European Community' (1982) 2 *OJLS* 393, 423.

[152] T Stein, '"Bananen-Split"? Entzweien sich BVerfG und EuGH über den Bananenstreit?' [1998] *EuZW* 261, 263; Case C-57/96 *Hermès v FHT* [1998] ECR I-3603, Opinion of AG Tesauro, para 14; Flemisch, *Umfang* (2002) (ch 2, fn 5) 14.

[153] Flemisch, *Umfang* (2002) (ch 2, fn 5) 137.

In addition, Member States suffer harm to the extent that retaliatory measures adopted as response to the EU's infringements of WTO law hit national companies.[154] While this factual adverse effect for companies does not fall into the scope of Article 4 para 3 TEU, which is limited to the relationship between the EU and the Member States (excluding private companies),[155] there remains the legal responsibility the Member States assume for the EU's unlawful conduct.

The duties involved in implementing an international agreement have already been identified by the CJEU in its early decision in *Kupferberg*. In that case, the Court stated that:

> in ensuring respect for commitments arising from an agreement concluded by the Community institutions the Member States fulfil an obligation not only in relation to the non-member country concerned but also and above all in relation to the Community which has assumed responsibility for the due performance of the agreement.[156]

From this statement of the Court, two observations can be inferred with regard to the principle of Article 4 para 3 TEU: first, the duty to ensure respect for the commitments arising from an agreement is mutual to the extent that both EU and Member States must respect their respective commitments, because the loyalty principle under Article 4 para 3 TEU is a common principle imposing duties on both the EU and Member States.[157] Second, the obligation to respect each other's commitments is even more evident in the case of mixed agreements, in which the ties between Member States and the EU are closer, given the shared responsibility each of them is exposed to on an international level.[158] In sum, the foregoing has shown that certain loyalty duties in the relationship between the EU and the Member States are violated, if one of the two does not abide by its obligations under international agreements. Thus, the EU violates its duty to loyal conduct under Article 4 para 3 TEU by not implementing DSB rulings under the WTO agreements.

In sum, the loyalty principle under Article 4 para 3 TEU—the third pillar on which the CJEU based its doctrinal move to delink liability from direct effect in *Francovich*—supports the establishment of liability for WTO infringements. The principle of ensuring the functioning of the EU coincides with the principle of practical effectiveness, as both principles require the EU to comply with its obligations under Article 216 para 2 TFEU. Moreover, liability ensures the EU's duty to

[154] Schoißwohl, 'Haftung' (ch 1, fn 8) 710.

[155] Case C-341/95 *Bettati v Safety Hi-Tech* [1998] ECR I-4355, para 77. Referring to the order of 13 July 1990 in *Zwartveld and Others* (n 131) para 17, and to the judgment of 13 October 1992 in Case C-63/90 and C-67/90 *Portugal and Spain v Council* [1992] ECR I-5073, para 52.

[156] *Hauptzollamt Mainz v Kupferberg* (ch 2, fn 7) 3662, para 13.

[157] This duty implies to take account of each other's interests *Luxembourg v European Parliament* (n 131) para 37; *Portugal and Spain v Council* (n 155) I-5156; see also A Hatje in J Schwarze (ed), *EU-Kommentar*, 3rd edn (Baden-Baden, Nomos, 2012), Art 4 TEU, para 24.

[158] Similarly Flemisch, *Umfang* (2002) (ch 2, fn 5) 137.

respect Member States' interests where issues of mixed agreements are concerned. In these cases, Member States assume international responsibility for unlawful acts committed by the EU. The loyalty principle requires the EU to act in line with mixed agreements, notably by implementing DSB rulings, in order to avoid adverse legal (and factual) consequences for the Member States.

# 4

# *DSB Ruling and the Protection of Individual Rights*

## I. THE REQUIREMENTS OF INDIVIDUAL PROTECTION UNDER ARTICLE 340 PARA 2 TFEU

THE ABOVE ANALYSIS sought to demonstrate that an analogy of the *Francovich* approach of the Court is possible in the context of liability for WTO violations—from a doctrinal perspective, this implies a de-linking of the concept of direct effect from violation of a 'norm intended to protect individual rights' (the German *Schutznorm* or 'protective norm'), as a requirement under Article 340 TFEU. A *Schutznorm* within the meaning of Article 340 TFEU does not necessarily have to be directly effective. Yet, it remains to be clarified which requirements a DSB ruling has to fulfil in order to meet the protective character of a *Schutznorm*. Violation of the duty to implement the DSB decision, based on Article 216 para 2 TFEU, can give rise to liability only if the decision intends to confer rights on individuals.[1]

How and to what extent must the DSB ruling protect individual interests? The wording chosen by the Court in damage suits brought under previous judgments offer a heterogeneous interpretation of the Court's criteria for a *Schutznorm*, even though, at least for WTO breaches, direct effect has constantly been required. In *Atlanta*, the General Court found that in areas 'involving choices of economic policy, the Community can incur liability only if a sufficiently-serious breach of a superior rule of law for the protection of individuals has occurred'.[2] Hence, in *Atlanta* the General Court still refers to the formula used since *Schöppenstedt*. In the subsequent damage suits in *Bocchi*, *T.Port*, *Cordis* and *Chiquita*, the General Court (as well as the Court) slightly modified its wording to require 'that the rule of law infringed be intended to confer rights on individuals and that the breach

[1] P Aalto, *Public Liability in EU Law*, 1st edn (Oxford, Hart Publishing, 2011) 39, for the parallel issue on the implementation of directives HD Jarass, 'Haftung für die Verletzung von EU–Recht durch nationale Organe und Amtsträger' [1994] *NJW* 881, 883; M Schimke, 'Zur Haftung der Bundesrepublik Deutschland gegenüber Bürgern wegen Nichtumsetzung der EG-Richtlinie über Pauschalreisen' [1993] *EuZW* 698, 700.

[2] Case T-521/93 *Atlanta AG and Others v Council and Commission* [1996] ECR II-1707, II-1738, para 83.

of such a rule be sufficiently serious'.[3] By referring to the Court's judgment in *Bergaderm*, the General Court suggests indicating a modification of its previous line of jurisprudence. The General Court uses the same wording and reference to *Bergaderm* in its judgement in *Biret*.[4]

We thus observe an alternation of the liability requirement to the effect that the established *Schöppenstedt* formula is used in *Atlanta*, while subsequently a conferral of individual rights is required. The wording used in recent judgments corresponds to the conditions set out in *Francovich*, according to which 'the result prescribed by the directive should entail the grant of rights to individuals'.[5] The structural convergence between liability of the EU and Member States offers a persuasive explanation for this modification in streamlining the *Schutznorm* for both EU and Member State liability.[6] As the Court stated in *Brasserie du Pêcheur*, the 'conditions under which the State may incur liability for damage caused to individuals by a breach of Community law cannot, in the absence of particular justification, differ from those governing the liability of the Community in like circumstances'.[7] The Court's effort to harmonise the two liability regimes also serves to ensure a uniform level of individual legal protection. This explains why the judgments related to WTO damage suits refer to the previous *Bergaderm* decision.

The standard necessary for a norm conferring rights on individuals remains unclear. The Court does not give an indication for a substantial difference between the *Schutznorm* under Article 340 TFEU, on the one hand, and the 'conferral of individual rights' pursuant to *Francovich*, on the other hand. Previous case law on the *Schutznorm* has been rather generous, deeming it sufficient that individual interests were protected only indirectly. The question then is whether this extensive reading of a *Schutznorm* requires modification, if reference to the wording used in *Francovich* would imply a more restrictive stance on the meaning of conferring individual rights.[8] An indication to that end could be seen in the fact that it is not sufficient if the directive would simply 'protect' individuals but—even stronger—to require that it confers 'rights' on individuals.[9]

[3] Bocchi *Food Trade International v Commission* (Introduction, fn 8) II-965, para 50; *Cordis Obst v Commission* (Introduction, fn 8) II-931, para 46ff; *Chiquita v Commission* (Introduction, fn 8) II-315, para 77; these judgements refer to *Bergaderm and Goupil v Commission* (ch 3, fn 2) I-5291, para 42; in Banatrading the General Court does not even identify the conditions for liablity, see Case T-3/99 *Banatrading v Council* [2001] ECR II-2123, II-2137, para 30; see also *FIAMM and FIAMM Technologies v Council and Commission* (Introduction, fn 8) paras 172f.

[4] *Biret International v Council* (ch 3, fn 6) II-17, para 52.

[5] *Francovich v Italy* (ch 3, fn 16) I-5415, paras 39f.

[6] See also Aalto, *Public Liability* (2011) (n 1) 3ff.

[7] *Brasserie du Pêcheur v Germany and Rv Secretary of State for Transport, ex parte Factortame III* (ch 3, fn 23) I-1029, para 42; confirmed in *Bergaderm and Goupil v Commission* (ch 3, fn 2) I-5324, para 41.

[8] Peers, 'WTO dispute settlement' (ch 2, fn 57) 612f.

[9] Therefore, scepticism was raised in the literature regarding the transferability of the extensive jurisprudence on Article 340 TFEU into the context of Member State liability Henrichs, *Haftung* (1995) (ch 1, fn 50) 28; Triantafyllou, 'Haftung' (ch 3, fn 137) 569; Eilmansberger, *Gemeinschaftsrecht* (1997) (ch 3, fn 119) 73.

In the literature, a broad understanding of the *Schutznorm* has largely been approved, provided that individual rights can be identified at least as a kind of reflex (or as 'the other side of a coin') accruing from a clear, unconditional obligation without discretion.[10] By contrast, a purely factual effect would not be captured by this extensive interpretation of the *Schutznorm*.[11] By way of interpretation, there must be a legally protected interest to be discerned. Thus the crucial question is: does the norm (at least among other goals) aim at protecting individual interests or not? This does not only refer to whether the primary objective of the norm is being considered in a narrow sense only, because that would ignore the reflex-like character of the protection.[12] Rather, the interpretation of the objective of the norm allows one to go beyond the explicit and primary protective goal of the norm and capture the indirect effect of the provision, which is sometimes only the secondary effect aimed at by the norm. In sum, in the area of EU liability, the standards set to determine the protective character of a violated norm should not be too high—in particular, the protective character is not precluded just because the norm also pursues other goals or aims at protecting individual rights on a secondary basis only.[13]

## II. THE PROTECTIVE CHARACTER OF WTO LAW AND DSB DECISIONS

Having clarified the standards to qualify as a protective norm under the EU liability regime, the quality of WTO law is to be examined on that basis.

### A. Lack of legal standing of individuals

The standing of individuals within the legal system of the WTO is one point of reference for the determination of its protective character. The limited role of individuals in this system militates against characterising the WTO as a legal order

[10] R Streinz, 'Staatshaftung für Verletzungen primären Gemeinschaftsrechts durch die Bundesrepublik Deutschland' [1993] *EuZW* 599, 601; Gellermann (ch 1, 48) Art 340, para 20; M Zuleeg, 'Umweltschutz in der Rechtsprechung des Europäischen Gerichtshofs' [1993] *NJW* 31, 37; A Bell, 'Enforcing Community Law Rights Before National Courts—Some Developments' (1994) 21 *LIEI* 111, 120; S Prechal, *Directives in EC Law*, 2nd edn (Oxford, Oxford University Press, 2005) 328.

[11] Triantafyllou, 'Haftung' (ch 3, fn 137) 569; Geiger, 'Staatshaftungsanspruchsrechts' (ch 3, fn 20) 470; Diehr, *Staatshaftungsanspruch* (1997) (ch 3, fn 19) 94.

[12] Similarly on the determination of legal positions afforded by directives M Ruffert, 'Dogmatik und Praxis des subjektiv-öffentlichen Rechts unter dem Einfluss des Gemeinschaftsrechts' [1998] *DVBl* 69, 72; M Ruffert, *Subjektive Rechte im Umweltrecht der Europäischen Gemeinschaft* (Heidelberg v Decker, 1996), 147ff, 157ff, 224.

[13] J Temple Lang, 'New Legal Effects resulting from the Failure of States to Fulfil Obligations under Community Law; the Francovich Judgment' (1992) 16 *Fordham Int'l L J* 1, 28f; D Simon, 'Droit communautaire et la responsabilité de la puissance publique: Glissements progressifs ou révolution tranquille' [1993] *AJDA* 235, 238; Cornils, *Staatshaftungsanspruch* (1995) (ch 3, fn 22) 125; Peers, 'WTO Dispute Settlement' (ch 2, fn 57) 613.

protecting individuals. Individuals are not explicitly endowed with rights in WTO agreements; they are neither the immediate subject of the rules, nor do they have a legal standing before the adjudicative bodies of the WTO. This may have been one of the main drivers for the Court's underlying reasoning to deny direct effect to the WTO provisions. The Court has stressed that the 'purpose of the WTO agreements is to govern relations between States or regional organisations for economic integration and not to protect individuals'.[14] The Court's statement is correct to the extent that WTO rules primarily provide a regulatory system for cross-border trade containing obligations for states. As such, the rules aim at restricting policy space by states rather than conferring direct and independent rights to individuals.[15] The genuine character as an inter-state legal order is due to its origin in an international law treaty constituting rights and obligations of states.[16] Formally, individuals are not (or only on a very limited scale) subject of this legal order, even if the individual has emerged as a subject of international law in some issue areas over the last decades. Under WTO law, individuals have no direct legal standing and do not formally participate in the dispute settlement proceedings[17]—individuals clearly do not enjoy 'subjectivity' under WTO law.[18]

### i. *Indirect protection of individuals under WTO law*

Different considerations apply if one replaces the strict formal approach and instead takes into account what the WTO rules are aiming at beyond their primary intention. Assessing the indirect and reflexive intentions of legal provisions is precisely what was analysed above as the standard to be applied to consider a *Schutznorm* under the purpose of Article 340 TFEU—besides the objective regulatory content of the norm, one must examine whether the norm also protects the interests of individuals. This approach is not alien to the Court's jurisprudence. For example, in the area of environmental directives, the Court dealt in *Commission/Germany*[19] with a directive requiring Member States to establish a surveillance system, in order to avoid the emissions of certain substances. This objective obligation addressed to Member States did not prevent the Court from accepting that this norm would also protect individual interests. Even if individual interests in such cases are protected only indirectly or as a reflex, this may suffice to establish certain rights.

[14] *Biret International v Council* (ch Introduction, fn 8) para 62; see R Schwartmann, *Private im Wirtschaftsvölkerrecht* (Tübingen, Mohr Siebeck, 2005), 159ff.

[15] Weiß, 'Verletzung des WTO-Rechts' (ch 2, fn 50) 292; Griller, 'Enforcement' (ch 2, fn 30) 296; Schwartmann (2005) (n 14) 159.

[16] See also H Kelsen, *Principles of International Law* (Clark, The Lawbook Exchange Ltd, 2012) 234; CA Nørgaard, *The Position of the Individual in International Law* (Kopenhagen, Munksgaard, 1962) 27f.

[17] P Backes, 'Die neuen Streitbeilegungsregeln der Welthandelsorganisation (WTO)' [1995] *RIW* 916, 916.

[18] Meng, 'Rechtsstellung der Individuen' (ch 2, fn 6) 65.

[19] Case C-131/88 *Commission v Germany* [1991] ECR I-825, I-867, para 7.

From an economic perspective, the WTO rules aim at generating positive welfare effects and, therefore, implicitly seek to set a regulatory framework conducive to the trading activities of private economic actors.[20] In that regard, states have laid down the principle of free trade as the fundamental goal of the WTO rules.[21] Even if WTO rules do not explicitly endow private actors with enforceable rights, trading companies are the main group intended to benefit from free trade rules.[22] They are not addressees of obligations, but they are the ones who act within the rules applicable and whose activities are to be promoted through the rules.[23] As main actors of transactions on the markets for goods, services and payments, the individual companies conducting their business in the world trading system under the rules of the WTO are at least indirectly protected by the WTO provisions. The self-restrictions by trade law, pertaining to a country's policy space, correspond to the extension of economic activities and freedoms of individual companies. In other words, individual benefits do not accrue from the explicit intention of the agreements to safeguard enforceable individual rights, but rather result from the states' obligation, as on the other side of the coin.

Moreover, by reference to individual provisions under the WTO rules, it is hard to argue that these rules would exclusively reflect states' interest in free trade. The WTO negotiation rounds aim at comprehensive reduction and elimination of barriers to trade.[24] The concessions are to be granted to importing companies, on the basis of the most-favoured-nation treatment,[25] including a prohibition of quantitative import restrictions.[26] These provisions are addressed to Member States, but their essential aim is to benefit companies.[27] Even if the WTO rules do not establish an enforcement mechanism for individual companies,[28] individual trading companies are the ones to be ultimately protected through the free trade rules.[29]

[20] P Behrens, 'Die private Durchsetzung von WTO-Recht' in C Nowak W Cremer (eds), *Individualrechtsschutz in der EG und der WTO: Der zentrale und dezentrale Rechtsschutz natürlicher und juristischer Personen in der Europäischen Gemeinschaft und der Welthandelsorganisation*, 1st edn (Baden-Baden, Nomos 2002) 202; Meng, 'Rechtsstellung der Individuen' (ch 2, fn 6) 65.

[21] See also the preamble of the WTO agreement.

[22] Berrisch and Kamann, 'Gemeinschaftsrecht' (ch 2, fn 30) 97; Petersmann, 'GATT/WTO-Recht' (ch 2, fn 35) 651; Meng, 'Rechtsstellung der Individuen' (ch 2, fn 6) 65; Schoißwohl, 'Haftung' (ch 1, fn 8) 714f; Reinisch, 'Opfer des Hormon- und Bananenstreites' (Introduction, fn 7) 45.

[23] MJ Trebilcock and R Howse, *The Regulation of International Trade*, 3rd edn (London, Routledge, 2005) 1ff; JH Jackson, *The World Trading System*, 2nd edn (Cambridge, MIT Press, 1997) 1; Oeter, 'Rechtsschutzdefizit' (ch 3, fn 121) 222f.

[24] Art II, XXVIIIff GATT.

[25] Art I GATT.

[26] Art XI GATT.

[27] E-U Petersmann, *The GATT/WTO Dispute Settlement System* (London, Kluwer Law International, 1997) 238: 'The formulation of international trade rules in terms of rights and obligations of states is therefore no convincing reason for preventing individuals from invoking precise and unconditional international guarantees of freedom and non-discrimination, such as the custom union rules of the EC Treaty and their underlying worldwide GATT rules'.

[28] See also Oeter, 'Rechtsschutzdefizit' (ch 3, fn 121) 221ff.

[29] Weiß, 'Verletzung des WTO-Rechts' (ch 2, fn 50) 292; *Biret International v Council* (Introduction, fn 8) Opinion of AG Alber, I-10497, para 116ff; Hörmann and Göttsche, 'Haftung' (ch 2, fn 37) 691; Schoißwohl, 'Haftung' (ch 1, fn 8) 714f; Zonnekeyn, 'EC Liability' (ch 1, fn 35) 263f; Meng, 'Rechtsstellung der Individuen' (ch 2, fn 6) 66; critical Sack, 'Weltordnung des Rechts' (ch 2, fn 29) 650.

Jurisprudence of WTO adjudicative bodies supports an interpretation of the WTO with a view to indirect protective nature. In *United States—Section 301–310 of the Trade Act of 1974*, the Panel elaborated on the importance of individual trading activities in the domain of world trade, as well as for the interpretation of WTO rules:[30]

> Many of the benefits to Members, which are meant to flow as a result of the acceptance of various disciplines under the GATT/WTO, depend on the activity of individual economic operators in the national and global market places. The purpose of many of these disciplines, indeed one of the primary objects of the GATT/WTO as a whole, is to produce certain market conditions, which would allow this individual activity to flourish.[31]
>
> The multilateral trading system is, per force, composed not only of States but also, indeed mostly, of individual economic operators. The lack of security and predictability affects mostly these individual operators. Trade is conducted most often and increasingly by private operators. It is through improved conditions for these private operators that Members benefit from WTO disciplines. The denial of benefits to a Member, which flows from a breach, is often indirect and results from the impact of the breach on the market place and the activities of individuals within it.

The Panel underscores the indirect effect of WTO law promoting the protection of individual interests. This supports the conceptual view on the WTO agreements as providing a regulatory framework enabling private activities on international markets to flourish.[32] Interpretation of WTO law should, thus, not account only for the expectation of states, but rather adopt the perspectives of individuals conducting their business within the WTO legal framework. The intrinsic link between public and private interests finds their expression also in the preamble of the WTO agreement, which refers to 'raising the standards of living, ensuring full employment and a large and steadily growing volume of real income and effective demand, and expanding the production of and trade in goods and services [...]'. Intentions related to macroeconomic and microeconomic purposes are thus hard to separate from each other. Rather, private interests are exploited for the purpose of public objectives, because the promotion of public interests can be accomplished through the advancement of private activities.[33] In this vein, individual rights pertaining to free trade are at least indirectly an inherent goal of the WTO agreements.

[30] *WTO: United States—Section 301-310 of the Trade Act of 1974—Report of the Appellate Body* (27 January 2000) WT/DS152/R, para 7.71ff.

[31] 'See also similar language in the second preambles to GATT 1947 and GATS. The TRIPS Agreement addresses even more explicitly the interests of individual operators, obligating WTO Members to protect the intellectual property rights of nationals of all other WTO Members. Creating market conditions so that the activity of economic operators can flourish is also reflected in the object of many WTO agreements, for example, in the non-discrimination principles in GATT, GATS and TRIPS and the market access provisions in both GATT and GATS.'

[32] Likewise Behrens, 'Durchsetzung' (n 20) 202 (referring to the 'utility' of WTO rules for individual companies); critical Bogdandy, 'Legal Effects' (ch 3, fn 11) 53.

[33] Meng, 'Rechtsstellung der Individuen' (ch 3, fn 6) 75.

*ii. Indirect protection of case group B: the example of hormones and bananas*

The transatlantic disputes surrounding the import of hormone-treated beef and bananas are among the most controversial trade disputes in WTO history.[34] From an individual company perspective, the EU banana import regime restricted business opportunities of companies of case group B, to the extent that imports of bananas from third countries were subject to higher duties than those applicable to Community and ACP bananas, and were also restricted through quantitative restriction differentiation concerning the origin of the imported bananas. The WTO adjudicative bodies found violations of Articles I,[35] II,[36] III,[37] XI,[38] XIII,[39] GATT and Art II[40] GATS. In the hormones dispute, violations were found of Articles 5 para 1, Art 5 para 5 and Art 3 para 1[41] of the SPS Agreement.

The general most-favoured-nation principle in Article I para 1 GATT is sufficiently clear and unambiguous, since both the requirements and legal consequences of this principle are precisely defined.[42] Given the clarity of this wording, there is no doubt as to the protective character of this provision favouring individuals. The provision grants the individual to claim 'any advantage, favour, privilege or immunity granted by any contracting party to any product originating in or

[34] See, inter alia, BL Brimeyer, 'Bananas, beef and compliance in the World Trade Organization: the inability of the WTO dispute settlement process to achieve compliance from superpower nations' (2001) 10 *Minn J Global Trade* 133, 133; Jackson and Grane, 'Banana Dispute' (Introduction, fn 7).

[35] GATT Doc DS 38/R, in: ILM XXXIV (1995), 180 and 224, para 159; under the WTO see *WTO:* EC Regime for the Importation, Sale and Distribution of Bananas—Report of the Appellate Body (22 May 1997) WT/DS27/R, para 7.241; WTO: *European Communities—Regime for the Importation, Sale and Distribution of Bananas—Report of the Appellate Body* (9 September 1997) WT/DS27/AB/R, paras 205ff; for a comprehensive discussion see JC Cascante and GG Sander, *Der Streit um die EG-Bananenmarktordnung* (Berlin, Duncker & Humblot, 1999), 75ff.

[36] Vgl GATT Doc DS 38/R, in: ILM XXXIV (1995), 180, 217f, paras 134ff; see also GG Sander, *Rechtsprobleme der EG-Bananenmarktordnung* (Marburg, Tectum Verlag, 1996), 36.

[37] WTO: European Communities—Regime for the Importation, Sale and Distribution of Bananas—Report of the Appellate Body (22 May 1997) WT/DS27/R/ECU, para 7.171ff; WTO: European Communities—Regime for the Importation, Sale and Distribution of Bananas—Report of the Appellate Body (22 May 1997) WT/DS27/R/GTM and WT/DS27/R/HDN, paras 7.216ff and paras 7.244 ff; WTO: *European Communities—Regime for the Importation, Sale and Distribution of Bananas—Report of the Appellate Body* (9 September 1997) WT/DS27/AB/R paras 208 ff.

[38] Cascante and Sander, *EG-Bananenmarktordnung* (1999) (n 35) 81f.

[39] WTO: European Communities—Regime for the Importation, Sale and Distribution of Bananas—Report of the Appellate Body (22 May 1997) WT/DS27/R/ECU, para 7.79; WTO: *European Communities—Regime for the Importation, Sale and Distribution of Bananas—Report of the Appellate Body* (9 September 1997) WT/DS27/AB/R, para 189ff.

[40] WTO: *European Communities—Regime for the Importation, Sale and Distribution of Bananas—Report of the Appellate Body* (22 May 1997) WT/DS27/R/ECU, WT/DS27/R/MEX and WT/DS27/R/USA, paras 7.353, 7.368, 7.393, 7.397; confirmed by the report of the Appellate Body, WTO: *European Communities—Regime for the Importation, Sale and Distribution of Bananas—Report of the Appellate Body* (9 September 1997) WT/DS27/AB/R, paras 244, 246, 248.

[41] WTO: EC Measures Concerning Meat and Meat Products (Hormones)—*Report of the Appellate Body* (13 February 1998) WT/DS48/R/CAN, para IX.1.

[42] Kuschel, 'EG-Bananenmarktordnung' (ch 3, fn 45) 690; Petersmann, 'GATT/WTO-Recht' (ch 2, fn 35) 652; Flemisch, *Umfang* (2002) (ch 2, fn 5) 253.

destined for any other country' to be 'accorded immediately and unconditionally to the like product originating in or destined for the territories of all other contracting parties'.[43] This principle is not formulated as an obligation or right accruing to states, but is rather drafted from the perspectives of the 'goods'. As such, the MFN principle is potentially directed towards the economic actors.[44] Some scholars even claim a direct effect of this norm due to the specificity and unambiguousness of this wording.[45] Similar considerations apply to the parallel provision in Article II para 1 GATS, the infringement of which had also been found in the banana dispute.[46]

Also, Article II para 1(a) GATT should be considered as protecting individual rights, since it is sufficiently precise in its formulation and confers, in combination with the schedules of concessions, the right of a 'treatment no less favourable than that provided for in the appropriate Part of the appropriate Schedule annexed to this Agreement'. The potential direct effect of Article III para 1 GATT has been discussed controversially.[47] Doubt arises not so much because of the lack of certainty of the rights entailed in Article III GATT, but rather because this provision has been interpreted as a political objective to which direct effect could not be accorded.[48] It seems convincing to argue that Article III para 1 GATT is sufficiently precise in its binding character[49] and to recognise the subjective character of the provision to give individuals the right that 'internal taxes and other internal charges [...] should not be applied to imported or domestic products so as to afford protection to domestic production'.[50]

Also, Article XI para 1 GATT stipulates the ban on import restrictions with great clarity and unambiguousness and has, therefore, been viewed as sufficiently precise and unconditional.[51] The judge can apply this provision without further legislative acts of implementation being necessary, if the individual company invokes this provision for the purpose of tackling quotas, import or export licences or other measures. Similarly, Article XIII para 1 GATT specifies unambiguously the

[43] Similarly Flemisch, *Umfang* (2002) (ch 2, fn 5) 259; Schoißwohl, 'Haftung' (ch 1, fn 8) 714; Reinisch, 'Opfer des Hormon- und Bananenstreites' (Introduction, fn 7) 45.

[44] Stoll, 'Freihandel und Verfassung' (ch 2, fn 34) 119.

[45] Flemisch, *Umfang* (2002) (ch 2, fn 5) 253; Petersmann, 'GATT/WTO-Recht' (ch 2, fn 35) 652.

[46] See also Flemisch, *Umfang* (2002) (ch 2, fn 5) 267; critical Krajewski, *Verfassungsperspektiven* (2001) (ch 2, fn 30) 190.

[47] While German courts have consistently denied to grant direct effect to GATT and WTO rules, Italian courts have ruled to the contrary. See Finanzgericht München, EFG 1970, 145; 'Art III des GATT ist nicht geeignet, unmittelbare Wirkungen zu erzeugen und individuelle Rechte des Einzelnen zu begründen, welche die nationalen Gerichte zu beachten haben.'

[48] Ott, *GATT und WTO* (1997) (ch 2, fn 5) 226.

[49] J Drexl, *Entwicklungsmöglichkeiten des Urheberrechts im Rahmen des GATT* (München, CH Beck 1990), 280; Flemisch, *Umfang* (2002) (ch 2, fn 5) 255; Petersmann, 'GATT/WTO-Recht' (ch 2, fn 35) 652.

[50] Likeswise Flemisch, *Umfang* (2002) (ch 2, fn 5) 261; Drexl, *Entwicklungsmöglichkeiten* (1990) (fn 49) 280; A Gerken, *Rechtsschutzmöglichkeiten europäischer Wirtschaftsteilnehmer gegen GATT-widrige Wirtschaftshemmnisse* (Frankfurt am Main, P Lang 2004), 167f; Zonnekeyn, 'WTO Law in the EC Legal Order' (ch 1, fn 7) 121.

[51] Petersmann, 'GATT/WTO-Recht' (ch 2, fn 35) 652; Flemisch, *Umfang* (2002) (ch 2, fn 5) 258f.

non-discriminatory application of import restrictions, which—by virtue of the non-discrimination principle—favours the interests of the individual.[52]

Regarding the SPS Agreement, the relevant sanitary and phytosanitary measures aim at protecting individual interests.[53] According to the first recital of the preamble, as well as Article 2 para 3 SPS, the agreement seeks to prevent measures constituting a disguised restriction on international trade. Restrictions of trade by adopting sanitary and phytosanitary measures can generally lead to discrimination between domestic and imported goods, thereby affecting the freedom of economic activities of the individual. Such restrictions of economic freedoms by the relevant EU directive have led the DSB to find a violation of Article 5 para 5 SPS, because the import restriction on hormone-treated beef constituted an unjustified discrimination and disguised restriction. Hence, the provisions of the SPS are designed to ensure market freedoms of the economic actors.

#### *iii. Protection of victims of retaliatory measures (case group C)*

Most evidently, there is an encroachment of economic freedoms in case of the companies hit by US retaliation, following authorisation through the DSB (case group C). Imposing a 100 per cent duty on selected products from the EU suspends the MFN treatment of these products, inflicting severe comparative damages vis-à-vis competing products. EU exporting companies' rights under Articles I and II GATT are being deprived by the imposition of retaliatory measures. There is a causality issue since the measures are the direct consequence of US authority decisions raising the question of attributability to the EU,[54] which, however, does not alter the infringement of the individual company's rights under the MFN principle. One could question the intention of WTO rules to grant the right not to be subject to retaliation, given that such measures can be in line with Article 22 para 6 DSU and are thus foreseen by the WTO. In that regard, a distinction must be made between the right, which the companies concerned are deprived of (ie, import opportunities at conditions like all other importing companies), on the one hand, and the rights under WTO law protecting the companies from being subjected to retaliatory measures approved by the DSB, on the other hand. The WTO rules were designed with the aim to promote free trade between Member States on the basis of frequent rounds of negotiations, as a result of which a specific level of trade restrictions is agreed on. Trade barriers beyond that agreed level are generally not permissible, unless authorised by the DSB or they are within the flexibility granted under the rules (eg, safeguarding clauses). Put differently, the WTO rules not just aim at reducing restrictions to trade, but also protect from

[52] Flemisch, *Umfang* (2002) (ch 2, fn 5) 262.

[53] *Biret International v Council* (Introduction, fn 8) Opinion of AG Alber, I-10497, para 116ff; with doubts Wiers, 'European Court of Justice in Biret' (ch 3, fn 14) 149.

[54] See below ch 6 III.

adopting trade-restrictive measures.[55] If the WTO rules primarily aim at inducing Members of the WTO to design their trade policies in line with the logic of reducing barriers in a binding way, then these rules must also protect from economic harm resulting from the violation of these norms, especially if they give rise to retaliation based on Article 22 para 6 DSU. The protective intention of the rules for case group C can thus be derived from a teleological interpretation of the WTO agreements.[56]

## III. INTERIM CONCLUSIONS ON THE QUALITY OF WTO LAW AS A *SCHUTZNORM*

On balance, taking account of the indirectly protective nature of WTO law one can conclude that, despite the lack of an explicitly individual-centred objective of trade promoting rules of the WTO, there are strong individual benefits intended with the application of the rules. Visually, these individual benefits and rights can be seen as the flipside of a coin, where WTO rules formally only impose obligations on states. Even if the relevant provisions of the WTO agreements primarily regulate inter-state obligations regarding the admissibility of trade restrictions, there are indirect beneficial effects for individual companies. In addition, the uniformity of the liability regimes for Union and Member States suggests that the criterion of the *Schutznorm* is not to be interpreted differently from the 'conferral of individual rights'—the criterion used in *Francovich* regarding the strength of the individual right enshrined in the infringed norm. This implies, in particular, that indirectly intended effects can meet this standard, even if individual benefits accrue only as reflexes of an otherwise objective obligation to states.

If the Panel or Appellate Body report finds that EU secondary law is incompatible with the WTO and GATT provisions entailing benefits and rights for individuals, the DSB decision then gains the character of a *Schutznorm*, non-implementation of which incurs liability. This holds, even if in practice the DSB decision typically only states the mere incompatibility or violation of the WTO by national measures, without specifying certain groups or individuals who suffered damages or who would be specifically protected by the violated norm. Identifiability of the right-holders is an issue to be assessed independently from the general suitability of the DSB decision to accord individual rights and benefits. More specifically, in the bananas and hormones disputes, the violated WTO norms met the requirements of a *Schutznorm* under Article 340 TFEU—this extends to both companies of the case groups B and C alike.

[55] Reinisch, 'Opfer des Hormon- und Bananenstreites' (Introduction, fn 7) 45 with reference to Petersmann, 'GATT/WTO-Recht' (ch 2, fn 35) 652.

[56] Similarly Höher, *Haftung* (2006) (ch 2, fn 5) 344f; Reinisch, 'Opfer des Hormon- und Bananenstreites' (Introduction, fn 7) 45.

# 5

# *Identifiability of an Individual Right*

IN CHAPTER 4 we discussed, on an abstract level, the suitability of WTO law to protect individual rights and create individual benefits. A different requirement for a liability to be well-founded is that the content of the rights of the DSB decision is sufficiently identifiable.[1] This requirement is more concrete and stems from the general legal requirement of legal certainty, according to which—applied in the liability context—there must be a 'normative minimum', a 'minimum right' to be identified in the DSB decision.[2] In other words, the legal position of the individual must be clearly discernible from the DSB decision.[3] The purpose of the identifiability is that the individual should not be able to invoke a right, which has not yet been sufficiently specified by the WTO Member States. Identifiability is lacking, if the content of the individual right is to a degree discretionary, such that it would be impossible to discern a minimum, non-disputable right.[4] It thus needs to be examined whether a normative minimum right can be derived from the individual WTO provisions, the violation of which is found in the DSB decision and which obliges the losing party of the dispute to create an individual right in its legal order.

## I. ADDRESSEE OF THE DSB DECISION

Besides the 'minimum right' requirement regarding the content of the DSB decision, legal certainty also extends to the identifiability of the right holders—in the context of WTO liability this means identifying those who are entitled by the DSB decision. In this regard, there may be a significant difference between the EU directive and the DSB ruling. The DSB decision typically limits its adjudication

[1] *Francovich v Italy* (ch 3, fn 16) I-5415, para 40.

[2] Case C-91/92 *Faccini Dori v Recreb* [1994] ECR I-3325, I-3325, para 17; Joined Cases C-283/94, C-291/94 and C-292/94 *Denkavit and Others v Bundesamt für Finazen* [1996] ECR I-5063, para 39f; Hailbronner, 'Staatshaftung' (ch 3, fn 119) 288; Ossenbühl, 'Staatshaftungsanspruch' (ch 3, fn 76) 996.

[3] For the implementation of directives into Member State law *Francovich v Italy* (ch 3, fn 16) I-5357, para 44; Case C-178/94, C-179/94, C-188/94, C-189/94 and C-190/94 *Dillenkofer and Others v Germany* [1996] ECR I-4845, para 43ff.

[4] U Klinke, 'Europäisches Unternehmensrecht und EuGH in den Jahren 1991–1992' [1993] *ZGR* 1, 28.

on stipulating the incompatibility of a specific measure with WTO rules. By contrast, *Francovich* was about a directive on the basis of which Member States were obliged to grant rights to individuals and, more specifically, to implement a legal entitlement to receive salaries over several months, in case of their employer's insolvency.[5] Typically, identification of those individuals that are intended by the directive to obtain a right, is rarely an issue in practice. And if there is still a lack of clarity, one could refer to the reasoning of the directive, which reveals the intention of the directive.

The DSB decision lacks a clear identification of beneficiaries of the decision. Yet, this lack of explicitness does not preclude the identifiability of the beneficiaries.[6] Unlike the EU directive, the ruling of the DSB does not constitute a legislative act, but rather a quasi-judgment in which the (non)-conformity of national measures with WTO law is stated.[7] Judgments rule on the lawfulness of a measure and, as such, often do not specify the beneficiaries of the statement—this is obviously different in legislative acts aimed at granting individual rights. It lies in the nature of the reflex-like and indirect protection of individual interests, that judgments limited to a finding of unlawfulness do not explicitly mention the beneficiaries. Rather, the beneficiaries must be assessed on a case-by-case basis in light of the specific WTO rules violated. As for the discussion above in chapter 4 on the protective nature of WTO provisions, the indirect protection of individuals through WTO law also allows determination of beneficiaries of the DSB ruling.

## II. THE DECLARATORY CHARACTER OF THE DSB DECISION

Determination of a sufficiently identifiable minimum right favouring an individual requires consideration of the particularities of the adjudicative practice. The Panel and Appellate Body undertake a legal assessment, leading to a finding on whether certain trade restrictions are in violation of WTO rules, in which case the losing party has to remove the measures pursuant to Article 19 DSU. Typically, the legal assessment leads to a declaratory finding on the violation of certain provisions, but normally does not entail clear commands on how the losing party has to bring its measures into compliance with WTO rules.[8] This is different in the case of EU directives, which are often very detailed and ease determination of a minimum right.[9] As an expression of the freedom of choice regarding the measures, the

[5] On the differences between granting rights directly and indirectly Eilmansberger, *Gemeinschaftsrecht* (1997) (ch 3, fn 119) 68ff.

[6] In this vein, Hörmann and Göttsche, 'Haftung' (ch 2, fn 37) 694.

[7] Thies, 'Biret and beyond' (ch 2, fn 6) 1678.

[8] Cottier, 'Streitschlichtungsverfahren in der WTO' (ch 2, fn 45) 186; Hinderer, *Rechtsschutz* (2004) (ch 2, fn 5) 442f; Gabler, *Streitbeilegungssystem der WTO* (1997) (ch 2, fn 45) 143; differently Flemisch, *Umfang* (2002) (ch 2, fn 5) 226.

[9] A Furrer and A Epiney, 'Staatliche Haftung für quantifizierbare Wettbewerbsnachteile aus nicht umgesetzten Richtlinien' [1995] *JZ* 1025, 1033.

losing party generally enjoys discretion as to which measures to adopt in order to comply with the DSB ruling.[10] Again, an EU directive and DSB ruling are structurally similar to the extent that both are mandatory as regards the objective, but leave discretion as to how to reach the objective. The freedom of choice is then necessarily limited by the mandatory character of the compliance command. Besides, on a number of occasions, the DSB decisions went beyond mere declaration and requested a specific conduct from the losing party. For example, the party can be barred from continuing the application of a measure,[11] or be required to terminate[12] or eliminate[13] the measure or to take immediate countermeasures.[14]

## III. IDENTIFIABILITY IN THE BANANAS AND HORMONES DISPUTES

The identifiability requirement for liability purposes can be assessed in light of the Panel and Appellate Body reports in the bananas and hormones disputes. Did the reports allow for the identification of both minimum rights and beneficiaries, on which grounds the EU Court could base a liability claim? The DSB decision must be sufficiently clear to the extent that it must contain unambiguous and complete provisions as regards the legal consequences and the beneficiaries of the decision.

### A. Case group B in the banana dispute

Although the Panel and Appellate Body reports typically do not command specific actions to the losing party,[15] in its report of 12 April 1999, the Appellate Body identified three options by which the EU could bring its banana import regime into compliance with WTO rules.[16] This report goes beyond mere declaration of unlawfulness of the banana regime and identifies the specific measure, which the Appellate Body considers suitable in reaching WTO compliance. The first option

[10] Gabler, *Streitbeilegungssystem der WTO* (1997) (ch 2, fn 45) 84.

[11] WTO: Brazil—Imposition of Provisional and Definitive Countervailing Duties on Milk Powder and Certain Types of Milk from the EEC –*Report of the Panel* (27 January 1994) SCM/153, para 369.

[12] WTO: United States—Measures affecting Imports of Softwood Lumber from Canada—Report of the Panel (19 February 1993) SCM/162, para 415; WTO: Canada—Imposition of Countervailing Duties on Imports of Manufacturing Beef from the EEC—*Report of the Panel* (13 October 1987) SCM/85, para 5.17.

[13] WTO: Japan—Import Restrictions on Imports from Certain Agricultural Products—Report of the Panel (22 March 1988) BISD 25S/163, para 6.10.

[14] WTO: *United States—Imports of Sugar from Nicaragua—Report of the Panel* (13 March 1984) BISD 31S/67, para 4.7.

[15] There are exceptions, notably where the Panel requested the refund of subsidies, see WTO: *Australia—Subsidies Provided to Producers and Exporters of Automotive Leather—Report of the Panel* (25 May 1999) WT/DS126/RW, para 6.42.

[16] WTO: *European Communities—Regime for the Importation, Sale and Distribution of Bananas—Report of the Panel* (12 April 1999) WT/DS27/RW/ECU, para 6.155.

is the elimination of all quantitative restrictions, and its replacement with a customs tariff in combination with the preferential custom treatment for traditional ACP bananas (so called 'tariff only' solution).[17] A second option would be the implementation of a customs duty in combination with a quota for traditional ACP bananas. And a third WTO-compatible solution would be the retention of the existing system quota, without country specific quotas, which would have been in line with Article XIII para 2 GATT.

For the purpose of assessing the EU liability, the three compliance options set out in the reports are the basis to identify a legal position of the individual claiming liability. The legal position—a 'minimum right' which the individual was deprived of due to non-compliance of the decision—must be the 'common smallest denominator' discernible from all three options, in order to be considered a non-contestable minimum right. The situation is comparable to the implementation of the insolvency directive in *Francovich*, and the freedom of choice granted under the directive in determining the point in time after which the entitlement of the employees would have to be guaranteed. In *Francovich*, the Court had to assess which point in time would constitute the smallest burden for the guarantee.[18] Analogously, in the case of the WTO liability, the decisive aspect is the import regime that creates the most favourable importing condition and which minimises the impact on the EU and its possibility to maintain preferential trade with ACP bananas. A hypothetical economic assessment of the importers' economic activities is thus indispensable, which obviously implies practical difficulties. In principle, however, the hypothetical assessment would allow the Court, on the basis of the compliance options set by the Appellate Body report, to determine the minimum legal position to which importers are entitled under this report.

The beneficiaries encompass those market participants who suffered damages because of the violation of those WTO provisions. It is precisely the avoidance of these damages which are intended by the relevant norms, indirectly and as a reflex of an objective obligation on Member States. It is true that the group of beneficiaries could be very large, but this issue is more appropriately dealt with by the legal requirement of the 'sufficiently serious breach', which requires a clearly definable group to be affected—as discussed here, a criterion to be distinguished from the identifiability of an individual right.

## B. Case group B in the hormone dispute

As discussed above in chapter 4, the rules protecting the exercise of economic freedoms and bans of discrimination, constitute provisions aiming at the

[17] This is the preferred option from the perspective of international trade, because all quantitative restrictions would be converted into tariffs, see Meier, 'Bananas IV' (ch 2, fn 23) 430; H-D Kuschel, 'Bananenstreit—und kein Ende?' [1998] *RIW* 122, 126f.

[18] *Francovich v Italy* (ch 3, fn 16) I-5410, para 19.

promotion of economic activities of the individual.[19] This also applies to the scope of application of sanitary and phytosanitary measures, as laid down in the SPS agreement. Article 2 para 3 SPS and the first recital of the preamble of the SPS agreement state that the rules seek to prevent disguised restriction of trade. The DSB found the EU directive banning the use of hormones[20] to constitute a restriction of economic freedoms and a violation of Article 5 para 5 SPS, because the import ban discriminated between hormone-treated beef and conventional beef and, hence, restricted the import of hormone-treated beef. Further, the EU violated Article 5 para 1 SPS by not having undertaken a proper risk assessment, which would have sufficiently substantiated the risk of cancer associated with the use of certain hormones. In its legislative risk assessment, the EU could not base its arguments on international norms or scientific justifications, which would have justified a higher level of sanitary protection. Pertaining to the issue of identifiability of an individual entitlement and the ascertainment of a 'minimum right', one can say that in the absence of scientific evidence suggesting otherwise, only an elimination of the import restriction could constitute a WTO compliant solution. This had been confirmed by the WTO arbitrator established under Article 21 para 3(c) DSU mandated to determine the reasonable compliance period. The arbitrator elaborated that it 'would not be in keeping with the requirement of *prompt* compliance to include in the reasonable period of time, time to conduct studies or to consult experts to demonstrate the *consistency* of a measure already judged to be *inconsistent*.'[21] Further doubts that the elimination of the import ban was the only remedy possible to be WTO-compliant, are resolved in light of Article 3 para 3 SPS granting Member States the opportunity to increase the level of protection above that of international norms.[22] Non-compliance with the non-discrimination principle is only permissible, if the EU were capable of demonstrating the relevant scientific evidence, which it failed to deliver. As long as there is no such evidence, there is an assumption that no sanitary justification existed to discriminate between hormone-treated and usual beef. Would the EU be capable of delivering the evidence at a later stage, the situation would change *ex tunc*. The only WTO compliant policy option at the moment of expiry of the implementation period was the removal of the import restriction. Would the EU have complied with this obligation, hormone-treated beef could have been imported without restrictions. Hence, with regard to the certainty and identifiability of an individual right, it can be concluded that the DSB decision must be interpreted to

[19] *Biret International v Council* (Introduction, fn 8) Opinion of AG Alber, I-10497, para 116ff.

[20] (EC) No 96/22 of 29 April 1996 concerning the prohibition on the use in stockfarming of certain substances having a hormonal or thyrostatic action and of ß agonists, and repealing Directives 81/602/EEC, 88/146/EEC and 88/299/EEC 1996, 3.

[21] WTO: EC Measures Concerning Meat and Meat Products (Hormones)—*Report of the Appellate Body* (29 May 1998) WT/DS26/15, WT/DS48/13, para 39.

[22] T Makatsch, *Gesundheitsschutz im Recht der Welthandelsorganisation (WTO)* (Berlin, Duncker & Humblot, 2004), 161ff.

the effect that the individual would have a 'minimum right' entailing unrestricted and non-discriminatory import of hormone-treated beef.

### C. Case group C

Finally, companies hit by US retaliation measures upon approval of the DSB constitute another kind of economic effect. The group comprising these companies can clearly be identified on the basis of the list of EU import products, which the US had published. It has been argued that this listing of products would not meet the certainty standard, because the list of products to be sanctioned was published only after the DSB ruling. This argument must be rejected on the basis of the Court's jurisprudence, according to which a specific group must not be clearly identifiable before the measure causing liability has been adopted.[23] Rather, it should suffice that the affected companies can be identified only after the damages have occurred. Likewise, a certain degree of vagueness of the provision when assessing the claim is acceptable, as long as the Court is in the position to derive a clear statement from the provision, in the specific case.[24] The crucial point in time for assessing the claim is when the Court reviews the case. Publication of the retaliation list of targeted companies by the winning party, and the imposition of retaliatory duties, necessarily precedes the launch of a suit for damages, and thus precludes the risk of insufficient identifiability at the moment of filing the suit. This is also in line with the purpose of identifiability, which is that the individual should not be able to invoke a right that is still at the discretion of the EU legislator—there is no such discretionary choice between the acceptance of retaliation and WTO-compliant conduct, after expiry of the implementation period.

As discussed above, WTO rules offer not only indirect protection for individuals' business opportunities as a result of the compliance with the WTO rules, but also (rather implicitly) the right to not being subjected to retaliation measures.[25] This also applies to the DSB ruling as such. Following the finding of unlawfulness and the consequently binding obligation, the losing party must comply within a reasonable period of time. On the flipside of this obligation is the inherent legal position of those who suffer damages as a consequence of the losing party not complying within the time limit. Such damages accrue to the victims of retaliatory measures—if the losing party does not comply with the DSB ruling within the time period, the winning party can request the suspension of concessions according to Article 22 para 6 DSU. Since the DSU aims at preventing retaliation, the relevant norms of the DSU also offer indirect protection for companies being hit

[23] Joined Cases T-195/94 and T-202/94 *Quiller and Heusmann v Council and Commission* [1997] ECR II-2247, para 67.

[24] *Dillenkofer and Others v Germany* (n 3) I-4845, para 30; *Francovich v Italy* (ch 3, fn 16) I-5357, para 17.

[25] Above ch. 4 II A c.

by the suspension of concessions.[26] Finally, the duty of WTO-compliant conduct had been initially inspired by the idea of avoiding trade-war like scenarios and associated damaging effects.

In conclusion, for previous and future incidents of companies being damaged following the imposition of retaliation duties, the Court should identify the absence of retaliation (and the individual damages accruing from it) as a normative 'minimum right' enshrined in the DSB ruling. In the banana and hormones episodes, identifiability of beneficiaries of the DSB rulings was sufficiently identifiable (both members of case groups B and C). However, for the companies belonging to group B, it must be added that identifiability depends on how the DSB determines WTO compliance in its rulings. In principle, determining a 'minimum right' as a result of compliance with the DSB requires some guidance from the ruling on possible potential modes of compliance. The more concrete the DSB dwells on the suitable measures, the more easily a minimum right can be discerned from these measures. By contrast, it would be more problematic, if the DSU confines itself to a mere statement, based on Article 19 para 1 sent 1 DSU, to request the losing party to bring its national laws in compliance with the decision. The degree and the possibility to establish minimum rights that could be the grounds for damage claims, thus depends on the adjudicative practice of the DSU organs and their inclination to move away from a mere statement of unlawfulness, and instead identify the measures to be adopted by national authority.

[26] Thies, 'Biret and beyond' (ch 2, fn 6) 1679.

# 6

# *Further Liability Requirements*

## I. THE 'SUFFICIENTLY SERIOUS BREACH' REQUIREMENT

ACCORDING TO ESTABLISHED case law, the EU's liability requires that in the case of legislative measures a 'sufficiently flagrant breach of a superior rule of law for the protection of the individual has occurred'.[1] The qualification of the mere standard of unlawfulness implies that not just any unlawful act can trigger liability, but rather there must be a certain gravity in the violation. The Court justifies the limitation of the EU's liability for legislative measures by reference to comparative legal arguments rooted in the legal order of the Member States. In this vein, in *HNL*, the Court observed that according to Member States' legal orders, 'public authorities can only exceptionally and in special circumstances incur liability for legislative measures, which are the result of choices of economic policy' and that 'this restrictive view is explained by the consideration that the legislative authority, even where the validity of its measures is subject to judicial review, cannot always be hindered in making its decisions by the prospect of applications for damages, whenever it has occasion to adopt legislative measures in the public interest, which may adversely affect the interests of individuals'.[2] A number of judgments the Court rendered following *Schöppenstedt* and *HNL* seeking to clarify the term 'sufficiently serious breach'.[3] To that end, the criteria of *gravity* and *effect* of the violations have been developed.[4] However, there is an overall perception that these terms lack precision and universality, and that the jurisprudence has ultimately been acting on a case-by-case basis.[5]

Further, in *Ireks-Arkady*, the Court introduced the elements of *delimitability* and *foreseeability* as a consideration applicable to judge the 'sufficiently serious

[1] Established case-law since *Schöppenstedt v Council* (ch 1, fn 25) 975, para 11; *Sofrimport v Commission* (ch 1, fn 17) I-2477, para 25; *Mulder and Others and Heinemann v Council and Commission* (ch 1, fn 17) I-3061, para 12; *Bergaderm and Goupil v Commission* (ch 3, fn 2) I-5291, para 43.

[2] *HNL and Others v Council and Commission* (ch 1, fn 27) 1209, para 5; this has largely been agreed to in the literature, see only Ruffert (ch 1, fn 27) Art 340 TFEU, para 11 with further references.

[3] Reinisch, 'Opfer des Hormon- und Bananenstreites' (Introduction, fn 7) 49; Gellermann (ch 1, fn 48) Art 340 TFEU, para 23 with further references.

[4] Herdegen, *Haftung* (1983) (ch 1, fn 22) 126ff; Gellermann (ch 1, fn 48) Art 340 TFEU, para 23; Schoißwohl, 'Haftung' (ch 1, fn 8) 716f.

[5] Czaja, *Außervertragliche Haftung* (1996) (ch 1, fn 15) 83; Herdegen, *Haftung* (1983) (ch 1, fn 22) 126ff; Grabitz, 'Haftung' (ch 1, fn 52) 222.

breach' requirement. The Court found that 'a limited and clearly defined group of commercial operators' was affected and that the damage 'goes beyond the bounds of the economic risks inherent in the activities in the sector concerned'.[6] Thus, the seriousness of the breach was assessed in light of the number of affected persons and the nature and magnitude of the damage. However, while *Ireks-Arkady* gave an indication for excluding a serious breach where a large group is affected, in *Mulder*, the Court abandoned such restriction and accepted damage suits from a group of 12,000 claimants.[7] In that case, the Court simply considered it sufficient that the affected group was clearly *delimitable* and could thus be distinguished from the general public.[8] The Court also added that the legal consequences had not been foreseeable[9] and did not fall 'within the bounds of the normal economic risks inherent in the activities'.[10]

The heterogeneous set of factors determining the sufficiently serious breach are supplemented by the Court's specification of the gravity of the violation—to that purpose, it referred to the significance of the provision concerned and to whether the decision 'was verging on the arbitrary'.[11] However, the Court subsequently abandoned the arbitrariness as a criterion for non-contractual liability[12] and rather sought guidance in the criteria developed in the context of Member States' liability. In *Brasserie du Pêcheur*, the Court developed conditions for Member States' liability for non-implementation of EU law, which also must apply to the EU liability regime under Article 340 TFEU, because of the necessary coherence between Member States liability and EU liability.[13] In that case, the Court went beyond the criteria of arbitrariness and the effects of the violation, and identified a number of further factors indicative for a sufficiently serious breach, by referring to the degree of clarity and certainty of the violated norm, the scope of discretion

[6] Case 238/78 *Ireks-Arkady v Council and Commission* [1979] ECR 2955, 2955, para 11.

[7] *Mulder and Others and Heinemann v Council and Commission* (ch 1, fn 17) I-3061, para 15.

[8] *Ireks-Arkady v Council and Commission* (n 6) 2955, para 12; *Mulder and Others and Heinemann v Council and Commission* (ch 1, fn 17) I-3061, para 16; see also F Ossenbühl, 'Die außervertragliche Haftung der Europäischen Gemeinschaft' in H-W Rengeling (ed), *Handbuch zum europäischen und deutschen Umweltrecht: Eine systematische Darstellung des europäischen Umweltrechts mit seinen Auswirkungen auf das deutsche Recht und mit rechtspolitischen Perspektiven*, 2nd edn (Köln, C Heymanns, 2003) § 42 para 54; Berg (ch 1, fn 47) Art 340 TFEU, para 48; Gellermann (ch 1, fn 48) Art 340 TFEU, para 22.

[9] In some judgments the Court refers to the unforseeability of the typical risks, see Case 59/83 *Biovilac v EEC* [1984] ECR 4057, para 29; Case 50/86 *Grands Moulins de Paris v Council and Commission* [1987] ECR 4833, para 21.

[10] *Mulder and Others and Heinemann v Council and Commission* (ch 1, fn 17) I-3061, para 17.

[11] *Amylum v Council and Commission* (ch 1, fn 43) 3567, para 18ff; Case T-481/93 and T-484/93 *Vereniging van Exporteurs in Levende Varkens and Others v Commission* [1995] ECR II-2941, para 128; Gellermann (ch 1, fn 48) Art 340 TFEU, para 22; *Koninklijke Scholten-Honig v Council and Commission* (ch 1, fn 43) 3583, para 16.

[12] Case C-220/91 P *Peine-Salzgitter v Commission* [1993] ECR I-2393, para 51.

[13] Aalto, *Public Liability* (2011) (ch 4, fn 1) 52; P Craig and G de Búrca, *EU Law*, 6th edn (Oxford, Oxford University Press, 2015) 588; M Herdegen and T Rensmann, 'Die neue Konturen der Gemeinschaftlichen Staatshaftung' (1997) 161 *ZHR* 522, 540.

granted under the norm, the justifiability of errors and the deliberateness of the violation.[14] These factors do not apply cumulatively but are rather elements of an overall assessment depending on the circumstances of the individual case.[15] In particular, *Brasserie du Pêcheur* could be a reference point in the present context, because the seriousness of the violation was tied to the clarity of the unlawfulness. According to the Court, the German import restrictions in that case could only be considered sufficiently clear and serious from the moment the measure was found by the Court to be unlawful—a finding the Court made in *Reinheitsgebot*.[16] Prior to that judgment, there was some ambiguity on whether the measure was unlawful, which rendered divergent views on the lawfulness at least arguable. Thus, one could give different interpretations to the norm before the judgment of the Court gave ultimate clarification.

If one applies the somehow fuzzy and inconsistent standards developed in the jurisprudence to the EU violations of WTO law during the hormones and bananas episodes, one has to apply the Court's standards in relation to both the EU's conduct and the effect on the respective case group. As regards the EU's conduct, the Court's general stance that the gravity of the violation must be higher the greater the scope of discretion enjoyed by the EU organs is decisive. In the bananas dispute, the EU constantly refused to bring its banana import regime into compliance with the orders of the DSB ruling.[17] In line with the approach in *Brasserie du Pêcheur*, one could argue that before adoption of the DSB ruling there is an ambiguous standard of lawfulness, and that the EU could interpret WTO rules to the effect that the EU measures were in line with WTO law. This scope for argumentation vanishes in the moment when the DSB makes its finding on unlawfulness. The EU's refusal to comply then stands in contrast to the fact that there is no discretion of the EU legislative organs as to 'whether' to comply with the DSB ruling or not.[18] Also, the obligation to comply formulated in the DSB ruling is unambiguous, and thus could not give rise to errors or misunderstandings. The decision was sufficiently clear on what was legally required from the EU in terms of the measures to be adopted.[19] Further, in the hormones dispute, over a period of five years the EU did not undertake any attempt to bring its import regime into compliance with the DSB decision. Given the clarity of the DSB ruling, there are

[14] *Brasserie du Pêcheur v Germany and Rv Secretary of State for Transport, ex parte Factortame III* (ch 3, fn 23) I-1150, para 56.

[15] Weiß, 'Verletzung des WTO-Rechts' (ch 2, fn 50) 293; Gellermann (ch 1, fn 48) Art 340 TFEU, para 46.

[16] Case 178/84 *Commission v Germany (Beer Purity)* [1987] ECR 1227.

[17] See Reinisch, 'Opfer des Hormon- und Bananenstreites' (Introduction, n 7) 49; Weiß, 'Verletzung des WTO-Rechts' (ch 2, fn 50) 293; Hinderer, *Rechtsschutz* (2004) (ch 2, fn 5) 467; Thies, 'Biret and beyond' (ch 2, fn 6) 1668.

[18] Above Ch. 2 II.

[19] H-D Kuschel, 'Auch die revidierte Bananenmarktordnung ist nicht WTO-konform' [1999] *EuZW* 74, 76; Schoißwohl, 'Haftung' (ch 1, fn 8) 718; Zonnekeyn, 'EC Liability' (ch 1, fn 35) 269; Cascante, *Rechtsschutz* (2003) (ch 2, fn 6) 272.

good reasons to apply the strict liability standard developed for the transposition of EU directives, also in the context of liability for non-implementation of DSB decisions—continuous inactivity of the EU then gives an indication of the seriousness of the breach.

Regarding the *effect* of the violation of the norm, which the Court referred to in order to assess the impact on a *delimitable* group of market participants, it is most evident in the case of the companies of group C, because the risk of being subject to retaliatory measures cannot be considered to be part of foreseeable market risks of an EU-based company exporting to the US. Also, the criterion of limitation is fulfilled in this group, as the punitive damages are imposed on the import of selected products by way of which the companies exporting these products can be ascertained.

More problematic is the assessment of the *effects* of the violation for the case group B, as it turned out that the claimed damages were not limited to importing companies but also extended to companies that were only indirectly involved with importing activities. The *delimitability* of the companies is likely to be hardly possible for case group B, because the disadvantages would practically extend to all companies somehow involved in trading bananas, even if only indirectly. However, this would not necessarily hinder acceptance of liability, as the Court relaxed its stance on the *delimitability*. More importantly, however, the disadvantages incurring to case group B must be considered to lie typically within the bounds of what constitutes the inherent market risks of importing activities. The basic right to economic freedom is a common principle of EU law and protects the individual against an arbitrary ban of the free exercise of economic activities. However, this right does not entail a guarantee on seizing certain market volumes or market shares, because such economic interest is part of the potential risk of economic activities.[20] Therefore, no market actor can claim a certain market share or a legitimate interest in maintaining the current legal and economic situation.[21] Modifications to import regimes are subject to policy decisions and every market participant has to anticipate certain fluctuations in the governance of trade policies. This applies particularly in the context of market organisations, such as agricultural markets which, by definition, must frequently be adapted to the changing

[20] *Atlanta AG and Others v Council and Commission* (ch 4, fn 2) para 62: 'It is settled case-law that freedom to pursue an economic activity is one of the general principles of Community law. It is not, however, an absolute prerogative and must be considered in relation to its social function. It confers the assurance that a trader will not be arbitrarily deprived of the right to pursue his activity but it does not guarantee him a particular volume of business or a specific share of a given market. The guarantees accorded to traders cannot in any event be extended to protect mere commercial interests or opportunities, the uncertainties of which are part of the very essence of economic activity [...]. It follows that restrictions may be placed on the freedom to pursue an economic activity, particularly in a common market organization, provided that they are required in order to meet objectives of general interest pursued by the Community and that they do not constitute a disproportionate and intolerable interference which entrenches upon the very substance of the right guaranteed.' Similarly in *FIAMM and FIAMM Technologies v Council and Commission* (Introduction, fn 8) paras 183, 184.

[21] *Germany v Council* (ch 3, fn 38) para 77.

economic situation. In sum, for members of case group C, the requirement of a sufficiently serious breach does not constitute an insurmountable barrier. As regards members of case group B, the circumstances of the concrete trade dispute are decisive. However, experience with the longest and most controversial trade dispute concerning bananas and hormones suggests that the high requirements would hardly be met, mainly because market participants cannot claim a legitimate interest in the continuity of certain policy decisions.

## II. DAMAGE

For a liability claim brought under Articles 235, 288 para 2 TFEU to be successful, there must be a damage. Given the silence of the Treaty on this requirement, the Court has specified the conditions for the kind of damage to be demonstrated.[22] It has developed an extensive interpretation of damages, capturing any disadvantage accruing to the wealth of the individual or the deprivation of any other legally protected goods.[23] This includes loss of profits, provided this can be sufficiently substantiated.[24] Substantiation is lacking, if the business operations were merely intended but have not yet become concrete.[25] In this vein, in *Kampffmeyer I*, it was not sufficient that the importers had requested import licences, but had not yet concluded the purchase contract on which basis they were going to carry out the import. Accordingly, it may appear questionable whether such business transactions, which do not come to the stage of implementation because of the 100 per cent *ad valorem* retaliation duty could constitute damage. This kind of damage would be tantamount to loss of profits, because the export would be realised at less favourable conditions, compared to a hypothetical situation without the WTO violation. In line with a restrictive interpretation, this kind of loss of profits could then be considered as merely envisaged export operations, without having reached the necessary stage of implementation.[26] However, in *Produits Bertrand*, the Court has already accepted the curtailing of sales opportunities, suffered due to state aid granted to competitors.[27] It cannot be ignored that the imposition of retaliation duties at the detriment of EU exporters creates positive business opportunities for other non-EU exporters, even though these advantages do not constitute state aid. The discriminatory punitive duty places EU exporters into a comparatively less

[22] Instructively AG Toth, 'The Concepts of Damage and Causality as Elements of Noncontractual Liability' in T Heukels and A McDonnell (eds), *The Action For Damages In Community Law* (The Hague, Kluwer Law International, 1997) 192.

[23] Case 40/75 *Produits Bertrand v Commission* [1976] ECR 1, para 4ff; Case 63-69/72 *Werhahn v Council* [1973] ECR 1229, para 2.

[24] *Ireks-Arkady v Council and Commission* (n 6) 2955, para 13f.

[25] *Kampffmeyer and Others v Commission* (ch 1, fn 49) 359.

[26] Reinisch, 'Opfer des Hormon- und Bananenstreites' (Introduction, n 7) 50; Zonnekeyn, 'EC Liability' (ch 1, fn 35) 270.

[27] *Produits Bertrand v Commission* (n 23) 1, para 9ff.

favourable position, which directly affects their sales opportunities. Moreover, the Court has on another occasion recognised damages upon losses induced by effects on competition because of a modification of agricultural policies.[28] Obviously, the EU import regime does not only have anti-competitive effects at the expense of importers, but also for those exporters who are subjected to retaliatory measures following DSB approval. The loss in turnover due to the WTO-incompliant measure is thus decisive.[29] According to the Court's judgment in *Mulders*, the quantitative evaluation of the damages then yields from the difference between the income, which the claimant would have generated if the WTO violations would not have occurred, and the income the company actually gained.[30] Hence, the General Court has approved damages that incurred to a company of group C on the basis of statistics of the European Commission, which showed that exports of the product concerned to the US declined following the adoption of retaliatory measures.[31]

By contrast, damages incurring to companies of group B do not meet the standards developed for damages to be recognisable, for the reasons mentioned above, concerning the requirement of a sufficiently serious breach. According to established case law, in cases of liability for legislative acts damages are only considered if they go beyond the risk that is typically inherently linked to a certain market activity.[32] Foreseeable damages cannot be claimed in a proceeding under Article 340 TFEU.[33] In fact, the damages suffered by companies of group B must be considered as risks typically associated with modifications of legislative acts, particularly in areas such as economic policies. In turn, the damages suffered by victims exporting to the US and hit by retaliation cannot be considered market risks. Moreover, retaliation typically occurs in business sectors entirely unrelated to the sector in which the initial violation took place. This kind of 'cross-retaliation' gives the retaliating country a margin of discretion to choose sectors, which may hurt the violating country the most. From the perspective of the market participants concerned, the choice of sectors of retaliation is unpredictable, without being related to the typical market risks of this sector.

## III. CAUSALITY

There must be causality between the unlawful conduct of an EU organ and the damage suffered.[34] The Court applies a rather restrictive notion of causality based

[28] *Werhahn v Council* (n 23) 1229, para 2.

[29] Similarly Reinisch, 'Opfer des Hormon- und Bananenstreites' (Introduction, n 7) 50; Zonnekeyn, 'EC Liability' (ch 1, fn 35) 270.

[30] *Mulder and Others and Heinemann v Council and Commission* (ch 1, fn 17) I-3061, para 26ff.

[31] *FIAMM and FIAMM Technologies v Council and Commission* (Introduction, fn 8) II-5393, para 169.

[32] *Biovilac v EEC* (n 9) 4057, para 28f; Case 62/83 *Eximo v Commission* [1984] ECR 2295, para 22; *Développement SA and Clemessy v Commission* (ch 1, fn 33) 1907, para 33.

[33] *Grands Moulins de Paris v Council and Commission* (n 9) 4833, para 21.

[34] Case C-55/90 *Cato v Commission* [1992] ECR I-2533, para 18; Case T-572/93 *Odigitria v Council and Commission* [1995] ECR II-2025, para 65; Case C-358/90 *Compagnia Italiana Alcool v Commission* [1992] ECR I-2457, para 47; *Produits Bertrand v Commission* (n 23) 9.

on the concept of adequacy.[35] Accordingly, attribution is limited to the kind of damages that were typically foreseeable, based on a normal course of action.[36] Put differently, the concept of adequacy limits causality to those violations and causes, which in light of their nature are not entirely unsuitable to cause such damages, and which do cause the damage not only because of an extraordinary combination of incidents.[37]

Applying this standard to the respective case group offers a heterogeneous picture: there is no doubt about causality of the ones directly affected by the EU measures (case group B), because as traders in the EU market they suffer immediate consequences from the WTO incompatible measures by the EU.[38] Far less clear is the situation of the victims of retaliatory measures (group C). Certainly, the conduct of the EU is *conditio sine qua non* for the damages they suffer, because the US would not have imposed sanctions, had the EU implemented the DSB ruling. However, the adequacy of the causality chain is in doubt, if there are various incidents contributing in a causal way to the damages.[39] In the case of group C, the damaging act (retaliation) is the immediate consequence of the conduct of US authorities, and can be attributed only indirectly to WTO-incompliant acts of the EU. The concept of adequacy thus requires some valuation in the assessment of the various causal contributions, which are led by considerations related to risk spheres.[40] Moreover, the Court found that, even if certain events interfere with the initially set causal act during the course of things, this does not preclude the attribution of a damage to the initial violating act.[41] Disruption of the causality chain would only be the case, if the national measures would constitute wrongful acts themselves, and if this wrongful act would have set a causal factor for the damage.[42] However, this is not the case, given that the retaliation of the US is approved by the DSB and is thus in conformity with WTO rules.[43] Although the immediate damage is not from an EU but a US act, the US conduct is only the direct consequence of non-implementation of the DSB ruling by the EU. There is no indication that the imposition of duties by the US rests on a decision independent from the preceding EU conduct. Also, the imposition of sanctions was foreseeable for

[35] Berg (ch 1, fn 47) Art 340 TFEU, para 62; Reinisch, 'Opfer des Hormon- und Bananenstreites' (Introduction, fn 7) 50f; Diehr, *Staatshaftungsanspruch* (1997) (ch 3, fn 19) 196.

[36] Ossenbühl, 'Haftung' (n 8) § 42, para 57.

[37] B Schoißwohl, *Staatshaftung wegen Gemeinschaftsrechtsverletzung*, 1st edn (Wien, Verlag Österreich, 2002) 453.

[38] Weiß, 'Verletzung des WTO-Rechts' (ch 2, fn 50) 294f; Schoißwohl, 'Haftung' (ch 1, fn 8) 719; on the hormones dispute *Biret International v Council* (Introduction, n 8) Opinion of AG Alber, I-10497, para 121ff.

[39] F Smith and L Woods, 'Causation in Francovich: The Neglected Problem' (1997) 46 *ICLQ* 925, 938ff; Toth, 'Damage and Causality' (n 22) 193ff.

[40] Schoißwohl, *Staatshaftung* (2002) (n 37) 453.

[41] Case C-182/91 *Forafrique Burkinabe v Commission* [1993] ECR I-2161; Case 175/84 *Krohn v Commission* [1986] ECR 753, para 18f; Berg (ch 1, fn 47) Art 340 TFEU, para 66.

[42] Joined Cases 89 and 91/86 *Etoile Commerciale and CNTA v Commission* [1987] ECR 3005, para 18ff.

[43] Zonnekeyn, 'EC Liability' (ch 1, fn 35) 271; Reinisch, 'Opfer des Hormon- und Bananenstreites' (Introduction, fn 7) 51.

the EU, as it could expect that following the expiry of the implementation period the US would request the suspension of concessions before the DSB.[44] In light of the explicit possibility to impose sanctions granted under the DSU, retaliatory measures constitute the logical next step in the escalation of the trade dispute.[45] The General Court seems to agree with this view. In a judgment dealing with the situation of a company pertaining to group C, the Court found that retaliation was an objective consequence of the WTO-incompatible banana regime of the EU, which is in line with the mechanisms provided under the WTO disputes settlement procedure.[46] For this reason, the US sanctions do not break the link initiated by the unlawful EU conduct, which constitutes the causal ground for the damages suffered due to US retaliation.[47]

[44] Likewise Thies, 'Biret and beyond' (ch 2, fn 6) 1679f; Görgens, *Außervertragliche Haftung* (2006) (ch 2, fn 5) 186.

[45] Schoißwohl, 'Haftung' (ch 1, fn 8) 719f; Hörmann and Göttsche, 'Haftung' (ch 2, fn 37) 696.

[46] *FIAMM and FIAMM Technologies v Council and Commission* (Introduction, fn 8) II-5393, para 183.

[47] ibid II-5393, para 185.

# 7

# *Damage Claims and Fundamental Rights*

FUNDAMENTAL RIGHTS COULD constitute another *Schutznorm*, a violation of which could give rise to liability under Article 340 TFEU. The respective WTO-incompatible EU directives and violations may be in violation of EU fundamental rights. Unlike under Article 216 para 2 TFEU as the legality standard, EU secondary law can be reviewed in light of fundamental rights and individuals can directly invoke these rights before a court both in proceedings for annulment and compensation.[1] Violation of fundamental rights can thus give rise to both primary and secondary legal protection.

Fundamental rights have been controversially discussed in the context of WTO violation, in particular as a consequence of the Court's judgment in *Germany v Council*, in which Germany had sought the annulment of the EU's banana market regulation.[2] The dispute had been brought even before the German Constitutional Court, claiming that certain fundamental minimum standards had been violated and that the EU secondary act would therefore constitute a so-called 'ausbrechender Rechtsakt'; that is, a legislative act falling beyond the scope of competences of the EU.[3]

Because of the deprivation of trade activities on the part of market participants, the corresponding right laid down in the European Chart of Fundamental rights would be the freedom to conduct a business (Article 16 EU Charter of Fundamental Rights). Further, fundamental rights can be concerned to the extent that they can be derived from the general principles common in the laws of Member States.[4]

[1] Hörmann and Göttsche, 'Haftung' (ch 2, fn 37) 697.

[2] See only M Nettesheim, 'Grundrechtliche Prüfdichte durch den EuGH' [1995] *EuZW* 106, 107; Stein, 'Bananen-Split' (ch 3, fn 152) 261; Everling, 'Will Europe Slip on Bananas?' (ch 1, fn 7) 412ff; J Coppel and A O'Neill, 'The European Court of Justice: Taking Rights Seriously?' (1992) 29 *CML Rev* 669, 691f; J Kokott, 'Die Grundrechte des europäischen Gemeinschaftsrechts' (1996) 121 *AöR* 599, 599.

[3] Referring order by Verwaltungsgericht Frankfurt, [1997] EuZW 186ff; however, the German Constitutional Court rejected the referral based on its established jurisprudence, BVerfGE 102, 147ff.

[4] For a comprehensive analysis of general principles of EU law to give rise to liability, see A Thies, 'The Impact of General Principles of EC Law on its Liability Regime Towards Retaliation Victims after FIAMM' (2009) 34 *EL Rev* 889, 889ff; Krajewski, *Verfassungsperspektiven* (2001) (ch 2, fn 30) 167.

In the Member States' legal orders the freedoms related to external trade activities are typically protected through the freedom to choose an occupation and the right to property.[5] The Court has not developed an autonomous right to conduct external trade, but has based such activities on the freedom to choose an occupation and the right to property,[6] the general freedom to do business[7] and freedom of competition.[8]

Past liability claims for WTO breaches show that the fundamental rights referred to above have an external trade dimension.[9] In its action for damages, *Atlanta* was claiming a violation of its freedom to do business.[10] *T Port* invoked the right to property in its liability claim.[11] Moreover, the enterprises *Bocchi* and *Chiquita* saw their right to choose an occupation violated by the EU banana market regulations.[12] Besides fundamental rights, claimants have often referred to general principles common in the Member States' laws. In *Biret* and in *Atlanta*, the importing company claimed infringement of legitimate expectations.[13]

As mentioned above, the political question doctrine and the general exclusion of legality review of certain acts related to external policies have not been accepted in the Court's jurisprudence.[14] From a functional perspective, the granting of a wide margin of discretion is, however, tantamount to a weak kind of judicial restraint. This is reflected in the Court's jurisprudence on WTO liability claims, in that it connects the review of fundamental rights violations to the scope of manoeuvre of the EU legislative organs.[15] Both the General Court and the Court of Justice have frequently referred, in suits regarding the bananas dispute, to the Court's statements for *Germany v Council*.[16]

[5] Stoll, 'Freihandel und Verfassung' (ch 2, fn 34) 91.

[6] *Germany v Council* (ch 1, fn 6) I-491, para 14; Case 240/83 *Procureur de la République v ADBHU* [1985] ECR 531, para 9.

[7] *Atlanta AG and Others v Council and Commission* (ch 4, fn 2) II-1707, para 62f; Case C-317/00 P *'Invest' Import und Export and Invest Commerce v Commission* [2000] ECR I-9541, I-9541, para 57.

[8] *Procureur de la République v ADBHU* (n 6) 531, para 15; *Germany v Council* (ch 1, fn 6) I-4973, para 63.

[9] Likewise Thies, 'General Principles of EC Law' (n 4) 889ff; Epping, *Außenwirtschaftsfreiheit* (1998) (ch 3 n 45) 577.

[10] *Atlanta AG and Others v Council and Commission* (ch 4, fn 2) II-1707, para 62f.

[11] *T Port GmbH & Co v Commission* (Introduction, fn 8) II-981, para 90ff.

[12] *Bocchi Food Trade International v Commission* (Introduction, fn 8) II-973, para 80; *Chiquita v Commission* (Introduction, fn 8) II-315, para 215ff.

[13] *P Atlanta AG v European Community* (Introduction, fn 8) I-7018, para 11.

[14] Above ch. 1 V.

[15] C Tomuschat, 'Aller guten Dinge sind III? Zur Diskussion um die Solange-Rechtsprechung des BVerfG' [1990] *EuR* 340, 356; Kokott, 'Grundrechte des europäischen Gemeinschaftsrechts' (n 2) 608f.

[16] *P Atlanta AG v European Community* (Introduction, n 8) I-7030, paras 46f; *Atlanta AG and Others v Council and Commission* (ch 4, fn 2) II-1730, para 56; *Bocchi Food Trade International v Commission* (Introduction, n 8) II-973, para 81.

The rights to economic freedoms are part of the general principles of EU law and the individual must not be arbitrarily deprived from these rights. However, a restriction of the freedom to pursue a trade or profession:

> may be restricted, particularly in the context of a common organisation of the market, provided that those restrictions in fact correspond to objectives of general interest pursued by the Community, and that they do not constitute disproportionate and intolerable interference, which infringes upon the very substance of the rights guaranteed.[17]

A similar wording is used by the General Court for accepting the restriction on the freedom to occupation as invoked by *Bocchi* in its liability claim.[18] In *Bocchi*, the General Court refers to *Germany v Council*, in which it stated that certain trade restrictive measures related to the establishment of a common organisation of the market is:

> inherent in the objectives of general Community interest pursued by the establishment of the common organisation of the market in bananas and, therefore, do not improperly impair the freedom of traditional traders in third-country bananas to pursue their trade or business.[19]

The Court does not see a violation of the right to property, because no company can trust in the continuity of the current market and legal conditions, which is particularly the case where the market organisations require the legislator 'to reconcile divergent interests and thus select options within the context of the policy choices'. This scope of discretion then is only violated 'if the measure is manifestly inappropriate in its regard to the objective that the competent institution is seeking to pursue'.[20]

Similar considerations apply to the general principle of legitimate expectations, which has been recognised by the Court as one of the fundamental principles of the Community legal order.[21] However, this principle does not extend to situations, which can be altered by the Community institutions in the exercise of their discretionary power. This is especially the case where constant adjustments to the market organisation are necessary, in order to meet changes in economic circumstances.[22] Similarly, in the context of the dispute regarding the import of hormone-treated beef disputes, the General Court referred to the practices of Member States' embargoes since the 1980s and the lack of assurances given by the EU on the outcome of the negotiations before the WTO. Besides its established reference

[17] Case 265/87 *Schräder v Hauptzollamt Gronau* [1989] ECR 2237, para 15; *Atlanta AG and Others v Council and Commission* (ch 4, fn 2) II-1730, para 62.

[18] *Bocchi Food Trade International v Commission* (Introduction, fn 8) II-973, paras 79ff.

[19] ibid II-973, para 81 with reference to *Germany v Council* (ch 1, fn 6) I-4973, para 87.

[20] *T Port GmbH & Co v Commission* (Introduction, fn 8) II-981, para 91ff.

[21] *Atlanta AG and Others v Council and Commission* (ch 4, fn 2) II-1730, para 55.

[22] ibid; Case C-133/93, C-300/93 and C-362/93 *Crispoltoni v Fattoria Autonoma Tabacchi and Others* [1994] ECR I-4863, I-4863, para 57.

to the discretionary powers of the EU institutions, which cannot be deprived by expectations of continuity of an existing situation, the General Court stressed that 'expectations in a future, hypothetical amendment of legislation, particularly in an area such as the common agricultural policy' could not be recognised, especially given that 'any legislative amendment depends on unpredictable developments in scientific knowledge and complex assessments to be made by the legislature' in this policy area.[23]

Given the lack of direct effect of WTO law and the limited reviewability of EU secondary law on the basis of WTO rules, the proportionality assessment remains the most important substantial review mechanism related to the appraisal of individual rights.[24] The above line of jurisprudence shows continuity in the Court's jurisprudence—it extends its restrictive approach to reviewing EU law in light of WTO rules in the context of fundamental rights by stressing—as in the context of the direct effect discussion of WTO law—the wide discretionary margin enjoyed by EU institutions in shaping their internal market organisations and external trade policies. This has led the Court also to apply a proportionality assessment within very narrow borders only. In its early *Germany v Council* judgment on the banana market organisation, its proportionality assessment concluded that it could not be shown that the EU measures were 'manifestly inappropriate or that it carried out a manifestly erroneous assessment of the information available to it at the time when the Regulation was adopted'.[25] In literature, criticism was voiced against this finding, in particular that the review of fundamental rights violations was limited to a review of the absence of arbitrariness and flagrant mistakes only, and that this stance would impair fundamental rights of their protective effects.[26] According to this view, the proportionality assessment would lose its function in a legality review, if the scope of the proportionality assessment would be entirely at the discretion of the EU legislator without the Court undertaking its own proportionality review—this would ultimately blur the lines between the review of discretion (which is naturally wide in the policy areas concerned) and the review of proportionality of the measure.[27] This criticism feeds into a broader argument

[23] Case T-210/00 *Etablissements Biret et Cie SA v Council* [2002] ECR II-47, II-47, paras 60, 62; see already Case C-331/88 *Fedesa and Others* [1990] ECR I-4023, para 10.

[24] Hörmann and Göttsche, 'Haftung' (ch 2, fn 37) 696.

[25] *Germany v Council* (ch 1, fn 6) I-5039, para 95.

[26] Epping, *Außenwirtschaftsfreiheit* (1998) (ch 3, fn 45) 582; Cascante and Sander, *EG-Bananenmarktordnung* (1999) (ch 4, fn 35) 57; Nettesheim, 'Grundrechtliche Prüfdichte' (n 2) 107; Everling, 'Will Europe Slip on Bananas?' (ch 1, fn 7) 412ff; Coppel and O'Neill, 'Taking Rights Seriously?' (n 2) 691f.

[27] G Berrisch, 'Zum 'Bananen'-Urteil des EuGH vom 05.10.1994' [1994] *EuR* 461, 467; Stein, 'Bananen-Split' (ch 3, fn 152) 261; Schmid, 'Status des GATT/WTO' (Introduction, fn 7) 191; Kokott, 'Grundrechte des europäischen Gemeinschaftsrechts' (n 2) 608.

that the 'wide discretion argument' would prevent the Court to evaluate the gravity of restrictions of fundamental rights, and would thus deprive the fundamental rights in their essential normative force.[28] As a consequence, the Court would curtail a proper evaluation of the interests and rights concerned, although the proportionality assessment would be the most appropriate tool to undertake such balancing.[29] By contrast, a proper proportionality assessment would weigh the objectives and consider the gravity of intrusion into individual rights.[30]

From a doctrinal perspective, applying the principle of proportionality, in combination with a WTO-consistent interpretation of EU law, provides an avenue to both appraise the fundamental rights of the companies concerned despite the lack of direct effect of WTO law and, at the same time, value the Union's interests as reflected in the discretionary margin on the part of EU institutions.[31] International treaties must be incorporated in the process of weighing within the proportionality assessment, because they have become an integral part of EU law and must, therefore, have an impact on the valuation of the Union's interests. If EU law is interpreted to the effect that the DSB ruling is accounted for, this may alter the assessment of the legitimacy of the conflicting interests. As a consequence, the individuals' freedoms related to business in external trade would be supported by a WTO-consistent interpretation of EU law given the protective intentions enshrined in the DSB ruling. A prerequisite for such a revised appraisal of fundamental rights would be the Court's willingness to undertake a proportionality assessment, taking into account the gravity of the encroachment with the rights of market participants and to lift its confinement to evident errors in the exercise of discretion.

In sum, we observe that the Court accepts the intrusions into fundamental rights by allowing a wide and virtually unlimited scope to manoeuvre in favour of EU institutions. Confining the proportionality assessment to merely reviewing arbitrariness and evident errors does not allow an appraisal of the conflicting interests concerned, even though the proportionality assessment is the genuine review stage for balancing individual and Union interests. The relevance and weight of fundamental rights must be assessed on a case-by-case basis.[32] Through WTO-consistent application of the proportionality assessment, a more comprehensive evaluation of both the fundamental rights and Unions' matters would

[28] P Selmer, *Die Gewährleistung der unabdingbaren Grundrechtsstandards durch den EuGH*, 1st edn (Baden-Baden, Nomos, 1998) 105; Hörmann and Göttsche, 'Haftung' (ch 2, fn 37) 692; Epping, *Außenwirtschaftsfreiheit* (1998) (ch 3, fn 45) 582.

[29] D Besse, 'Die Bananenmarktordnung im Lichte deutscher Grundrechte und das Kooperationsverhältnis zwischen BverfG und EuGH' [1996] *JuS* 396, 401; Hörmann and Göttsche, 'Haftung' (ch 2, fn 37) 696; Everling, 'Will Europe Slip on Bananas?' (ch 1, fn 7) 417f; Nettesheim, 'Grundrechtliche Prüfdichte' (n 2) 107f.

[30] F Schwab, *Der Europäische Gerichtshof und der Verhältnismäßigkeitsgrundsatz* (Frankfurt am Main, P Lang, 2002), 95.

[31] Wünschmann, *Gemeinschaftsrecht* (2003) (ch 2, fn 5) 232ff; Hermes, *TRIPS* (2002) (ch 2, fn 58) 177f; Flemisch, *Umfang* (2002) (ch 2, fn 5) 235ff; Cascante, *Rechtsschutz* (2003) (ch 2, fn 6) 301ff.

[32] See also Thies, 'General Principles of EC Law' (n 4) 899.

thus be possible. This does not necessarily alter the Court's conclusions to safeguard the Union's margin of discretion, particularly if, as in the case of the hormones dispute, considerations related to health policy are at stake. By contrast, a proportionality assessment weighing the interests concerned would allow identifying and rejecting protectionist intentions as unsuitable to permit encroachments with fundamental rights. Only those Unions' interests that can be traced to legally substantiated valuations can override intrusions into fundamental rights. Finally, and from the perspective of a uniform level of individual rights protection, a proper proportionality assessment would ensure that barriers for intrusions into freedoms related to external trade activities do not seem to be lower, compared to other individual rights under EU law.[33]

[33] E-U Petersmann, 'Wie kann Handelspolitik konstitutionalisiert werden?' [1989] *EA* 55, 57; E-U Petersmann, *Constitutional Functions and Constitutional Problems of International Economic Law* (Fribourg, Switzerland, University Press 1991), 299ff.

Part Two

# Economic Analysis of Liability for WTO Violations

# 8

# *Analytical Foundations*

## I. ECONOMIC ANALYSIS AND LIABILITY

DO THE LEGAL results of this work find support in economic reasoning? This part of the analysis will adopt an economic perspective, studying in particular the welfare implications and the desirability of a liability design for WTO violations. Methodologically, the economic analysis of law is a well-established branch in literature, whose methods aim at exploring the law by using economic insight. This can be done as a positive analysis (what are the economic efficiency implications of a certain legal arrangement?) or from a normative angle, seeking to make concrete proposals on how law should be designed.[1] However, adopting an economic view does not mean that the efficiency objective enjoys legal primacy over other normative goals, and that the efficiency considerations applying to damage claims would be the overarching goal of liability law, besides its function to render fair damage compensation.[2] The added value of an economic analysis of law is seen in extending the scope of arguments and making use of economic methods to solve legal problems.[3] This adds a perspective neglected by lawyers, in particular in light of the incentives set by legal norms on their addressees. Hence, this study does not discuss the pros and cons of an economic analysis of law, but rather accepts its heuristic utility for the study of law and applies certain methods to the liability issues at stake here.[4]

[1] Among the basic literature see only RA Posner, *Economic Analysis of Law*, 9th edn (New York, Wolters Kluwer Law & Business, 2014); R Cooter and T Ulen, *Law and Economics*, 6th edn (London, Pearson, 2012); RP Malloy and CK Braun (eds), *Law and Economics* (New York, P Lang, 1995). On the difference between positive and normative analysis, see MF Grady, 'A New Positive Economic Theory of Negligence' (1983) 92 *Yale L J* 799, 799f; M Kelman, *A Guide to Critical Legal Studies* (Cambridge, Harvard University Press, 1987), 115ff; S Shavell, *Foundations of Economic Analysis of Law* (Cambridge, Harvard University Press, 2004), 1ff.

[2] MA Geistfeld, 'Compensation as a Tort Norm' in J Oberdiek (ed), *Philosophical Foundations of the Law of Torts*, 1st edn (Oxford, Oxford University Press, 2014); Shavell, *Economic Analysis* (2004) (n 1) 267.

[3] RA Posner, *The Problems of Jurisprudence* (Cambridge, Harvard University Press, 1990) 454ff; D Kennedy, 'Cost-Benefit Analysis of Entitlement Problems: A Critique' (1981) 33 *Stanford Law Review* 387, 444; OE Williamson, 'Franchise Bidding for Natural Monopolies—in General and with Respect to CATV' [1976] *Bell Journal of Economics* 73, 74.

[4] For a comprehensive discussion see B Hsiung, 'Economic Analysis Of Law: An Inquiry of its Underlying Logic' (2006) 2 *ELER* 1; AM Polinsky, *An Introduction to Law and Economics*, 4th edn (New York, Wolters Kluwer Law & Business, 2011) 2ff.

This analysis connects both the positive and normative perspectives of the economic analysis on the liability issue:[5] For the purpose of analysing the policymaker's decision-making, a descriptive and positive approach is chosen with a view to assessing the welfare losses due to WTO violations, and the incentives associated with legal regimes with or without liability. In turn, statements regarding the preferability of certain liability rules or designs based on their respective incentives is in line with normative approaches focusing on the question of how the liability rule should be designed in order to optimise welfare effects. More specifically, the choice of the liability rule may vary between the no-liability rule as argued by the CJEU and a liability rule tied to a negligence standard—both regimes are distinct as to their effect in internalising welfare losses in the EU legislator's decision-making.

Focusing on the incentive structure inherent to a certain liability rule underscores the deterrence function, which the liability is supposed to perform from an economic perspective. By contrast, lawyers typically see the function of liability in providing compensation for damages suffered, while deterrence has a rather auxiliary function.[6] The economic analysis of liability, in turn, seeks to analyse liability regimes in light of their suitability in reaching social welfare optima[7]—since the economic analysis identifies liability as a cost to the wrongdoer, any costly liability rule has a steering and deterrence effect on the wrongdoer's actions. Ideally, the liability rule incentivises the wrongdoer to choose a level of activity securing the social welfare optimum. Thus, for the wrongdoer to know that he will *ex post* be obliged to compensate the injured party, will induce the wrongdoer to take measures that increase the likelihood of avoiding damages. From an economic perspective, individual behaviour should then be incentivised towards a level of action that optimises the costs related to both damages prevention and actual damage.[8]

Since there is virtually no literature on the economic assessment of a liability for WTO violations,[9] it is worthwhile to seek orientation in the established strand

[5] Generally on positive and normative aspects of the economic analysis of law see Posner, *Economic Analysis* (2014) (n 1) 24ff; Grady, 'Theory of Negligence' (n 1) 799f.

[6] J Coleman, S Hershovitz and G Mendlow, 'Theories of the Common Law of Torts' in EN Zalta (ed), *The Stanford Encyclopedia of Philosophy* (Stanford, Stanford University 2014) Section 3; S Sugarman, 'Tort Reform through Damages Law Reform: An American Perspective' (2005) 27 *Sydney Law Review* 507; Shavell, *Economic Analysis* (2004) (n 1) 3; while liability thus performs an *ex ante* function from an economic perspective, the legal concept rather pursues an *ex post* function of the liability regime. However, following the Court's *Francovich* judgment, there have been voices in literature stressing the deterrence and steering function of liability: I Saenger, 'Staatshaftung wegen Verletzung europäischen Gemeinschaftsrechts' [1997] *JuS* 865, 872.

[7] Shavell, *Economic Analysis* (2004) (n 1) 178ff.

[8] ibid 267.

[9] Similar analytical considerations apply, for example, in the work by *van den Bergh* and *Schäfer* dealing with an economic analysis of the liablity of EU Member States for violations of EU law; see H-B Schäfer and R van den Bergh, 'Member States Liability for Infringement of the Free Movement of Goods in the EC: An Economic Analysis' 2001 *German Working Papers in Law and Economics*; H-B Schäfer and R van den Bergh, 'State Liability for Infringement of the E.C. Treaty: Economic Arguments in Support of a Rule of "Obvious Negligence"' (1998) 23 *EL Rev* 552, 552ff. On the redistributive effect of the refusal to grant compensation see Hoekman and Mavroidis, 'Bite the Bullet' (ch 2, fn 28) 327.

of literature on economic analysis of civil liability. Initiated by the works of *Coase* and *Calabresi*,[10] civil liability is one of the core issues in economic analysis of law.[11] The analysis aims at identifying liability design to incentivise potential wrongdoers in undertaking the optimum level of precaution.[12] Based on fault-based liability, the wrongdoer can be held liable, if he does not take the necessary care and attention.[13] If a damage occurs, although the responsible person has performed the required level of care, he cannot be held liable. From an economic perspective, the wrongdoer is ideally incentivised to set his level of care at a welfare optimum (ie, cost-minimising) point.[14] The ratio between the prevention costs and damages is essential—although the probability of damages decreases the higher is the prevention effort, the optimum normally does not correspond to the maximum prevention effort.[15] Put differently, the optimum lies where the sum of prevention costs and expected damages is at a minimum.[16]

The relevant norm for our analysis, Article 340 TFEU, generally applies the fault-based liability standard. Although the norm is silent in this regard, the Court's well-established *Schöppenstedt* formula and the requirement of a 'sufficiently-serious breach' apply similar criteria for the purpose of evaluating the sufficiently-serious breach,[17] whereby the criteria applied lie significantly above the standard typically applied for negligence—a breach must have 'manifestly and gravely disregarded the limits on the exercise of its powers'.[18] As has been discussed above in chapter 6, this criterion is partly interpreted by reference to the effect (ie, its impact on the 'injured' party), but also depends on certain conduct on part of the EU as the wrongdoer. Partly, this criterion was referred to as a 'non-excusable' violation.[19] Another criterion developed in the case law is that the threshold-triggering liability is lower the smaller the scope of discretion. If the scope to manoeuvre is limited, the mere unlawfulness of the measures can suffice to establish liability—in turn, a wide margin of discretion requires an especially

[10] R Coase, 'The Problem of Social Cost' (1960) 3 *J L Econ* 1, 1; G Calabresi, *The Costs of Accidents* (New Haven, Yale University Press, 1970).

[11] Shavell, *Economic Analysis* (2004) (n 1) 175ff; FJ Vandall, *Strict Liability* (New York, Quorum Books, 1989); JP Brown, 'Toward an Economic Theory of Liability' (1973) 2 *J Legal Stud* 323, 323ff; WM Landes and RA Posner, *The Economic Structure of Tort Law* (Cambridge, Harvard University Press, 1986); S Shavell, 'Strict Liability versus Negligence' (1980) 9 *J Legal Stud* 1, 1ff.

[12] See also generally S Shavell, *Economic Analysis of Accident Law* (Cambridge, Harvard University Press, 1987), 5–47; JL Coleman, 'The Economic Structure of Tort Law' (1988) 97 *Yale L J* 1233, 1234ff.

[13] Shavell, *Economic Analysis* (2004) (n 1) 180f.

[14] HB Schäfer and A Schönenberger, 'Strict liability versus negligence' in GD Geest and B Bouckaert (eds), *Encyclopedia of Law and Economics II: Civil Law and Economics* (Cheltenham, Edward Elgar Publishing, 2000) 600.

[15] B Trautmann, *Die Konkurrenz von Haftpflicht- und Versicherungsanspruch* (Frankfurt am Main, P Lang, 2002), 107.

[16] Brown, 'Economic Theory of Liability' (n 11) 325.

[17] See also Ipsen, *Gemeinschaftsrecht* (1972) (ch 3, fn 53) 538ff.

[18] *HNL and Others v Council and Commission* (ch 1, fn 27) 1209, para 6.

[19] *Peine-Salzgitter v Commission* (ch 6, fn 12) I-2393, para 51.

qualified breach.[20] While fault (in the concept of civil liability) and 'sufficiently-serious breach' (within EU liability) rest on a distinct conceptual basis, there is a certain resemblance between both criteria from their functional perspective, that is to allow liability only if the conduct of the wrongdoer fulfils a certain qualification tied to the severity of the misconduct.

## II. INSTITUTIONAL ECONOMICS AND EU LIABILITY

A crucial barrier for simply transferring the insight from the economic analysis of the civil law context to EU liability for WTO violations is the involvement of political stakeholders. While under civil law only private parties are concerned with justifying a microeconomic perspective of their individual decision-making, liability of a public authority involves collective actors and opens the door to integrate the insight provided by institutional economics. This area of the economic discipline examines, *inter alia*, institutions in the market (applying, for example, transaction cost economics and the principal-agent theory), the structure of political institutions and constitutional economics.[21] The main distinctive feature of institutional economics compared to classical theory is that, unlike the latter, it does not ignore institutions or consider them neutrally. Institutional economics studies—positively—the effects resulting from institutions and—normatively—how institutions should be designed.

Unlike under civil liability situations, public liability involves non-market institutions in the political sphere, which is the subject of the political economy. Applying this subdivision of the institutional economic branch to our present analysis requires integrating public choice theory and, in particular, principal-agent considerations, as well as abandoning the maxim of complete information regarding the threshold of unlawfulness under the liability regime.[22] A central tool is transaction costs analysis.[23] Transaction costs appear in all market and non-market areas.[24] For the purpose of this analysis, it is relevant that not only economic transactions but also 'social conduct' can be integrated into the transaction cost analysis.[25]

[20] *Bergaderm and Goupil v Commission* (ch 3, fn 2) I-5291, para 44.

[21] N Mercuro, 'Toward a Comparative Institutional Approach to the Study of Law and Economics' in N Mercuro (ed), *Law and Economics* (Dordrecht, Springer Netherlands, 1989) 1ff; EG Furubotn and R Richter, *Institutions and Economic Theory*, 2nd edn (Ann Arbor, University of Michigan Press, 2005) 1ff; M Erlei, D Sauerland and M Leschke, *Neue Institutionenökonomik*, 2nd edn (Stuttgart, Schäffer-Poeschel, 2007), 27ff.

[22] Unlike classical theory, institutional economics accepts that individuals act under incomplete information and do have problems processing available information, see DC North, 'Structure and Performance: The Task of Economic History' (1978) 16 *J Econ Lit* 963, 972ff.

[23] OE Williamson, 'The Economics of Organization: The Transaction Cost Approach' (1981) 87 *AJS* 548, 552. According to Williamson, 'a transaction occurs when a good or service is transferred across a technologically separable interface. One stage of activity terminates and another begins'.

[24] Furubotn and Richter, *Institutions* (2005) (n 21) 47ff.

[25] ibid 50.

This includes political transactions, that is decisions taken in the exercise of public authority, and allows a study of the way how political decisions are made, especially having regard to the interaction between politicians and interest groups. The 'rent-seeking' performed by interest groups in order to influence political decisions is a core subject of the political economy seeking to provide an explanatory pattern of political decision-making processes.

It is the theory of public choice,[26] which deals with non-market institutions in the political sphere. It offers descriptive explanations on why and how decisions are made, and has developed concepts to examine the interaction between the decision-maker and rent-seeking companies. Considering the harmful effects for welfare resulting from trade restrictions,[27] it is generally surprising that the EU would not pursue free-trade policies and eliminate trade barriers. Rather, virtually all countries pursue protectionism in at least certain sectors through tariff-based or non-tariff restrictions.[28] The discrepancy between economic theory of free trade and the actual external trade policy is dubbed the 'paradox of protectionism',[29] raising the question of how and why such 'government failure' occurs, which in most cases would harm consumers.[30]

The basic premise of public choice theory is to give up the assumption of a welfare maximising politician, and rather extend the insight of the utility maximising *homo oeconomicus* to the political decision-making process and construe a bargaining process.[31] In this process, there is an interaction between the suppliers (government) and demanders (producers and consumers) of political decisions.[32] The specific interests and bargains occurring in this process can explain protectionist

[26] On the various terms 'New Political Economy', 'Public Choice', 'Constitutional Economics', see L van den Hauwe, 'Public Choice, Constitutional Political Economy and Law and Economics' in GD Geest and B Bouckaert (eds), *Encyclopedia of Law and Economics I: The History and Methodology of Law and Economics* (Cheltenham, Edward Elgar Publishing, 2000).

[27] See only D Salvatore, *International Economics*, 11th edn (Hoboken, Wiley, 2014), 213ff.

[28] J Williamson and C Milner, *World Economy* (New York, New York University Press, 1991), 139ff; L Schuknecht, *Trade Protection in the European Community* (Chur, Switzerland, Harwood Academic Publishers, 1992) 17ff; Petersmann, *Constitutional Functions* (1991) (ch 7, fn 33) 100ff; AV Deardoff, 'Why do goverments prefer nontariff barriers?' *University of Michigan Research Seminar in International Economics Seminar* Discussion Paper no 186, 14.

[29] V Vanberg, 'A Constitutional Political Economy Perspective on International Trade' (1992) 43 *ORDO* 375, 378.

[30] H Hauser and others, 'Der Beitrag von Jan Tumfir zur Entwicklung einer ökonomischen Verfassungstheorie internationaler Handelsregeln' (1988) 39 *ORDO* 219, 224ff; Schuknecht, *Trade Protection* (1992) (n 28) 17ff; H Hauser, 'Domestic Policy Foundation and Domestic Policy Function of International Trade Rules' (1986) 41 *Aussenwirtschaft* 171, 175; Petersmann, *Constitutional Functions* (1991) (ch 7, fn 33) 112.

[31] JM Buchanan, 'From Private Preferences to Public Philosophy: The Development of Public Choice' in JM Buchanan (ed), *Constitutional Economics* (Cambridge, Blackwell, 1991) 42: '… All of public choice or the economic theory of politics may be summarised as the "discovery" or "re-discovery" that people should be treated as rational utility-maximisers in all of their behavioural capacities'.

[32] DC Mueller, *Public Choice III* (Cambridge, Cambridge University Press, 2003), 333ff; Furubotn and Richter, *Institutions* (2005) (n 21) 420ff; B Frey, 'The Public Choice View of International Political Economy' (1984) 38 *International Organization* 199, 201.

measures adopted as a result of rent-seeking processes. On the political market, demanders of certain political decisions offer political support or personal advantages in return for favourable political decision.[33] In the area of international trade, a further characteristic of the bargaining process is that interests of protectionist sectors are opposed to consumer interests, as the latter typically benefit from free trade through competition. This adds to a general asymmetry to the extent that protectionist interest groups are better organised and can push their particular interests more effectively in the political process than consumers could. In turn, the political decision-maker does not care about the overall welfare, but rather adopts decisions in a way that maximises his own utility function (eg, increase chances to be re-elected).

An example for the representative course of action of political decision-making in the arena of international trade is illustrated by the steel dispute between the US and the EU, in which the US imposed safeguarding import duties on steel from the EU. According to a study of the manufacturing industry, these measures harmed domestic industries, for example, the processors of steel General Motors and Caterpillar. The protectionist move by the US was mainly induced by the pressure of the 'steel states' Pennsylvania and West Virginia, and aimed at releasing the pressure on the steel industry. A small, strong interest group managed to push its interests through despite its comparatively little significance from an economic point of view—according to the study, the steel dispute led to a loss of 200,000 jobs in the US industry, while the overall number of employees in the US steel industry is lower than 190,000.[34] A similar phenomenon prevails in the case of the EU agricultural policy. The particular recognition of agricultural interests and the privileges and monetary subsidies granted to the agricultural sector can (largely) be attributed to the influential and well-organised agricultural interest groups, even though their economic significance both in terms of contribution to GDP and employees is marginal.[35]

If the EU legislator adopts decisions ignoring the welfare losses accruing to consumers and its constituency, and which overrate the interests of the domestic industry,[36] there is a discrepancy between the social welfare and the utility function maximised by the politician. Analytically, this can be captured by using principal-agent concepts, according to which the EU legislator acts as the agent of the

[33] W Mitchell and MC Munger, 'Economic Models of Interest Groups: An Introductory Survey' (1991) 35 *AJPS* 512, 520; Furubotn and Richter, *Institutions* (2005) (n 21) 482f.

[34] See A Oldag, 'Zölle wider alle Vernunft' (12 November 2003) *Süddeutsche Zeitung*.

[35] AF Cooper and GD Skogstad, 'Introduction: Domestic Pressures, International Tensions, and the MTN' in GD Skogstad and AF Cooper (eds), *Agricultural Trade: Domestic Pressures and International Tensions: Papers presented at a conference held at the University of Toronto in January 1989* (Halifax, Institute for Research on Public Policy, 1990) 6f.

[36] The term 'discounting' is used in the present context to underscore that interests of consumers and importers have only a reduced weight in their incorporation into the welfare function maximised by the policy-makers.

European citizen as the principal.[37] More broadly, this relationship may explain the interdependency of those involved in the political process. The democratic system may then be represented as a network of relational principal-agent relationships between citizens (principals) and representatives (agents).[38] The political election leads to matching suppliers and demanders on the political market, and constitutes the command of the principal to the agent to act in the interests of the principal. Under two conditions the instability of this relationship and the potential for interest groups pushing their individual interests becomes visible: first, the conceptualisation of the political decision-maker as an individual utility maximiser makes deviations from the principals' interests likely. Second, the absence of an efficient monitoring and sanction mechanism hinders detection and deterrence of such conduct. The control of citizens over the European Commission is even weaker than on the national level, which is further exacerbated by an underdeveloped European public and the very limited possibilities to suspend individual EU Commissioners. In the absence of individual protection in external trade, the only sanction mechanism would be the voting out of the EU legislator, which in the case of the European Commission is not practical. The particularities of the political market in the area of external trade thus promote a principal-agent relationship, in which political influences by interest groups are particularly likely given the lack of control mechanisms of citizens over the EU legislator.

The concept of transaction costs also extends to social behaviour.[39] It encompasses political transactions, which take into account the exercise of political authority by decision-makers, and the transactions between politicians and interest groups. Rent-seeking requires resources, which cannot be used otherwise for possibly more productive activities.[40] Lobbying activities aim at yielding profits, which are not used for the production of goods or services and are, therefore, considered as unproductive profit-seeking activities.[41] The use of unproductive resources and the striving for this kind of rent is rational from an individual company's perspective, because the company invests in the area in which it generates the highest profit, even though this may not be desirable from a social perspective and the company continues seeking rent, as long as the individual company's profits from rent-seeking exceed the profit from alternative uses of resources.

[37] Generally JW Pratt and RJ Zeckhauser (eds), *Principals and Agents* (Boston, Harvard Business School Press, 1985).

[38] Furubotn and Richter, *Institutions* (2005) (n 21) 476.

[39] ibid 50.

[40] It should also be mentionned that governments often cooperate with companies in conducting WTO proceedings. While the dispute settlement mechanism is a inter-state procedure, private actors play an increasingly important role, which is referred to as a 'public-private partnership', see GC Shaffer, *Defending Interests* (Washington, DC, Brookings Institution Press 2003). Participation of private parties in WTO proceedings offers interest groups an additional channel for rent-seeking activities by way of cooperating with the government.

[41] JN Bhagwati, 'Directly Unproductive, Profit-Seeking (DUP) Activities' (1982) 90 *JPE* 988.

Concerning the relationship between the level of rent-seeking and the level of protection, this analysis assumes a positive correlation which implies a high degree of protectionisms if the rent-seeking activities are high. In a state of policymaking, that is largely free of interest group influence, politicians are more likely to maximise the welfare function rather than accounting for particular interests. By contrast, in order to achieve and maintain a high level of protectionism, it is assumed that high rent-seeking activities are necessary. Further, one can assume that the marginal costs from each additional rent-seeking activity is increasing, because with each increase in rent-seeking activity, it becomes more difficult to convince politicians to engage in even more protectionism, as this would lead further away from the welfare optimum and because the resistance of groups interested in free trade (consumers and importing industry) increases too.[42] In other words, the higher the level of protection and the greater the ensuing welfare losses, the more rent-seeking a company has to undertake in order to reach an even higher level of protection. Eventually, the assumption of decreasing marginal utility of rent-seeking activity implies that rent-seeking is particularly effective in situations and sectors in which the trade is fairly liberalised, because marginal costs are comparatively small.[43] Also, opportunity costs are a relevant factor to be considered, as each resource going into rent-seeking cannot be used for other productive purposes.

## III. INCOMPLETE INFORMATION AND THE COMPLIANCE STANDARD

Incomplete information is an empirical phenomenon prevalent, *inter alia*, in the conduct of external trade policy. It alludes to the difficulty to possess all relevant information that would give the EU legislator certainty whether or not a specific measure is in line with WTO rules and whether this measure would give rise to liability. There is factual and legal uncertainty in several regards: uncertainty extends to the question of whether another WTO Member State would bring the alleged WTO violation before the dispute settlement mechanism. If a proceeding is initiated, the EU legislator may lack the necessary legal clarity on whether the measures will be found to be in violation of WTO rules. Thus, there is uncertainty about the standard of lawfulness, which is further exacerbated by the vague und unprecise provisions of the WTO agreements. Following a finding of a violation by the DSB, there is uncertainty about how the winning party will react to

[42] The example of the steel dispute confirms this assumption: Following the increase in prices for steel, a number of car suppliers struggled in their operative business leading to layoff. Consequently, resistance occurred in the car industry and among consumer representatives triggering protests which were ultimately supported by senators in some states, see Oldag, 'Zölle wider alle Vernunft' (n 34).

[43] To what extent rent-seeking activities are profitable from the perspective of the individual company depends on a number of factors including whether and to which magnitude the company is involved in foreign trade.

non-implementation of the DSB, that is whether the winning party will seek approval for retaliation measures, eventually giving raise to potential liability claims of case group C. Further, on the level of EU law, the legislator cannot anticipate under what conditions the Court will consider the legislator's conduct as a 'sufficiently-serious breach' as prerequisite for an action for damages—the criteria determining these requirements have been described above as rather vague and dependent on the specific case. Despite the multiple deficits of information, the legislator must set the regulation and determine the desired level of protection.

The economic analysis of law has explored extensively how uncertainty affects the incentives resulting from sanction-based legal norms.[44] This applies particularly to situations in which sanctions are tied to a certain standard of care, as under fault-based liability. It is well researched that in liability settings, the wrongdoer does not know the precise standard of fault and lawfulness that the court is going to apply.[45] Given factual and legal uncertainties, the wrongdoer can only estimate the establishment of liability with a certain probability. It is well-established that from the perspective of the potential wrongdoer, it is rational to exceed the optimal level of precaution by the probability of being exempted from liability.[46] Hence, under fault-liability rules, uncertainty usually does not lead to an optimal but rather too high a level of precaution.[47] In the present context, the EU legislator as a potential wrongdoer faces uncertainty: the necessary standard of care corresponds to the degree to which the trade regime is designed in a liberal fashion—higher caution means less trade restriction; less caution implies higher trade barriers. The standard of permitted trade restriction is *ex ante* unclear, and gains certainty only later by the DSB decision on the finding of WTO infringement and, subsequently in an action for damages, through the review of liability conditions by the CJEU. At the point in time of legislating, the policy-maker can make its probability assessment of potential liability only on the basis of previous case law of the WTO adjudicative bodies (regarding the WTO legal standards) and the CJEU case law (regarding liability standard under EU law). Given the vague

[44] See, inter alia, R Craswell and J Calfee, 'Deterrence and Uncertain Legal Standards' (1986) 2 *JLEO* 279; H-B Schäfer and C Ott, *Lehrbuch der ökonomischen Analyse des Zivilrechts*, 5th edn (Berlin, Springer, 2012), 173ff; DG Baird, RH Gertner and RC Picker, *Game Theory and the Law* (Cambridge, Harvard University Press, 1994), 48; see also Shavell, *Economic Analysis* (2004) (n 1) 479ff.

[45] R Craswell and J Calfee, 'Some Effects of Uncertainty in Compliance with Legal Standards' (1984) 70 *Va L Rev* 965, 976; Shavell, *Accident Law* (1987) (n 12) 79.

[46] CD Kolstad, T Ulen and GV Johnson, 'Ex post Liability for Harm vs. ex ante Safety Regulation: Substitutes or Complements?' (1990) 80 *AER* 888, 894; F Mueller-Langer and H-B Schäfer, 'Strict Liability versus Negligence' in M Faure (ed), *Tort Law and Economics* (Cheltenham, Edward Elgar Publishing 2009) 13; Craswell and Calfee, 'Legal Standards' (n 44) 299.

[47] Kolstad, Ulen and Johnson, 'Substitutes or Complements?' (n 46) 895.

judicial standard, the wrongdoer assigns a certain probability to the finding of liability and, hence, the level of protection chosen is likely to be higher or lower than the optimum level.

Besides the factual uncertainty on whether other WTO Members will request the establishment of a panel and, following a DSB finding, continue the case towards seeking the suspension of concessions, the lack of clarity in most WTO provisions does not allow an unambiguous forecast on the finding of lawfulness. This lack of clarity does not even necessarily vanish once the DSB ruling has been rendered, because the ruling is typically confined to the mere finding as to whether a certain measure is in violation of WTO law or not—the ruling does not give clear guidance regarding the measures to comply with the ruling.[48] Thus, even after the DSB ruling, there is scope for discretion regarding the appropriate measure to comply with the ruling.[49] The same applies to the standards applied by the CJEU regarding the liability and the 'sufficiently-serious breach' requirement, in particularly the criteria of gravity and effects referred to by the Court. Despite several attempts to give precision to these criteria through the case law,[50] *ex ante*, there is no certainty about the standards applied. Again, the legislator can determine lawfulness on a probabilistic basis only.[51] The lack of precision of judicial legal standards is of relevance in view of the incentives of the legislator, because under this condition liability can lead, as the discussion will show below, to over-deterrence in the legislative activity, and imply the choice of an inefficiently low regulatory level.[52]

Can the decision-maker exert care by gathering the missing information and reduce factual and legal uncertainty about the lawfulness? The economic analysis of civil law liability rests on the assumption that the wrongdoer can reduce the expected value of damage claims by increasing the standard of care, which in the present case would correspond to an increase in the information-gathering effort.[53] Damage prevention is directly correlated to the probability of the occurrence of a loss. The transferability of civil law considerations into the context of WTO liability is, however, limited, as the standard of care under civil liability cannot easily be compared to the decision structure of European policy-making.[54] There may be a number of situations in which public liability generally depends on the level of care undertaken by the public authority, and are thus directly comparable with situations under civil liability, given the immediate relationship between the level of care and occurrence of damage. As regards WTO violations, it is difficult to

[48] Cottier, 'Streitschlichtungsverfahren in der WTO' (ch 2, fn 45) 186; Hinderer, *Rechtsschutz* (2004) (ch 2, fn 5) 442f.

[49] Steinbach, 'WTO-Streitbeilegungsentscheidungen' (ch 2, fn 3) 332.

[50] See above ch 6 I.

[51] More generally, on the scope of building expectations based on jurisprudential case-law A Endres, 'Allokationswirkungen des Haftungsrechts' (1989) 40 *Jahrbuch für Sozialwissenschaft* 115, 124.

[52] Schäfer and Bergh, 'State Liability' (n 9) 555. See below ch 9 II.

[53] Craswell and Calfee, 'Legal Standards' (n 45) 980f.

[54] Schäfer and Bergh, 'State Liability' (n 9) 557.

establish such a relation. There is no compelling relation between the legislator's information gathering exercise to increase the likelihood of lawfulness, on the one hand, and the occurrence of damages, on the other hand. Certainly, the assessment of the prospective conformity of the envisaged measures with WTO law requires a factual understanding as well as a legal analysis of the decision-maker. It is doubtful, however, whether it is feasible to simply increase the information effort to the end that the violation of WTO law could ultimately be precluded. It is precisely the vagueness of legal standards under WTO rules that make a certain forecast on the lawfulness rather difficult, even if the decision-maker undertakes a comprehensive factual and legal assessment of the case.

The example of the EU's compliance efforts in the banana dispute gives an indication for a relationship between information gathering and occurrence of damages. In this sense, one could consider that the WTO violations of the respective regulations No 1637/98 and No 2362/98, which had been found to infringe WTO law already shortly after their entering into force on 19 April 1999,[55] were due to an insufficient level of knowledge on the part of the Commission, which could have been avoided by better information gathering. But even if one would presume that the Commission did not fully appraise and understand the findings of the panel, there remains doubt as regards the relations between information gathering and WTO violation in light of the obvious WTO violation of the modified regulations.[56] It is more likely that political rationality (and the interest group pressure at work) is driving the decision not to comply with the DSB ruling.

In the hormones dispute, the relationship between information gathering and compliance with the standard of lawfulness is maybe even more fragile. In this dispute, the EU undertook comprehensive attempts to support its ban on hormone-treated beef by scientific evidence, none of which ultimately proved the risk asserted by the EU. That is, although the EU offered comprehensive scientific information gathering on the impact of hormone-treated beef on consumers' health, the breach of WTO law could not be avoided. In sum, the civil law liability assumption of the duality of an increasing standard of care with a decreasing likelihood of occurrence of damages does not hold. Again, this may have reasons rooted in the political nature of liability related to WTO law and the relevance of the political decision-making process, including the rent-seeking mechanisms at work. Also, the vagueness and lack in clarity of judicial standards under WTO rules and under the EU liability regime add to the limited transferability of the civil liability insight.

Moreover, for the purpose of this analysis, the costs for information can be considered negligible. Even if one would assume that EU breaches of WTO law would

[55] WTO: EC—Regime for the Importation, Sale and Distribution of Bananas—Recourse to Arbitration by the EC under Article 22.6 of the DSU—Report of the Appellate Body (9 April 1999) WT/DS27/ARB, para 5.79f. and 4.8.

[56] Kuschel, 'Bananenmarktordnung' (ch 6, fn 19) 76; Schoißwohl, 'Haftung' (ch 1, fn 8) 718; T Jürgensen, 'WTO-Konformität der reformierten Gemeinsamen Marktorganisation für Bananen' [1999] RIW 241, 241ff; Zonnekeyn, 'EC Liability' (ch 1, fn 35) 269; Cascante, Rechtsschutz (2003) (ch 2, fn 6) 272.

at least partially be caused by limited information, the information costs occurring for a careful review of factual and legal issues would be insignificant compared to the actual welfare costs and rent-seeking costs. Also, the resources bound within the European Commission for the purpose of the dispute at stake are comparatively small, so that it seems appropriate to assume that information costs and administrative costs are low.[57] This renders the insight gained in the economic analysis of civil law irrelevant in this case.

If information-gathering costs are hardly a determinative criterion for the expected damage, it remains to be examined as to which incentives have determinative impact on compliance. In line with the public choice arguments developed above, the policymakers' decision on whether to comply or not with DSB rulings heavily depends on the extent to which the legislator maximises the welfare function, which, in turn, depends on his individual utility function and the pressure interest groups can make in maximising his utility. In the utility function, compliance and non-compliance thus correspond to certain political costs. One essential observation then is that under a system without liability, the legislator does not bear the costs associated with the unlawful conduct. In the absence of primary and secondary legal redress, due to a lack of direct effect of WTO rules, the EU legislator does not have to internalise the costs of damages which remain under no liability with the injured party. For the legislator as the wrongdoer, these costs are external costs and constitute social costs inflicted on the injured parties. They are not taken into account by the legislator, because he does not have to fear that his laws will be challenged and possibly annulled, nor does he face compensation claims as a monetary way to incorporate the social costs into the policymaker's decision. This would be different under fault-liability, if the legislator can be held liable under certain conditions.[58]

[57] See also Schäfer and Bergh, 'Member States Liability' (n 9) 3f expressing doubts as to the comparability of the precautionary costs under the civil liability model and the costs incurred on increasing the probability of legal compliance.

[58] See below ch 9 II.

# 9

# *Compensation of Financial Losses and Over-deterrence*

## I. THE LEVEL OF WELFARE MAXIMISING PROTECTIONISM

A PRINCIPAL INSIGHT from the economic analysis of civil law is that, under certain conditions, compensation of financial losses can lead to over-deterrence of the wrongdoer. We will highlight the relevance of this insight and the ensuing paralysing effect on the EU legislator. At first, however, the legislative scope of the EU institutions regarding protectionist measures should be considered. In principle, this economic analysis relies on the insight of classical trade economics, according to which involvement in international trade is generally welfare-increasing, and that establishing trade barriers virtually always has adverse effects for the society as a whole.[1] A pure free trade focus, however, neglects certain welfare effects, which are not accounted for by the concepts of consumer and producer surpluses.[2] In fact, it is recognised that situations may occur in which it can be favourable for the overall welfare to restrict trade for specific purposes.[3] For example, a purely free trade focus may give rise to negative externalities as a consequence of certain production and consumption patterns, which justify an intervention even if trade restrictions are the consequence. This alludes in particular to environmental, health and consumer protection standards, often related to the production process or the product as such, which constitute legitimate reasons for restricting trade.[4]

In situations in which external costs are supposed to be internalised with a view to maximising overall welfare, certain WTO-consistent restrictive measures can

[1] See only PR Krugman, M Obstfeld and M Melitz, *International Economics*, 10th edn (Boston, Pearson, 2015) 241ff; H Thompson, *International Economics*, 3rd edn (Hackensack, World Scientific, 2011) 63ff.

[2] Krugman, Obstfeld and Melitz (2015) (n 1) 246.

[3] While safeguarding measures pursuant to Article XIX GATT are hardly justifiable by welfare gains, measures protecting human beings, animals and plants are more likely to generate welfare gains; see C Nowak, 'Subventionen' in S Oeter and M Hilf (eds), *WTO-Recht: Rechtsordnung des Welthandels*, 2nd edn (Baden-Baden, Nomos, 2010) § 3, para 1.

[4] See, inter alia, M Matsushita and others, *The World Trade Organization*, 3rd edn (Oxford, Oxford University Press, 2015) 724ff; M Herdegen, *Principles of International Economic Law*, 1st edn (Oxford, Oxford University Press, 2013) 203ff.

generate social benefits. If, for example, a rule aims at protecting public health, this can create certain disadvantages to consumer (eg, higher prices), but at the same time protect their physical integrity. Trade-restrictive measures may, for such purposes, create positive welfare effects. The WTO agreements account for such situations by allowing exceptions to free trade rules under certain conditions.[5] This creates scope for WTO Members to manoeuvre and generate positive welfare effects exceeding the potential adverse effects of trade restrictions. Problematic, however, is the fact that the size of the optimum level of protection is difficult to determine.[6] Moreover, the interventions on these grounds must not be used for implementing disguised trade barriers.[7]

Regarding the efficient level of protection in trade policies, we thus assume that a certain minimum level of import restrictive measures may be admissible and welfare-increasing, if they are based on the exceptions provided under WTO rules.[8] This implies, in turn, that the admissible limits of welfare increasing but trade-restrictive measures is exceeded, if the WTO adjudicative bodies have found an infringement of WTO law. In this vein, the import ban on hormone-treated beef cannot claim to generate additional social benefits through health protection, because the relevant scientific evidence could not show that consumption of hormone-treated beef led to adverse health effects.

For the purpose of determining the optimum welfare level, besides the possibly positive effects generated through trade restrictions, one must consider the rent-seeking costs accruing in the course of trade policy, since these activities imply expenses that cannot be used otherwise for productive purposes and which thus incur opportunity costs. Above (cp 8 II) we assumed that the level of trade protection raises with increasing rent-seeking activities and that it is comparatively low if rent-seeking activities are not considerable. At the same time, the marginal utility of each additional rent-seeking activity is decreasing. As a consequence, rent-seeking costs are assumed to be minimised at a corresponding level where there is no protection. From an overall welfare perspective, the optimum lies where the sum of welfare damages from trade restriction and rent-seeking activities is at a minimum.[9] The determination of this minimum then rests on two premises: first, lobbying costs have their minimum at zero and increase with the level of

[5] Herdegen, *International Economic Law* (2013) (n 4) 203ff.

[6] On welfare costs and benefits of non-tariff measures in trade: J Beghin et al, 'Welfare Costs and Benefits of Non-tariff Measures in Trade: A Conceptual Framework and Application' (2012) 11 *World Trade Review* 356; HH Glismann and others, *Weltwirtschaftslehre* (München, dtv wissenschaft, 1980) 76.

[7] Herdegen, *International Economic Law* (2013) (n 4) 204; S Oeter, 'Welthandelsordnung im Spannungsfeld von Wirtschaft, Recht und Politik' in S Oeter and M Hilf (eds), *WTO-Recht: Rechtsordnung des Welthandels*, 2nd edn (Baden-Baden, Nomos, 2010) § 1 para 29f.

[8] A similar assumption is made regarding the economic analysis of Member States' violations of EU law, see Schäfer and Bergh, 'Member States Liability' (ch 8, fn 9) 7ff and Schäfer and Bergh, 'State Liability' (ch 8, fn 9) 558.

[9] As discussed above, the information costs incurred by the EU legislator are considered marginal and can thus be disregarded for the purpose of welfare maximisation.

protection; and second, the welfare damages are the lowest at a protection rate slightly above zero. Consequently, the welfare optimum will lie somewhere between this level and zero.

## II. THE PARALYSING EFFECT RESULTING FROM WTO LIABILITY CLAIMS

The following analysis will highlight that recognising a liability regime for WTO violations will lead claimants to ask for compensation of financial losses, which will go beyond the overall social damages incurred from the WTO violation—the result is that individual damage claims exceed social losses. The literature on the economic analysis of liability has examined the consequences of compensation of financial losses for the incentive structure between the wrongdoer and the injured party.[10] The issue is that if a claimant asks for damages, the size of which exceeds the overall social costs, this will lead to overcompensation of the injured parties and over-deterrence of the wrongdoer. In fact, in many national legal orders, compensation of purely financial losses is precluded.[11] In *Brasserie du Pêcheur*, the Court dealt with the principles in national legal orders after the German Federal High Court of Justice (*Bundesgerichtshof*) had stated, in its request for a preliminary ruling, that a limitation of the liability claim to damages which have accrued to specific, legally protected interests (ie, excluding financial losses) should be justified. The *Bundesgerichtshof* argued that loss of profits should not be captured by the duty to compensate, because the mere opportunities to market products from other Member States would not be protected under the German legal order.[12] The CJEU contradicted this view and found it inadmissible to generally exclude the loss of profits from the compensable damages upon EU law being infringed. In this vein, the CJEU ruled on another occasion that compensation of financial losses should not be excluded from compensable damages.[13] The jurisprudence thus suggests a wide interpretation of the term damages within the meaning of Article 340 TFEU, so that every disadvantage could constitute a compensable damage.[14]

From an economic perspective, this wide understanding in the CJEU's jurisprudence raises concerns: a comprehensive compensation of financial losses typically

[10] I Gilead, 'Tort Law and Internalization: The Gap between Private Loss and Social Cost' (1997) 17 *IRLE* 589, 591ff; Posner, *Economic Analysis* (2014) (ch 8, fn 1) 196ff; T Ulen, 'Rational Victims—Rational Injurers: Cognition and the Economic Analysis of Tort Law' in RP Malloy and CK Braun (eds), *Law and Economics: New and Critical Perspectives* (New York, P Lang, 1995) 413ff; Schäfer and Bergh, 'Member States Liability' (ch 8, fn 9) 4f.

[11] W Bishop, 'Economic Loss in Tort' (1982) 2 *Oxford Journal of Legal Studies* 1, 1; VP Goldberg, 'Accountable Accountants: Is Third-Party Liability Necessary?' (1994) 23 *J Legal Stud* 1, 1; Landes and Posner, *Tort Law* (1986) (ch 8, fn 11) 251ff.

[12] *Brasserie du Pêcheur v Germany and Rv Secretary of State for Transport, ex parte Factortame III* (ch 3, fn 23) I-1157, para 86.

[13] *Produits Bertrand v Commission* (ch 6, fn 23) 1, para 4ff.

[14] M Jacob and M Kottmann in E Grabitz, M Hilf and M Nettesheim (eds), *Das Recht der Europäischen Union*, 58th edn (München, CH Beck, 2016); Art 340 TFEU, para 116.

has adverse effects on incentives because financial losses can exceed the overall damage to the society.[15] If the damages incurring to the individual are greater than to the society as a whole, full compensation may set incentives for an overly high level of damage avoiding activities.[16] At any level of damage-avoidance activity chosen by the wrongdoer, he has to expect with a certain probability to be held liable and to compensate for damages above the overall damage. Given this uncertainty, the wrongdoer is induced to increase his cost-avoiding activities to a level above the efficient level, in order to escape fault and the duty to compensate the overly high damages. The phenomenon particularly prevails if there is uncertainty about the necessary threshold of care, that is if the judicial legal standard is ambiguous.[17] If the wrongdoer were in the position to clearly anticipate the threshold of care, the risk of over-deterrence would be low, because the wrongdoer could choose the required level of care and damage avoiding activity. The purpose of non-recognition of purely financial losses is, therefore, not to oblige the wrongdoer to pay for damages, which would otherwise induce an inefficiently high level of care and damage avoidance on the part of the wrongdoer.[18]

Applying the above reasoning developed in the context of an economic analysis of civil law liability, the phenomenon of over-deterrence of the wrongdoer also occurs regarding the legislative activity of the EU legislator—the threat of over-compensation paralyses the political decision-maker in his legislative task.[19] In order to assess the risk of over-deterrence and paralysis of the legislator, it is necessary to examine the positive and negative effects of WTO violations on the respective affected group (ie, case groups A, B, and C), with a view to whether there is an identity of the social damages with the damages claimed by the individual groups.

More specifically, in order to assess the possibility of over-compensation in the case of damage claims for WTO violations and the risk of paralysation of the EU legislator, the respective damage positions resulting from WTO violations have thus to be put in relation to the social damages. In this regard, a distinction should be made between private damages—those suffered by the companies in case groups A, B and C—and social damages, which are reflected in the damages accruing to the society as a whole.[20] Assessing the congruency of these categories of damages is important, because any divergence may induce an undesirable deterring effect on the EU legislator, who could be paralysed due to the risk of being exposed to liability claims, if this goes together with an unprecise standard of lawfulness.

[15] Schäfer and Bergh, 'State Liability' (ch 8, fn 9) 556.

[16] Bishop, 'Economic Loss in Tort' (n 11) 1ff.

[17] M Adams, *Ökonomische Analyse der Gefährdungs- und Verschuldenshaftung* (Heidelberg v Decker, 1985), 128ff; Schäfer and Bergh, 'State Liability' (ch 8, fn 9) 553.

[18] Gilead, 'Tort Law and Internalization' (n 10) 597; Schäfer and Bergh, 'Member States Liability' (ch 8, fn 9) 4.

[19] In relation to the liability of Member States' liability for violations of EU law Schäfer and Bergh, 'State Liability' (ch 8, fn 9) 553.

[20] For a more general distinction between compensation and damages see, I Marboe, 'Compensation and Damages in International Law' (2006) 7 *JWIT* 723.

The respective damage position can be illustrated by the example of an import tariff. Import duties are the main tariff-based trade barrier. The economic implications of quantitative restrictions are similar.[21] Also, non-tariff barriers share the commonality that they raise the price of the protected domestic good,[22] so that the insight to be developed on the divergence of private and social damages can be applied to other trade policy instruments as well.

## A. The effect of tariffs and optimal tariff policy

If the EU introduces a tariff in violation of WTO law, a number of effects ensue, as illustrated in Figure 1.[23]

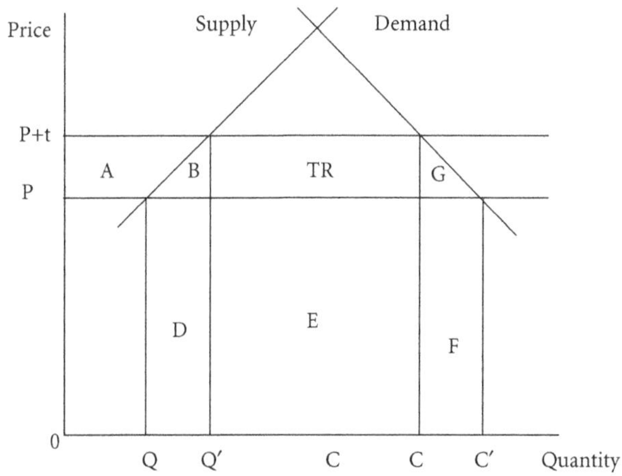


**Figure 1: Losses in turnover of groups A and B**

First, there is a protection effect allowing domestic producers to increase the supply of their products (Q→Q') and to raise the price of the products concerned, without having to fear being driven out of the market from foreign competitors. In parallel, demand for the product concerned decreases (consumption effect: C'→C), because the consumers have to pay more for the concerned products. In addition,

[21] Thompson, *International Economics* (2011) (n 1) 67f; however, an essential difference lies in the fact that revenues from quotas only accrue to the government if import licenses under quotas are distributed through auctions. Otherwise, revenues from quotas accrue to the importers: Krugman, Obstfeld and Melitz (2015) (n 1) 252.

[22] Salvatore, *International Economics* (2014) (ch 8, fn 27) 248ff; Thompson, *International Economics* (2011) (n 1) 68.

[23] For the following see Thompson, *International Economics* (2011) (n 1) 63ff; Krugman, Obstfeld and Melitz (2015) (n 1) 241ff.

public revenues are generated (government revenue gain: TR). These three effects altogether amount to a redistributive effect leading to losses for consumers and benefits to domestic producers and the government. However, not the entire loss borne by the consumer surplus (A+B+TR+G) is transferred to the producer surplus (A) and government revenue (TR). The domestic industry is working comparatively less efficiently than the foreign industry, implying 'production costs of protection' (B), which do not translate into the redistribution and thus lead to a loss of welfare. On the part of the consumers, they renounce consumption leading to consumption costs (G). These two kinds of costs are dubbed 'dead-weight losses' because they are lost during the redistribution without compensation. In balance, the losses of the consumer surplus are greater than the gains for the domestic industry and the government—and the overall welfare decreases.

A particularity results from the possibility to influence the world market price due to the tariff-induced decline in demand in the EU. Because of the size of the EU as a large trading block, the welfare effect is not necessarily negative.[24] On the one hand, there are the described welfare losses resulting from allocative inefficiencies; on the other hand, there are welfare gains due to improvement of the terms of trade. The terms of trade reflect the real relation between export prices of a country and its import prices. A term of trade improvement results from a decrease in import prices, and means that a country can import more in return for its export than previously. Because of the size and the economic potential of the EU, the tariff-induced decline of the demand in the EU leads to an expansion of the supply on the world market and creates a surplus of supply, which, in turn, leads to a decrease in world market prices. On that basis, one might argue that by establishing trade barriers, the EU would act rationally with a view to the maximisation of welfare, even if there were negative consequence for the welfare of other countries. This policy referred to as 'optimal-tariff policy'[25] employs the terms of trade effect. Importantly though, gains accrue to a country, only if other countries do not likewise adopt an optimal-tariff policy. In practice, as can be seen under the mechanism of the WTO, other countries will react by imposing retaliation tariffs to reduce the losses suffered as far as possible.[26] This would typically lead to a tariff war, in the course of which each country pursues national welfare maximisation goals, but at the end of it all the countries suffer welfare losses and are worse off compared to the initial situation. It is thus realistic to assume that any EU

[24] Krugman, Obstfeld and Melitz (2015) (n 1) 274f; M Chacholiades, *International Economics* (New York, McGraw-Hill, 1990) 168; K Bagwell and RW Staiger, 'An Economic Theory of GATT' [1997] *NBER Working Paper* No 6049, 1; F Breuss, 'WTO Dispute Settlement in Practice: An Economic Assesssment' in F Breuss, S Griller and E Vranes (eds), *The Banana Dispute: An Economic and Legal Analysis* (New York, Springer, 2003) 151ff; J Kennan and R Riezman, 'Do Big Countries Win Tariff Wars?' (1998) 29 *IER* 81, 81ff.

[25] HG Johnson, 'Optimum Tariffs and Retaliation' (1953–54) 21 *Review of Economic Studies* 142; DR Appleyard, AJ Field and SL Cobb, *International Economics*, 7th edn (New York, McGraw-Hill, 2010) 331f.

[26] Krugman, Obstfeld and Melitz (2015) (n 1) 275.

optimal-tariff policy would trigger a response by other countries eliminating potential improvements in EU welfare. This assumption is confirmed by empirical results showing that the optimal tariff lies well above the level laid down in the *Schedules of Concession* achieved in the WTO negotiation rounds.[27] Consequently, there is no scope for a WTO-compliant optimal-tariff policy. If a country tries to achieve positive welfare gains through an optimal-tariff policy, one can expect disputes before the WTO and retaliation to ensue. Consequently, there is a strong indication that an EU optimal-tariff policy would not even produce additional welfare effects and that the potential gains through an improvement of the terms of trade would not compensate the dead-weight losses.[28]

### B. Private versus social damages

For the efficiency analysis of the liability, consideration must be given to both private and social damages—by nature of the trade restrictive effect of the import tariff, damages incur to private traders, while from a welfare perspective overall damages are crucial. As analysed above, divergence of private and social damages may lead to inefficient results under a liability regime in which financial losses are compensated, as this may imply compensation exceeding social damages and imply over-deterrence of the legislator. Therefore, the size of damage positions of private parties must be assessed and compared to the overall welfare damage to society. More specifically, in our context we ask whether the damages claimed by case groups A, B and C are equivalent to the overall social damages. To that end, it needs to be examined as to what extent the respective case groups benefit or lose from the effects of the tariff on consumers and producers surpluses.

#### *i. Damages incurring to case groups A and B*

From an economic perspective, the trading activities by case group A (non-EU exporters who are impaired in their exporting opportunities) and case group B (EU traders being affected directly or indirectly by the EU import restriction) are the same. From a legal perspective, the above discussion has shown that group A does not have the necessary need for legal redress to establish liability, provided that the home countries offer a compensatory mechanism to mitigate the damages suffered due to the EU's violation of WTO law. While this is a purely legal reasoning, it does not have economic relevance—companies of group A suffer

[27] According to Whalley, the optimal uniform tariff for the EU and Japan lies at 150% and for the US at 145%, see J Whalley, *Trade Liberalization among Major World Trading Areas* (Cambridge, MIT Press, 1985) 248.

[28] This rests on the assumption that welfare maximisation is only possible through a WTO-compliant trade policy.

from restricted export opportunities. Companies of case group B are directly or indirectly (as was the Atlanta AG) dependent on the import of the good so that the tariff affects their business. Both groups A and B are equally impaired in their trading activities as a result of the import restriction. Thus, from an economic perspective the nature of the damages suffered by these groups is identical.

Graphically, the aggregated losses of case groups A and B are represented by the difference between the amount QC′, which was initially imported in the WTO-consistent situation and the reduced imported amount Q′C following the imposition of the tariff. The losses of case groups A and B are illustrated by the area D and F. Case groups A and B will claim damages by this amount as this corresponds to the private losses incurred by these groups due to the import restriction. The graph also underscores that compensation of these damages exceeds the overall welfare losses of the areas B and G. Variance in price elasticities may modify the relation between the actual monetary sizes. Also, the actual amount of overall welfare losses depends on the respective price level of the product concerned. However, a price increase of up to 100%, induced by an *ad valorem* duty, cannot lead to a scenario in which the surfaces D and F would be smaller than the welfare damages illustrated by areas B and G. This allows one to infer that if the damage claims are successful, there is a divergence between private and social damages.

A further relevant aspect, which is not reflected in the partial analysis of the tariff effect is that the partial analysis only accounts for the bilateral trade effects between the import restricting country and the country from where the good is exported. The effects on the world market remains disregarded.[29] There is the general assumption underlying the classical analysis of tariff effects that the world market price would decline due to the higher supply of the good on the world market, which means that a part of the welfare losses can be passed on abroad.[30] However, the model does not accurately reflect third-country effects and substitution effects.[31] Such effects result from a change of the demand and supply situation on the world market.[32] If the EU restricts the import of hormone-treated beef and bananas, this can lead to an excess of supply on the world market, which, in

[29] On the welfare effects for other countries see M Borchert, *Aussenwirtschaftslehre*, 7th edn (Wiesbaden. Gabler-Lehrbuch, Gabler, 2001) 267.

[30] See only K Rose and K Sauernheimer, *Theorie der Außenwirtschaft*, 14th edn (München, Vahlens Handbücher der Wirtschafts- und Sozialwissenschaften, Vahlen, 2006) 584. For the purpose of simplification, this effect is not depicted in the graph. The consequence for the domestic price would be that the difference between the new equilibrium price p' and the old equilibrium price p is smaller than t because of the decline in world market price.

[31] As will be shown below, WTO arbitrators are mainly guided by the sales volume in the bilateral trade relation when determining the magnitude of retaliatory measures pursuant to Article 22 para 7 DSU, see J Bernstein and D Skully, 'Calculating Trade Damages in the Context of the World Trade Organization's Dispute Settlement Process' (2003) 25 *Review of Agricultural Economics* 385, 391.

[32] For a comprehensive discussion of these effects see K Anderson, 'Pecularities of Retaliation in WTO Dispute Settlement' [2002] *CIES Discussion Paper* no 0207, 7ff.

turn, leads to lower world market prices of these goods.[33] At the same time, however, European consumers will demand substitutes due to the reduced import—this in turn will raise the price of the substitute and, hence, raise the demand for the import-restricted goods from third countries on the world market.[34] In sum, the effect could stimulate trade on third markets and, therefore, partially compensate the losses induced by the initial import restriction. However, trade with third countries takes place at lower prices and, therefore, for less favourable conditions than on the European market because supply and the consumers' willingness to pay would be higher in the absence of a trade restriction. The substitution effect thus cannot overcompensate the losses.

In balance, parts (but not all) of the dead-weight losses and the damages suffered by EU importers and foreign exporters, as caused by the import restriction, can be compensated due to third country and substitution effects. This effect is not reflected in the partial analysis of the tariff. Intuitively, this means that the areas D and F, which reflect the decline in trade volume in the bilateral relationship, should be smaller because of the compensation resulting from third country and substitution effects. If the size of damage claims is made on the basis of the areas D and F, a divergence between private and social damages is inevitable. As discussed above, this implies an over-deterrence effect on the legislator, leading to a paralysis of legislative activities. This effect could be avoided, if the damage analysis would not be limited to the companies' losses in sales volume on the European market only. However, there are significant impediments to measuring the actual welfare effect and the limitation of companies' claims to reflect third country and substitution effects, especially if the partial compensation caused by the higher demand on third market does not benefit the companies concerned, but other exporters/importers of the good. The third countries would then benefit from a positive externality caused by the tariff increase.[35] Under these circumstances, there is no optimal damage regulation, if the suing company would obtain a compensation award of the size of all the damages it suffered on the European market, leaving the positive effects on overall welfare disregarded—an inefficiently high level of damage compensation would ensue and over-deterrence of the EU legislator would be the consequence.

### *ii. Damages of case group C*

How are the damages of case group C to be judged? This group encompasses non-EU traders hit by US retaliation following approval by the DSB. Retaliation is typically imposed through tariffs. However, this does not have the same effect as

[33] Krugman, Obstfeld and Melitz (2015) (n 1) 196f.

[34] Anderson, 'Pecularities of Retaliation' (n 32) 7ff.

[35] This implies that the losses suffered by some importers can partially be compensated by gains accruing to other market operators. On the compensation of such damages through positive externalities more generally, see also Gilead, 'Tort Law and Internalization' (n 10) 594.

the initial WTO-inconsistent import restriction of the EU. Regarding the potential divergences between social and private damages, similar considerations are as pertinent to the other case groups. Awarding damages by the size of the decline in sales volume of the company targeted by retaliation would exceed the actual welfare losses.

The retaliation measures imposed have the effect that US consumers redirect their demand towards substitutes, raising the world market price of the substitute, and thus also increasing the demand and price of the product subject to retaliation and stimulating trading of the product in third country markets (as counter-effect to lower prices due to higher supply of the goods on the world market). If this leads to an increase of sales volumes of the product concerned in third country markets outside the US, the damages suffered due to US retaliation are partially compensated and thus reduce the actual loss of the overall welfare.

### *iii. The method of damage calculation by WTO arbitrators*

Congruence between social and private damages also depends on the extent to which the party winning against the EU before the DSB is entitled to impose retaliation measures. This alludes to the question of how the level of suspension of concessions is determined by the DSB prior to the permission to retaliate.[36] Article 22 para 4 DSU is the legal basis for the suspension of concessions. Accordingly, the level of suspension of concessions 'shall be equivalent to the level of the nullification or impairment'. This principle is also to be followed by the arbitrators pursuant to Article 22 para 7 DSU.

It is well researched that courts typically have difficulty to determine the optimal level of precaution under fault liability.[37] It is thus very likely that the level of precaution required by the court will be somewhere above or below the optimal level.[38] However, in the case of WTO arbitrators determining the level of suspension of concessions, additional complications result from the fact that WTO arbitrators are typically led by bilateral trade effects, rather than the overall welfare effect.[39] This approach can be observed in the impairment assessment in the hormones dispute.[40] From an economic perspective, this is problematic because a large share of the losses suffered by EU exporters on the EU beef market were recouped through sales in third country markets.[41] Thus, the issue at stake is that

[36] Matsushita et al, *WTO* (2015) (n 4) 33.

[37] Craswell and Calfee, 'Legal Standards' (ch 8, fn 45) 1000; Cooter and Ulen (2012) (ch 8, fn 1) 217f; TJ Miceli, *Economics of the Law* (New York, Oxford University Press, 1997) 46.

[38] Craswell and Calfee, 'Legal Standards' (ch 8, fn 44) 282f.

[39] In general, see the contributions in CP Bown and J Pauwelyn (eds), *The Law, Economics and Politics of Retaliation in WTO Dispute Settlement* (Cambridge, Cambridge University Press, 2010).

[40] WTO: *EC—Regime for the Importation, Sale and Distribution of Bananas—Recourse to Arbitration by the EC under Article 22.6 of the DSU—Report of the Appellate Body* (9 April 1999) WT/DS27/ARB, para 6.12.

[41] Bernstein and Skully, 'Calculating Trade Damages' (n 31) 391.

the determination of WTO retaliation based on Article 22 para 7 DSU disregards third country effects. More specifically, the approach adopted by the WTO arbitrators in the hormones case was the following: first, the arbitrators made a hypothetical forecast on what the quantitative size of imports would have been in a scenario without WTO violation. In a second step, a comparison was made with the actual imports based on figures provided by the US and the EU.[42] The difference constituted the trade losses due to the import restriction, and was also set to correspond to the level of nullification and impairment pursuant to Article 22 para 4 DSU.[43] The result of this method of assessing the level of suspension of concession corresponds to the areas D and F in Figure 1, as these areas depict the decline in imports on the national market.

We have seen that this method ultimately disregards third country effects and substitution effects of the countries concerned,[44] even though these effects lead to a reduction of the actual damages.[45] The consequence of the restriction of the nullification assessment to bilateral trade effects is that the damages suffered by the exporting/importing companies typically exceed actual welfare losses.[46] This hinders congruency between the welfare effects induced by the WTO-incompatible measures and the retaliation measures authorised by the DSB, because the

[42] WTO: *European Communities—Measures Concerning Meat and Meat Products (Hormones)—Recourse to Arbitration by the European Communities under Article 22.6 of the DSU—Report of the Appellate Body* (12 July 1999) WT/DS48/ARB, para 43; F Breuss, 'WTO Dispute Settlement in Action: An Economic Analysis of four EU-US Mini Trade Wars' [EcoMod2003] *Paper presented at the International Conference on Policy Modeling*, 4ff.

[43] For a comprehensive assessment of the damages in the hormones dispute see Breuss, 'WTO Dispute Settlement' (n 24) 164; T Sebastian, 'The law of permissible WTO retaliation' in CP Bown and J Pauwelyn (eds), *The Law, Economics and Politics of Retaliation in WTO Dispute Settlement* (Cambridge, Cambridge University Press, 2010) 101; see also CP Bown and M Ruta, 'The economics of permissible WTO retaliation' in CP Bown and J Pauwelyn (eds), *The Law, Economics and Politics of Retaliation in WTO Dispute Settlement* (Cambridge, Cambridge University Press, 2010) 164ff.

[44] Because of the lack of a welfare-orientated assessment of the damages it has been argued that WTO arbitrators are generally led by the plausibility of the figures presented by the parties rather than efficiency considerations. Bernstein and Skully, 'Calculating Trade Damages' (n 31) 396; Breuss, 'WTO Dispute Settlement' (n 24) 162; it is not surprising that the arbitrators also found a significant degree of discretion for WTO Members in carrying out retaliation. The Arbitrators in EC—Hormones argued: 'qualitative aspects of the proposed suspension touching upon the 'nature' of concessions to be withdrawn … fall outside the arbitrators' jurisdiction' (WTO: *European Communities—Measures Concerning Meat and Meat Products (Hormones)—Recourse to Arbitration by the European Communities under Article 22.6 of the DSU—Report of the Appellate Body* (12 July 1999) WT/DS26/ARB, WT/DS48/ARB, para 19).

[45] Anderson, 'Pecularities of Retaliation' (n 32) 7f; Bernstein and Skully, 'Calculating Trade Damages' (n 31) 397.

[46] Anderson, 'Pecularities of Retaliation' (n 32) 6ff. As a consequence of the method applied by the WTO arbitrator, there is a comparatively greater incentive to comply with the DSB ruling, because the magnitude of the retaliatory measures will be higher than by applying a welfare orientated standard. Bernstein and Skully, 'Calculating Trade Damages' (n 31) 397. On the integration of multilateral rather than only bilateral effects on trade for the purpose of determining nullification see Sebastian, 'WTO retaliation' (n 43) 108.

approved retaliation exceeds the actual welfare losses. This implies that retaliation generates more serious disadvantages than the preceding WTO violation.[47]

This finding is confirmed by a number of empirical analyses examining the welfare effects of the bananas and hormones disputes. These studies find that in both episodes of WTO disputes, the US retaliation against EU products have led to greater welfare losses than the EU had initially inflicted on the US through its import restrictions on hormone-treated beef and bananas.[48] The dis-equivalence between the impairment caused by the initial WTO violation and the level of retaliation must be distinguished from the previously discussed divergence between social and private damages. However, what both cases of incongruence have in common is that they set a certain incentive scheme for the party infringing WTO rules, because there is a threat to be exposed to retaliation above the level that the infringing party had initially caused.[49] This incentive mechanism not only affects the level of national liability as seen above, but it already applies on the preceding level regarding the implementation of WTO rules in the inter-state relation. However, the overly high fixing of retaliation feeds into the successive liability issues, because these damages are claimed by the case group C before the CJEU. We thus observe that retaliation victims would expose the EU legislator to liability claims exceeding the initial level of harm caused by the EU. In sum, because of the missing equivalence between the impairment due to WTO violation, on the one hand, and the retaliation measures, on the other hand, inefficient incentives are set: first, because retaliation creates greater economic harm than was previously caused, and second, because the over-compensation leads to over-deterrence of the EU legislators. We can thus conclude that for all case groups, the damages suffered do exceed the actual welfare effects and should not be compensated from an economic perspective. This is mainly due to the third country and substitution effects, which typically reduce the actual damages suffered but remain disregarded for the liability claims. In the case of group C, this effect is further exacerbated by the overestimation of the level of impairment (and thus the level of retaliation) by the WTO arbitrators, which increases the damages suffered by case group C above damages initially caused by the EU, which, in turn, implies a threat for the EU legislator of being subject to over-deterring damage claims.

[47] See also J Pauwelyn, 'Calculation and design of trade retaliation' in CP Bown and J Pauwelyn (eds), *The Law, Economics and Politics of Retaliation in WTO Dispute Settlement* (Cambridge, Cambridge University Press, 2010) 1ff.

[48] Breuss, 'WTO Dispute Settlement' (n 42) chart 2 and 3.

[49] On the inherent incentive to comply with WTO rules see also Bernstein and Skully, 'Calculating Trade Damages' (n 31) 397.

## III. INTERIM CONCLUSIONS

The purpose of this chapter was to gain insight into the divergence between social and private damages in the context of liability claims for WTO violations—this insight then informs us on the incentive structure for the EU legislator. Import restricting tariffs have different impacts on traders, which makes it difficult to achieve congruence on the kind of damages. Rather, there is some indication that both the damages claimed by case groups A and B, as well as those claimed by case group C, are subject to inefficient misevaluations that lead to undesirable incentives for the EU legislator.

If the member of the respective case group is awarded damages based on lost sales in the bilateral relation, without taking into account other third country and substitution effects, there will a discrepancy between social and private damages—this phenomenon distorts the damages claimed by all case groups. For case group C, there is also the effect caused by the WTO arbitrator acting within the impairment assessment of Article 22 para 7 DSU to overstate the level of suspension of nullification compared to the original effect of the WTO violation.

In balance, in a situation of unclear and unforeseeable standards of lawfulness, as well as an overstatement of damages by claimants compared to actual welfare effects, damage suits for WTO breaches may lead to paralysing the legislator. Any legislative decision determining the level of (admissible or not admissible) protection poses a threat that the EU legislator is obliged with a certain probability to pay damages exceeding actual social damages. Given the uncertainty about the standard of unlawfulness, this threat creates incentives to set legislative activities at an inefficiently low level, in order to make sure not to legislate inconsistent with WTO law and to avoid liability. If the legislator does not precisely know the standard of lawfulness, it can only vaguely guess whether the WTO adjudicative bodies will find a certain trade restrictive measure to be in line with WTO rules—from the perspective of the legislator, he acts based on certain probabilities of being held liable.[50] The expected value of damages is a function of the probability of unlawfulness (ie, the incompatibility with WTO law) and the amount of damages. Since the amount of damages lies above that corresponding to the overall social damage, the expected value is inefficiently high and the legislator will set its level of legislation too low. Renouncing legislative activities due to liability threats deprives the EU of the possibility to generate positive welfare effects, for example, by regulating environmental and health issues within the scope provided by the WTO agreements.

[50] On EU Member States' violations of EU law see Schäfer and Bergh, 'Member States Liability' (ch 8, fn 9) 16.

# 10

# *Liability Rule and Incentives*

## I. NO-LIABILITY RULE AND MALINCENTIVES

THE RESULTS OF the preceding chapters allow a comparison of the incentives for the EU legislator in two situations: 1) in which damages must be borne entirely by the respective companies (corresponding to the CJEU's current position) and 2) in which the duty of compensation is generally accepted (as argued throughout this analysis), with the caveat of the preceding chapter on the potential effect of over-deterrence. An obligation of the injured party to bear the damage entirely is referred to as the no liability rule.[1] The Court recognises WTO law as grounds for liability in very limited cases only, due to the lack of direct effect.[2] In principle, individual companies cannot invoke WTO rules, and these rules cannot serve as a legal standard for the review of EU secondary law.

From an economic perspective, preclusion of liability is inefficient, because it does not create incentives for the EU legislator to choose the welfare-optimising level of legislation. The bananas dispute has been characterised as an example for an evidently welfare-reducing trade policy.[3] One source of distortion of welfare-orientation in policymaking lies in the biases caused by rent-seeking and the influence of interest groups, which lead the policymaker to adopt welfare reducing decisions favouring individual interests. Generally, policymakers are obliged to shape policies in the public interest, which means maximising social welfare. Import restrictions and unproductive rent-seeking activities imply welfare costs, and are thus undesirable. To that end, a legality review and invocability of individual rights can generally be seen as instruments to hinder the policymaker from taking biased decisions in favour of powerful interest groups. If the legislator is, however, legally not restrained in that his legal acts are not reviewable, and that those suffering damages from its policy conduct are not able to hold the legislator liable for taking unlawful decisions favouring only certain lobby groups, an important tool ensuring the policymaker's compliance with its public mandate

[1] Shavell, *Economic Analysis* (2004) (ch 8, fn 1) 179.

[2] As seen above in ch 2, liability is only recognised within the narrow exception of the *Nakajima* and *Fediol* exceptions. The scope of these exceptions has been further narrowed in the Court's jurisprudence on the bananas and hormones disputes; see Steinbach, 'WTO-Streitbeilegungsentscheidungen' (ch 2, fn 3) 333ff.

[3] F Breuss, 'WTO Dispute Settlement: An Economic Analysis of Four EU–US Mini Trade Wars—A Survey' (2004) 4 *Journal of Industry, Competition and Trade* 275.

remains weak. One way to explain this in economic terms, is to argue that the EU legislator discounts the damages he inflicts on others. Recalling insight from civil liability, every wrongdoer determines his decision as a function of the prospective damage and the probability of being sanctioned.[4] Discounting the damage of third parties means setting the probability of being held liable equal to zero. Consequently, the legislator does not care about the damage and its size and chooses an inefficiently high level of protection.

Similarly, inefficiency of the no liability rule can be made plausible using the concept of external effects.[5] Causing damages without liability, constitutes an external effect in the sense that damages imply impairment of a good without paying a price. Damages caused by the wrongdoer have an impact on the injured party, without being internalised in the cost–benefit analysis of the injuring party. That is, without a price mechanism, market failure occurs. A negotiation based solution between the parties is in these settings typically unrealistic, because coordination and transaction costs are too high. And in the absence of liability, the wrongdoer cannot be forced to internalise the cost of his conduct but is rather able to produce externalities because the injured party has to bear the consequences. These considerations can also be applied in the current context: the EU legislator maximises its utility function largely ignoring the external costs it inflicts on importing traders. Hence, the legislator diminishes the trading values of the good and thus harms the economic operators trading this good. Since import restrictions produce dead-weight losses, the damages cannot be compensated by those economic operators benefiting from the import restriction.[6] Given the lack of liability (or even an annulment procedure) as a tool to internalise the costs, the policymaker maximises a biased welfare function, because the probability of being punished for the unlawfulness under EU law is equal to zero.[7]

## II. INCENTIVE SCHEME AND LIABILITY FOR WTO BREACHES

### A. Internalisation of damages through political costs

In light of the previous chapters, conclusions can be inferred to determine the incentives associated with establishing a liability rule for WTO violations.

[4] See the analysis provided by Schäfer and Bergh, 'Member States Liability' (ch 8, fn 9) 12f, analysing the context of EU Member States' liability for breaches of EU law.

[5] Generally on market failure due to external effects Cooter and Ulen (2012) (ch 8, fn 1) 38ff; Furubotn and Richter, *Institutions* (2005) (ch 8, fn 21) 101f.

[6] This means that the conditions of the welfare criteria of Pareto (describing a state in which at least one participant is better off and nobody else worse off) and Kaldor-Hicks (allowing for a hypothetical compensation of the losers) are not met.

[7] On the relationship between liability and internalisation generally, I Englard, 'Victor Mataja's Liability for Damages from an Economic Viewpoint: A Centennial to an Ignored Economic Analysis of Tort' (1990) 10 *IRLE* 173, 173.

For analytical purposes, we assume the EU legislator makes its decision on the basis of a cost–benefit rationale—whether and to what extent a liability rule influences this rationale, depends on the transformation of monetary financial liability into political costs relevant to the policymaker. One could argue that even when liability exists, the policymaker would still be able to externalise the costs by passing monetary liability payments on to taxpayers. While under no-liability, externalisation would occur because victims of trade restriction bear the damage, under a liability regime monetary obligations would be borne by taxpayers. In both cases, the legislator would thus not consider liability as a cost, which, in turn, would as in the case under no-liability create inefficient incentives, because the policymakers could continue to reap the (personal) benefits associated with favouring interest groups' interest, without being affected by the damage suits.

It seems more realistic, however, to attach a specific political cost to damage suits, particularly through negative political signalling for citizens and the public.[8] The public can take damage suits as an indicator for the legislator's biased policy favouring certain interest groups over the common good. In theory, this signalling effect has consequences for voting decisions of citizens. Monetary financial damages are thus translated into political costs. The steel dispute between the US and the EU may illustrate this reasoning. In this dispute, the US imposed tariffs on steel imports from the EU.[9] Following the DSB finding on violation of WTO rules, the EU threatened to impose retaliation tariffs one year before the presidential elections on products that had their origin in states where polls showed a close race between Republicans and Democrats. The purpose of this retaliation strategy was to make voters sensitive to the economic disadvantages associated with a protectionist trade policy. If citizens bear not only the large parts of the welfare losses of tariffs, but also monetary damages resulting from the tariff policy, this may have adverse political repercussions. In turn, political costs from damage claims feed into the expected utility function of the policymakers, which differs from the no-liability scenario in the sense that the probability of damages (and political costs) is much higher. Put differently, the legislator can no longer externalise the social costs of his trade restrictive policy, and incorporate liability claims as political costs into his decision-making rationale.

## B. Liability for 'sufficiently serious breaches' to avoid paralysis of the legislator

While the above underscores the desirability of a liability regime in order to reduce negative external effects, we have also seen that liability is problematic if social and

[8] Likewise Schäfer and Bergh, 'State Liability' (ch 8, fn 9) 559.

[9] M Jacobs, 'Smart Threats and Success in WTO Dispute Settlement: The Bush Steel Tariffs' (24 March 2016): www.e-ir.info/2016/03/24/smart-threats-and-success-in-wto-dispute-settlement-the-bush-steel-tariffs.

private damages diverge, because they can give rise to over-deterrence and paralysis of the legislator. As seen, financial losses incurring to the trading companies exceed social welfare costs and (in combination with the uncertain standard of lawfulness) induce the EU legislator to choose an inefficiently low level of legislative activities in order to escape liability.

In this situation, the principles developed by the Court under Article 340 TFEU and as articulated in its *Schöppenstedt*-formula, may seem as appropriate mechanism to counter the potentially paralysing effect of liability. The *Schöppenstedt*-criterion of requiring a 'sufficiently serious breach' amounts to qualified breaches, which do not let simple unlawfulness suffice, but impose additional legal qualifications regarding the nature and gravity of the breach.[10] In fact, the reasons for this qualification of the infringement are rooted in general considerations regarding the policy scope of the EU institutions.[11] The Court typically refers to the scope of manoeuvre enjoyed by the institutions where legislative measures are concerned. In this vein, in HNL, the Court observed that:

> this restrictive view is explained by the consideration that the legislative authority [...] cannot always be hindered in making its decisions by the prospect of applications for damages, whenever it has occasion to adopt legislative measures in the public interest, which may adversely affect the interests of individuals.[12]

In other words, the Court's approach implies that the gravity of the violation must be higher, the greater the scope of discretion enjoyed by the EU organs. The Court's reasoning alludes to considerations made in the context of the economic analysis. Recognising liability may have a paralysing effect on the legislator and impede his freedom to legislate without fearing the risk of being exposed to overstated damage claims. Hence, the 'sufficiently serious breach' requirement can serve as an adjusting factor in order avoid over-deterrence by the legislator.[13]

One condition for the plausibility of the qualified legality standard from an economic perspective is the existence of an unprecise standard of lawfulness. If the legislator could clearly foresee the compatibility or incompatibility of his measure with WTO rules, there would be no risk of over-deterrence. As shown above, WTO rules are vague and unspecific (justifying their lack of direct effect) and do not allow one to foresee with certainty the lawfulness of a policy measure. Since the standard of lawfulness is *ex ante* uncertain, the 'significantly serious breach' requirement allows the legislator to adopt trade measures potentially producing welfare gains without fearing the risk of liability. The 'significantly serious breach' requirement offers legal security to the legislator, in availing of his policy scope, knowing that no simple breach of WTO law would establish liability under

[10] Schäfer and Bergh, 'State Liability' (ch 8, fn 9) 552ff.
[11] *HNL and Others v Council and Commission* (ch 1, fn 27) 1209, para 5.
[12] ibid.
[13] Schäfer and Bergh, 'State Liability' (ch 8, fn 9) 560.

EU law.[14] In sum, the 'significantly serious breach' requirement ensures *de lege lata* to avoid undesirable incentives resulting from liability.

Further, it has been proposed that an alternative tool to avoid over-deterrence of the wrongdoer's activities, would be to assess the damage to overall welfare on an individual case basis and to recognise the damage claim at this amount only.[15] This would require an economic assessment of the specific case at hand, and would have to ascertain to what extent the claimants and their competitors have benefitted from an increasing demand in third country markets. This individual case study would further have to assess the size of the dead-weight loss, which would be an extremely cumbersome empirical exercise, as supply and demand-side price elasticities would have to be determined. Even if the objective of limiting liability to the size of the actual welfare losses would ensure—on a theoretical basis—a non-distortionary incentive scheme for the legislator, there are doubts whether the welfare losses resulting from WTO breaches can be estimated without a certain degree of arbitrariness. In any case, such an exercise would probably overburden judges and courts facing such technical tasks.

## III. CONCLUSIONS

From an economic perspective, the well-established jurisprudence of the Court on denying liability claims for WTO infringements leads to undesirable results. Under current jurisprudence, the EU legislator inclines not to act in the welfare-optimising sense—as an individual utility maximiser, he is concerned about other issues than welfare and is thus susceptible for rent-seeking activities by interest groups. In the absence of a liability regime, he externalises the costs associated with his trade restrictive and welfare-reducing decisions, which have to be borne entirely by those suffering damages as a result of his policymaking decisions. Legally, the Court has justified this by referring to the wide margin of manoeuvre the legislator necessarily enjoys for legislative actions. Economically, the discounting of damages in the individual cost–benefit decision leads to welfare distortions and an overly high level of protection.

By contrast, recognising liability forces the legislator to internalise the costs associated with trade restrictions. The main channel through which internalisation occurs are political costs, which the policymaker seeks to minimise. The threat of liability and the monetary costs involved for the public alter the policymaking rationale. However, liability simply tied to lawfulness also produces an inefficient outcome. This is so for two reasons: first, the standard of unlawfulness

[14] A distinction must be made between the conformity with WTO law and the 'sufficiently serious breach' requirement pursuant to Article 340 TFEU. Legal security for the EU legislator is limited to the EU liability regime but does not extend to the WTO compliance standard. There is not similar criterion like the 'sufficiently serious breach' requirement in the assessment of unlawfulness under WTO rules.

[15] Gilead, 'Tort Law and Internalization' (ch 9, fn 10) 249ff.

is necessarily vague as both the standard under WTO and the requirements for EU liability are *ex ante* not foreseeable for the legislator. Second, private damages typically exceed social damages associated with WTO violations, leading to overrated damage claims and, as a consequence, to over-deterrence and paralysing effects on the legislator. However, the Court's jurisprudence has developed an effective tool to deal with this problem—the 'sufficiently serious breach' requirement developed by the Court to shield the legislator from intrusions into his scope of discretion by liability claims. This requirement can counterbalance the undesirable effect of over-deterrence and paralysis. From an economic perspective, we can summarise: the Court should generally accept liability for WTO breaches (as has been argued from a legal doctrinal perspective in Part One), but it should apply its well-established regime on requiring certain qualifications for the damage claim going beyond mere unlawfulness of the measure concerned.

# Part Three

# EU Liability and Investment Treaties

# 11

# *Introduction*

INTERNATIONAL INVESTMENT LAW can be visualised as a grid of multiple interstate agreements—by February 2017, there were 2,964 bilateral investment treaties (BITs)[1] and 368 multilateral agreements containing investment law provisions.[2] The EU Member States maintain 1,250 BITs with third countries as well as 450 bilateral investment agreements among each other. For decades, investment agreements were a genuine part of national economic policies, with the Member States maintaining bilateral relationships according to national preferences. This has changed with the entry into force of the Lisbon Treaty—ever since, competences related to investment law have been transferred from the Member State to the EU level.[3] This led the EU Commission to announce that it is going to replace the existing Member States' BITs by EU BITs.[4] From a policy perspective, the EU BITs will aim at establishing market access provisions, in order to allow investments on a mutual basis both in the EU and for EU companies in third countries. The general market access strategy adds to the provisions common to BITs, protecting investments already made in the EU and third countries.

Regarding the kind of investments concerned, the Commission seeks to extend the scope of EU BITs to market operations related to direct investments as well as portfolio investments—the competence of the EU for the latter is controversial, with the Commission claiming to hold competence for portfolio investments.[5] By definition, direct investments are generally considered to include any foreign

[1] UNCTAD, 'International Investment Agreement Navigator' (2016) http://investmentpolicyhub.unctad.org/IIA.

[2] On the relevance of multilateral investment treaties see T Wälde, 'The "Umbrella" Clause in Investment Arbitration—A Comment on Original Intentions and Recent Cases' (2005) 6 *JWIT* 183, 183ff; S Schill, *The Multilateralization of International Investment Law* (Cambridge, Cambridge University Press, 2009), 8ff.

[3] J Chaisse, 'Promises and Pitfalls of the European Union Policy on Foreign Investment: How will the New EU Competence on FDI affect the Emerging Global Regime?' (2012) 15 *JIEL* 51, 54; M Klamert and N Maydell, 'Lost in Exclusivity: Implied Non-Exclusive External Competences in Community Law' (2008) 13 *EFA Rev* 493, 493; on the regime of competences prior to LW Shan, 'Towards a Common European Community Policy on Investment Issues' (2001) 2 *JWIT* 603, 603.

[4] European Commission, 'Towards a comprehensive European international investment policy' (Communication) COM (2010) 343 final, 6. See also A Reinisch, 'The EU on the Investment Path QuoVadis Europe? The future of EU BITs and other Investment Agreements' (2014) 12 *Santa Clara Journal of International Law* 111.

[5] ibid 8.

investment, which serves to establish lasting and direct links to an undertaking, which is provided with capital for carrying out an economic activity.[6] By contrast, portfolio investments are referred to when investments take the form where there is no intention to influence the management and control of an undertaking.[7] Prospective EU BITs are not intended to be confined to rules governing a direct investment itself—the acquisition of a foreign enterprise or the establishment of one—but also to all operations that accompany that investment and make it possible in practice, such as payments and the protection of intangible assets like intellectual property rights.[8]

From a substantive law perspective, the provisions enshrined in BITs typically encompass bans on discrimination, notably a 'most-favoured national treatment' and 'national treatment', the 'fair and equitable treatment' after admission and 'full security and protection' treatment, the protection of contractual rights granted by a host government to an investor ('umbrella clause'), as well as clauses regulating the conditions for expropriations.[9]

Procedurally, future EU BITs will be accompanied by interstate dispute settlements (as incorporated in the more recent free trade agreements by the EU),[10] and investor–state dispute settlement mechanisms (ISDS) as implemented in the Member States' BITs. ISDS allows investors to bring a claim of infringement of the provision of the BITs before an independent tribunal. Individuals bringing legal claims against a state before a tribunal is still fairly unique under international law. There are regional human rights agreements offering (in a more or less stringent and binding way) possibilities for individuals to submit their claims—the European Convention on Human Rights probably provides the most advanced system for individuals to bring suits against states. By contrast, in the area of international economic law, there is an evident discrepancy between the role of the individual in investment law by virtue of ISDS in BITs, on the one hand, and the WTO law, on the other hand, where individuals play only a marginal role and have no standing before the WTO adjudicative bodies.[11] More generally, this fits into the broader phenomenon that the rise of the individual as a subject of international

[6] ibid 2.

[7] ibid 3 referring to Judgment of 26 September 2008, Case C-282/4 and C-283/04 *Commission v Netherlands* [2008] ECR I-9141, para 19, where the Court mentioned 'the acquisition of shares on the capital market solely with the intention of making a financial investment without any intention to influence the management and control of the undertaking'.

[8] ibid 9.

[9] On the standards of protection under investments agreements see only R Dolzer and C Schreuer, *Principles of International Investment Law*, 2nd edn (Oxford, Oxford University Press, 2012), 130ff; M Sornarajah, *The International Law on Foreign Investment*, 3rd edn (Cambridge, Cambridge University Press, 2010), 201ff; Subedi, *Investment Law* (2008) (Introduction, fn 2) 83ff.

[10] I Garcia Bercero, 'Dispute Settlement in European Union Free Trade Agreements: Lessons Learned?' in L Bartels and F Ortino (eds), *Regional Trade Agreements and the WTO Legal System* (Oxford, Oxford University Press, 2006) 383.

[11] See only A Alemanno, 'Private Parties and WTO Dispute Settlement System' [2004] *Cornell Law School Inter-University Graduate Student Conference Papers* Paper 1.

public law is rather recent. Traditionally, the protection of individuals' interests have been intermediated on the state–state level through diplomatic protection.[12]

Also, while ISDSs have initially been a practice in the relationship between developing countries and industrialised countries, in recent years investment disputes abound within the framework of BITs between industrialised countries.[13] On several occasions, investments suits have been brought in the recent past before a tribunal against EU Member States because of measures adopted by the EU or Member States, for example in relation to measures countering the financial crisis in Cyprus,[14] the bans on fracking in Europe,[15] or the debt haircut in Greece.[16] Such suits have hitherto been made on the basis of bilateral investment treaties or the Energy Charter Treaty. In future, prospective EU investment treaties will be the basis for ISDS mechanisms, especially where such mechanisms will be incorporated into fully fledged trade agreements, like those with Canada and the US.[17]

## I. INVESTMENT AGREEMENTS AS MIXED AGREEMENTS

A premise of the following analysis (and a particularity of the liability issues surrounding EU investment agreements) is that investment agreements can be concluded by the EU and Member States as mixed agreements only.[18] This corresponds to the predominent view in literature (and among most policy actors), according to which the EU is solely competent for virtually all provisions related to direct investments regarding market access issues and to concessions and intellectual property issues. By contrast, despite the EU Commission's view, the EU is generally seen to lack competence to govern portfolio investments.[19] This competence

[12] More general, A Clapham, 'The Role of the Individual in International Law' (2010) 21 *EJIL* 25.

[13] Sattorova, 'European BITs' (Introduction, fn 3) 230; M Bronckers, 'Is Investor–State Dispute Settlement (ISDS) Superior to Litigation Before Domestic Courts? An EU View on Bilateral Trade Agreements' (2015) 18 *JIEL* 655, 673.

[14] International Arbitration Law, 'The Cypriot Debt Crisis and Recourse to International Arbitration' (1 May 2013) www.internationalarbitrationlaw.com/the-cypriot-debt-crisis-and-recourse-to-international-arbitration.

[15] Corporate Europe Observatory, 'The Right to say no: EU-Canada trade agreement threatens fracking bans' (6 May 2013) www.corporateeurope.org/climate-and-energy/2013/05/right-say-no-eu-canada-trade-agreement-threatens-fracking-bans.

[16] Financial Times, 'Germans seek lawsuits over Greek debt swap' (12 March 2012) www.ft.com/cms/s/0/79ed422c-6c67-11e1-bd0c-00144feab49a.html.

[17] N Lavranos, 'In Defence of Member States' BITs Gold Standard: The Regulation 1219/2012 Establishing a Transitional Regime for Existing Extra-EU BITs—A Member State's Perspective' (2013) 10 *TDM*, 13.

[18] On the numerous legal questions arising if the EU concludes investment agreements without Member States see A Dimopoulos, 'The Involvement of the EU in Investor-state Dispute Settlement: A Question of Responsibilities' (2014) 51 *CML Rev* 1671, 1684ff.

[19] This corresponds to the leading opinion in literature, see Chaisse, 'Foreign Investment' (n 3) 61; J Ceyssens, 'Towards a Common Foreign Investment Policy? Foreign Investment in the European Union' (2005) 32 *LIEI* 259, 289; M Krajewski, 'External Trade Law and the Constitution Treaty:

cannot be derived from implicit external competences therefore, the EU does not have the competence to conclude an agreement implementing an ISDS system, which comprehensively covers all substantial areas of investments. Given the EU's intention to set up comprehensive investment agreements, there is a strong indication that such investment agreements will be crafted as mixed agreements. This is even more likely in light of the political turbulences surrounding the negotiation of investment agreements in some countries of the EU. Indeed, past experience has shown that the EU has concluded mixed agreements, not only when there was uncertainty regarding the delineation of competences but also when political circumstances made an involvement of both EU and Member States desirable.[20]

From a legal perspective, mixed agreements become an integral part of EU law to the extent that the agreements fall within the competence of the EU.[21] Under international law, however, all parties to an agreement are bound by their agreement, unless it is explicitly stated therein that the binding effect governs only certain parts of the agreement.[22] Only if the EU and Member States explicitly allocate certain parts of the agreements to each individual scope of competence, the binding effect is limited to that specific part of the agreement.

Towards a Federal and More Democratic Common Commercial Policy?' (2005) 42 *CML Rev* 91, 112; T Eilmansberger, 'Bilateral Investment Treaties and EU law' (2009) 46 *CML Rev* 383, 395; M Bungenberg, 'Going Global? The EU Common Commercial Policy After Lisbon' (2010) 1 *EYIEL* 123, 147; JA Bischoff, 'Just a Little BIT of 'Mixity'?, The EU's Role in the Field of International Investment Protection Law' (2011) 48 *CML Rev* 1527, 1568f; G Villalta Puig and B Al-Haddab, 'The Common Commercial Policy after Lisbon: An Analysis of the Reforms' (2011) 36 *EL Rev* 289, 295; for a different view see S Hindelang and N Maydell, 'Die Gemeinsame Europäische Investitionspolitik: Alter Wein in neuen Schläuchen?' in M Bungenberg, J Griebel and S Hindelang (eds), *Internationaler Investitionsschutz und Europarecht vol* 2, 1st edn (Baden-Baden, Nomos, 2010) 77ff; W Shan and S Zhang, 'The Treaty of Lisbon: Half Way toward a Common Investment Policy' (2011) 21 *EJIL* 1049, 1059.

[20] A Rosas, 'The European Union and Mixed Agreements' in A Dashwood and C Hillion (eds), *The General Law of EC External Relations* (London, Sweet & Maxwell, 2000) 201f; P Eeckhout, *EU External Relations Law*, 2nd edn (Oxford, Oxford EU law library, Oxford University Press, 2011) 219.

[21] Case C-459/03 *Commission v Ireland* [2006] ECR I-4635, para 84; Case 12/86 *Demirel v Stadt Schwäbisch Gmünd* [1987] ECR I-3719, para 9; Case C-13/00 *Commission v Ireland* [2002] ECR I-2943, para 14; Case C-239/03 *Commission v France* [2004] ECR I-9325, para 25; *Hermès v FHT* (ch 3, fn 152) para 24; see also C-D Ehlermann, 'Mixed Agreements: a List of Problems' in D O'Keeffe and HG Schermers (eds), *Mixed Agreements* (Deventer, Kluwer Law and Taxation Publishers, 2009) 18; MacLeod, Hendry and Hyett, *External Relations* (1996) (ch 3, fn 45) 157; A Dimopoulos, *EU Foreign Investment Law* (Oxford, Oxford University Press, 2011) 263, 289ff.

[22] C Tomuschat, 'Liability for Rechtswirkung' in D O'Keeffe and HG Schermers (eds), *Mixed Agreements* (Deventer, Kluwer Law and Taxation Publishers, 2009) 130; J Heliskoski, *Mixed Agreements As a Technique for Organizing the International Relations of the European Community and Its Member States* (The Hague, Kluwer Law International, 2001) 147–149; A Bleckmann, 'Mixity in Public International Law' in D O'Keeffe and HG Schermers (eds), *Mixed Agreements* (Deventer, Kluwer Law and Taxation Publishers, 2009) 160; E Neframi, 'International Responsibility and Mixed Agreements' in E Cannizzaro (ed), *The European Union as an Actor in International Relations* (The Hague, Kluwer Law International, 2002) 195ff; M Cremona, 'External Relations of the EU and the Member States: Competence, Mixed Agreements, International Responsibility, and Effects of International Law' *EUI Working Paper* LAW No 2006/22, 20ff; L Mola, 'Which Role for the EU in the Development of International Investment Law?' *SIEL Working Paper* No 26/2008, 19; Bischoff, 'Just a Little BIT of 'Mixity'?' (n 19) 1562ff.

## II. NEW EU RULES ON INVESTOR–STATE DISPUTES

ISDS under EU governance is a new and evolving field. Following long discussions and amendments over two years, the first legal act dealing with the implications of the new EU competence in the area of investment law was enacted through Regulation No 912/2014.[23] In principle, the Regulation allocates financial responsibility for claims brought by non-EU investors for harm done to their investment within the EU. The new regime will only be applied to investor–state disputes brought under agreements to which the EU itself is a party and which foresees an ISDS mechanism. The importance of this regulation will be increasing, as the EU and third states are currently negotiating new agreements, in some cases with a view to replacing the current BITs between EU Member States and third states. The rules establish both the principles on monetary compensation awards, the dispute coordination procedure and negotiation of an agreement.

The new regime reflects the different roles the EU and Member States can play in issues arising under investment agreements and which necessarily impact the question of competence for investment issues. Initially, the EU Commission opined that it would be solely competent to conclude comprehensive investment agreements. From that perspective, as laid down in the Commission's initial proposal for the regulation, an investor could bring a suit against the Commission as the only respondent, no matter whether the measure contested was adopted by the EU or a Member State.[24] Following long discussions and the obvious objections of Member States to this approach, the final version of the regulation could not hold this position and only stated, 'the Union has exclusive competence with respect to the common commercial policy'.[25] The shared competence and the various possible contributions of EU and Member States to a violation of an investment agreement are now reflected in Regulation No 912/2014, which explicitly recognises the possibility that a claimant can notify a request for consultations to both the EU and the Member State.[26]

In principle, both the EU and Member States can be the author of a violation of an investment provision, and Regulation No 912/2014 provides different ways to allocate financial responsibility. Accordingly, financial responsibility should be allocated to the entity responsible for the treatment found to be inconsistent

[23] See Dimopoulos, 'Investor-state Dispute Settlement' (n 18) 1671ff.

[24] European Commission, 'Towards a comprehensive European international investment policy' (Communication) COM (2010) 343 final, 12; European Commission, 'Proposal for a Regulation of the European Parliament and of the Council establishing a framework for managing financial responsibility linked to investor-state dispute settlement tribunals established by international agreements to which the European Union is party' COM (2012) 335 final, 3.

[25] (EU) No 912/2014 of the European Parliament and of the Council of 23 July 2014 establishing a framework for managing financial responsibility linked to investor-to-state dispute settlement tribunals established by international agreements to which the European Union is party (Introduction, fn 5), para 1.

[26] ibid, Art 7 para 1.

with the relevant provisions of the agreement. This implies four principles of allocation. First, the Union itself should bear the financial responsibility, where the treatment concerned is afforded by an EU institution. Second, the Member State concerned should bear the financial responsibility, where the treatment concerned is afforded by that Member State. Third, where the Member State acts in a manner required by Union law, for example, in transposing a directive adopted by the Union, the Union itself should bear financial responsibility in so far as the treatment concerned is required by Union law.[27] Importantly, the term 'required by Union law' refers to treatment where the Member State concerned could only have avoided the alleged breach of the agreement by disregarding an obligation under Union law, such as where it has no discretion or margin of appreciation as to the result to be achieved.[28] Fourth, allocation of financial responsibility should also account for causal contributions by both Member States and the Union, and financial responsibility should account for the specific treatment afforded by either of them.

## III. LIABILITY ISSUES UNDER THE NEW EU INVESTMENT POLICY

What are the liability issues emerging from the evolving regime of EU investment agreements? The expansion of EU competence in dealing with investment issues (and the willingness of the Commission to use its new competences) implies a number of legal questions. It is already unclear, whether and to what extent the Union may enter into an international arrangement foreseeing an autonomous dispute settlement mechanism. The EU would be bound under international law, by virtue of the international agreement as well as the decisions rendered by a tribunal established on basis of that agreement. The CJEU has dealt on a number of occasions with the question, whether and to what extent the Union may accede to such an agreement.[29] Moreover, the Union cannot participate in all dispute settlement systems currently used by Member States, as not all of them allow international organisations to act as a party. Moreover, it is also questionable and highly controversial, as to how the weaknesses in current dispute settlement rules and the perceived lack of legitimacy will be addressed.[30]

[27] ibid, para 7.

[28] ibid, Art 2 para 1. See also Dimopoulos, 'Investor-state dispute settlement' (n 18) 1679.

[29] Opinion 1/91 EWR I [1991] ECR I-6079, I-6079ff; Opinion 1/92 EWR II [1992] ECR I-2821, I-2821ff; Opinion 2/94 ECHR [1996] ECR I-1759, I-1759ff; Opinion 1/00 GELR [2002] ECR I-3493, I-3493ff; Opinion 1/09 European and Community Patents Court [2011] ECR I-1137, I-1137ff.

[30] On the discussion of the constitutional requirements for ISDS see A Steinbach, 'Investor-Staat-Schiedsverfahren und Verfassungsrecht' (2016) 80 RabelsZ 1; see further G van Harten, *Investment Treaty Arbitration and Public Law* (Oxford, Oxford University Press, 2007), 175ff; on the ongoing discussion on establishing a permanent investor-state tribunal see R Mackenzie and P Sands, 'International Courts and Tribunals and the Independence of the International Judge' (2003) 44 *Harv Int'l L J* 271, 271; CJ Tams, *An Appealing Option?* (Halle (Saale), Inst für Wirtschaftsrecht, 2006).

For the purpose of this analysis, liability issues are of interest. In the context of international investment law, liability issues are of a different nature from the liability issues discussed above in relation to WTO law. Regarding the latter, the main issue resulted from the nature of WTO law as state-to-state regime under which the individual must claim the direct effect of decisions of the DSB before domestic courts. The doctrinal exercise dealt with the question of whether liability for WTO breaches is possible even without any direct effect. The intention of the WTO rules to protect individual rights was decisive in that regard. Given the nature of the WTO agreements and its dispute settlement mechanism as a purely interstate mechanism, investment agreements are fundamentally different, the most notable difference being that investment treaties are specifically designed to allow individuals to bring claims against states through ISDS.[31] The individual as investor is the core subject of international investment treaties. The individual company can enforce the rights granted under these agreements against the host country and seek financial redress—enforcement occurs outside the domestic legal order rendering the debate about direct effect irrelevant, even though most investment-related provisions of international investment treaties contain sufficiently clear and precise obligations of the state parties.[32] Unlike under the WTO rules, there is no scope for negotiating solutions for the parties as a temporary alternative to compliance with the DSB ruling. Under investment treaties, the individual company can claim the violation of its rights before the tribunal and claim damages—the states as parties to the agreement have no space in reaching certain inter-state solutions for an individual case, as it is the case under WTO law.

While there is vast literature on procedural and substantial issues under international investment law,[33] there is virtually no contribution dealing with liability issues arising under the future EU regime of investment agreements, which have recently been dealt with partly through Regulation No 912/2014. In particular, liability issues accrue from the nature of investment agreements as mixed agreements. One question is whether international responsibility occurs on the part of the EU, the Member State or jointly. This, in turn, may also depend on who is the respondent of the tribunal judgment. It thus needs to be discussed whether the EU or the Member States are responsible under international law, and whether they could be exposed to damage claims by the investor. A different set of liability-related questions concerns the internal relationship between the EU and Member

[31] SS Haghighi, *Energy Security*, 1st edn (Oxford, Hart Publishing, 2007) 217ff; Dimopoulos, *EU Foreign Investment Law* (2011) (n 21) 301f.

[32] Also, the provisions on market access possibilities and the protection of property and capital transfers typically grant specific rights to individuals. Dimopoulos, *EU Foreign Investment Law* (2011) (n 21) 301f; J Ahner, *Investor-Staat-Schiedsverfahren nach Europäischem Unionsrecht*, 1st edn (Tübingen, Mohr Siebeck, 2015) 341f.

[33] See, inter alia, RD Bishop, J Crawford and WM Reisman, *Foreign Investment Disputes*, 2nd edn (The Hague, Kluwer Law International, 2014); Dolzer and Schreuer, *Principles* (2012) (n 9); Z Douglas, *The International Law of Investment Claims* (Cambridge, Cambridge University Press, 2009).

States, because the distribution of liability internally may be different from external responsibility under international law. Clarifying internal liability may also offer insight into which party should be the respondent in the dispute proceedings, to what extent internal financial liability claims exist for the party obliged under international law and how internal claims can be enforced in the relationship between the EU and Member States.

There are other issues connected to the relationship between EU liability and the financial responsibility governed by the Regulation, but which are not addressed in this study. This particularly concerns the involvement of the EU in ISDS, in its very diverse contexts (under an agreement concluded by the EU, the EU and its Member States together or its Member States alone),[34] but also extends to the discriminatory standards of liability under investment agreements and EU legal standards. Regarding the latter, investment agreements typically offer third-country investors higher standards of protection than EU investors, leading to a parallel system of responsibility.[35] In this context, third-country investors may be eventually in a position to avail of the annulment proceedings under Article 263 TFEU to bring a decision of the Commission (eg, the choice of the respondent to a dispute or the allocation of responsibility to the EU for Member State conduct) before the CJEU.[36]

## A. State-to-State dispute settlement as under WTO law?

One may wonder why international investment law does not offer the same tools of individual legal enforcement as under WTO law. This question may be reasonable from the perspective of ensuring a coherent regime of legal protection across international economic law. Indeed, in the policy arena some commentators argue that investment protection rights enshrined in investment agreements should not be enforceable through international tribunals, but rather through state-to-state disputes as under the WTO regime.[37]

There are at least two problematic consequences: first, referring private entities to a state-to-state dispute settlement in order to seek legal protection would render enforcement of investment agreements a political issue as under WTO law.

[34] See Dimopoulos, 'Investor-state Dispute Settlement' (n 18) 1672.

[35] J Kleinheisterkamp, 'Financial Responsibility in European International Investment Policy' (2014) 63 *ICLQ* 449, 463–467. In this regard, the Regulation provides that 'Union agreements should afford foreign investors the same high level of protection as Union law and the general principles common to the laws of the Member States grant to investors from within the Union, but not a higher level of protection. Union agreements should ensure that the Union's legislative powers and right to regulate are respected and safeguarded', see Recital 4 of Regulation 912/2014. See also Dimopoulos, 'Investor-state dispute settlement' (n 18) 1706.

[36] ibid 1708.

[37] The Economist, 'Free-trade agreements: A better way to arbitrate' (11 October 2014) www.economist.com/news/leaders/21623674-protections-foreign-investors-are-not-horror-critics-claim-they-could-be-improved.

Experience with the WTO compliance system shows that both legal review and compliance with DSB rulings are largely determined by political components while, for example, the compliance mechanisms at work in the EU legal order are designed to minimise the political impact on legality review. More specifically, whether or not a Member State of the WTO will ultimately bring a claim before the DSB depends on many non-legal factors—there is no institution enforcing legality review of non-WTO-compliant measures, unless a Member State suffering damages launches proceedings under the DSU. By contrast, the European Commission acts in the EU as the monitoring body and can bring Member States' unlawful conduct before the CJEU. The state-to-state investment dispute settlement would likely follow the WTO mechanisms, at the detriment of legality and individuals' rights protection. Not surprisingly, past experience with state-to-state dispute settlement pertaining to investment law underscores the limited effectiveness from an individual claimant's perspective. Only a few cases were brought by governments for intergovernmental dispute resolution. As under the WTO system, political considerations decide on whether a case is brought.[38]

Second, as under the WTO scenario without recourse to international tribunals private claimants will seek to bring their case before domestic courts, raising the issue of direct effect as under WTO law. There is some indication that a similar line of jurisprudence as pertaining to WTO law would emerge, even though provisions of investment agreements have greater clarity and unconditionality compared to WTO rules. As we saw above, the Court frequently rejected the direct effect of WTO law, and extended this jurisprudence to other kinds of multilateral international treaties (UN Convention on the Law of the Sea (UNCLOS),[39] and the Aarhus Convention).[40] One could argue that a pivotal difference to the WTO setting lies in the fact that investment treaties are typically bilateral in nature, and the Court has shown a more lenient stance on the direct effect of bilateral agreements.[41] However, given the wide-reaching consequences of the direct effect of international norms in the domestic legal order (ie, annulment and compensation) the reciprocity considerations applicable to WTO law would be relevant in the investment context too. Treaty obligations would turn out to be unbalanced, if some countries would deny the direct effect of investment provisions favouring EU investors in their domestic legal order, while the EU would grant individual rights to foreign investors. Against this background, it is not surprising that there is a tendency that EU institutions and Member States insert clauses into bilateral agreements seeking to deny their applicability or the direct effect before domestic courts.

[38] Bronckers, 'Is Investor–State Dispute Settlement (ISDS) Superior to Litigation Before Domestic Courts?' (n 13) 667.

[39] *Intertanko and Others v Secretary of State for Transport* (ch 3, fn 103) I-4057.

[40] Joined Cases C-404/12 P and C-405/12 P *Council v Stichting Natuur en Milieu* (judgment of 13 January 2015) ECLI:EU:C:2015:5.

[41] Bronckers, 'Is Investor–State Dispute Settlement (ISDS) Superior to Litigation Before Domestic Courts?' (n 13) 662.

More specifically, such clauses have been incorporated in the agreements with Canada, Columbia, Georgia, Korea, Moldova, Peru, Serbia, Singapore, and Ukraine, amongst others.[42] There is thus a policy-driven desire to limit the legal force of investment rights to the level of international dispute settlement, and shield the domestic legal order (and domestic courts) from being overdriven by individual rights enshrined in investment agreements. The CJEU has stated that contracting parties are free to determine the legal effects of international agreement in their respective internal legal orders. The Court would thus have to give weight to the clauses explicitly excluding the direct effect of the agreement when individuals invoke the agreements before the Court. The legal assessment of direct effect is likely to concur with the policy-driven exclusion of the direct effect in bilateral investment rights.

Moreover, seeking settlement of a private–public dispute through an international court has the advantage that it reduces concerns about reciprocity, which are prevalent when legal redress is sought on the domestic level. Under the international dispute settlement system, national legal orders could continue to deny legal redress before domestic courts by refusing direct effect and could, at the same time, be ensured that both the EU and the foreign investor would have the same access and standing before the international court.[43] Concerns regarding the reciprocal character of treaty obligations thus do not impair individual legal protection.

As a consequence, designing individual protection under investment agreements as a state-to-state mechanism, sidelined by the possibility of invoking the provision before domestic courts, would not only significantly reduce the level of individual legal protection compared to the current practice under international tribunals. It would also lead to incoherence in legal protection, because domestic courts would have to decide on the direct effect of investment provisions on an individual basis; that is, each norm would have to be assessed in line with the regular standard under international law, in light of the wording, clarity and unconditionality.

## B. 'Regulatory chill'—comparison with the WTO case

The analysis of liability for WTO breaches has shown that the impact of liability on the legislator has played a role both for the legal and economic assessment. First, the space for the legislator to manoeuvre is the argument put forward by the Court to deny a direct effect under WTO law. The Court interprets the DSU rules in a way that, even after expiry of the period of implementation of the DSB

[42] Semertzi, 'The preclusion of direct effect' (ch 1, fn 45).

[43] Bronckers, 'Is Investor–State Dispute Settlement (ISDS) Superior to Litigation Before Domestic Courts?' (n 13) 671.

rulings, parties would continue to enjoy the scope to manoeuvre for certain solutions, such as the negotiation of monetary compensation and the adoption of retaliatory measures (Article 22 para 2 DSU), as well as the possibility laid down in Article 22 para 8 DSU to come to a 'mutually satisfactory solution'. Denying the direct effect aims at maintaining the policy space for finding a mutually agreeable solution. Second, high liability thresholds shield the scope to manoeuvre for legislative organs against liability. In the domain of economic policy, the CJEU has established the requirement of a 'sufficiently serious breach of a superior rule of law for the protection of the individual'.[44] In the Court's view, this restriction is justified by the wide discretion, which the legislative organs must enjoy and which is necessary in order not to impede the decision-making process.[45] Thus, on two levels of the legal assessment (direct effect of DSB decisions and the 'sufficiently serious' breach) the legislator's policy space is a crucial factor for the analysis.

Also, the economic analysis has shown that high liability thresholds shielding the legislator from liability are economically sound. Private damages typically exceed social damages associated with WTO violations, leading to overrated damage claims and, as a consequence, to over-deterrence and paralysing effects on the legislator. However, the Court's 'sufficiently serious breach' requirement can counterbalance the undesirable effect of over-deterrence and paralysis by shielding the legislator from intrusions into his scope of discretion by liability claims.[46]

'Regulatory chill' is a term associated with the above phenomenon in the WTO context and refers, in the context of investment agreements, to scepticism vis-à-vis ISDS and the alleged restrictive effect that it has on the scope of actions of national legislators. One prominent case frequently mentioned is *Vattenfall*, which concerns the construction of a new power plant near Hamburg. Being exposed to a liability suit of 1.4 billion euros, the German authorities had issued a modified water-use permit. This case is typically referenced to illustrate the risks of international tribunals.[47] ISDS is viewed as limiting the policy space of governments, who will be reluctant to introduce regulations that could expose them to challenges and financial claims of foreign private parties.[48] It is hard to accept that democratically enacted environmental legislation on consumer protection and public health at the European or national level would be thwarted by an international

[44] *Schöppenstedt v Council* (ch 1, fn 25) para 11, confirmed in *Mulder and Others and Heinemann v Council and Commission* (ch 1, fn 17) I-3061; *Oleifici Italiani v Commission* (ch 1, fn 26) II-1239; regarding safeguarding measures against imports *Faust v Commission* (ch 1, fn 26) 3745; *T Port GmbH & Co v Commission* (Introduction, fn 8) 1000, para 45; see also Ossenbühl and Cornils, *Staatshaftungsrecht* (2013) (ch 1, fn 23) 598.

[45] *HNL and Others v Council and Commission* (ch 1, fn 27) para 5; *Lefebvre v Commission* (ch 1, fn 27) para 38; Ruffert (ch 1, fn 27) Art 340 TFEU, para 16; Ossenbühl and Cornils, *Staatshaftungsrecht* (2013) (ch 1, fn 23) 596; Reinisch, 'Opfer des Hormon- und Bananenstreites' (Introduction, fn 7) 49.

[46] See above ch 6 I.

[47] See only Pernice, 'L'accès á la justice' (ch 1, fn 15) 139ff.

[48] Bronckers, 'Is Investor–State Dispute Settlement (ISDS) Superior to Litigation Before Domestic Courts?' (n 13) 656.

tribunal lacking democratic legitimacy. In the legal debate, this has stimulated the debate about the 'right to regulate' and how policy space for the legislator can be safeguarded.[49] However, it must be stated that jurisprudence has established such safeguard measures pertaining to WTO law, while they seem to be missing in international investment disputes.[50] In particular, the 'sufficiently serious' breach requirement has been a threshold characteristic for liability claims related to economic policy measures, which raise the liability threshold—this established tool of the EU liability regime is alien to international investment law (where simple inconsistency with the rules suffices), and thereby marks a significant difference in the liability regimes.

The described differences are particularly problematic in terms of their discriminatory effects. There is indication that future EU investment agreements will only allow claims of foreign investors on EU or national measures before international tribunals.[51] Accordingly, EU investors cannot bring their treaty-based claims addressing EU or national measures before the international court. Rather, unlike foreign investors they must take recourse to the established EU liability regime under Article 340 TFEU. Some view this as undermining the exclusive powers of EU courts under Article 340 TFEU.[52] However, not only foreign investors will have access to exclusive investor–state litigation (enjoying greater procedural rights than domestic investors), but also the applicable legal standard differs (EU law versus international investment treaty), and the EU liability system imposes more restrictive limitations ('sufficiently serious breach').[53] The concern is that the investment protection standards laid down in investment agreements offer foreign investors greater private property rights than those foreseen in national constitutions or EU law.[54]

[49] A parallel is then often drawn to the exceptions under Article XX GATT, see only A Titi, *The Right to Regulate in International Investment Law*, 1st edn (Baden-Baden, Nomos, 2014) 169ff.

[50] Occasionally, public interest is taken into account without, however, a clear doctrinal basis. See in relation to human rights M Jacob, 'Faith Betrayed: International Investment Law and Human Rights' in R Hofmann and CJ Tams (eds), *International Investment Law and its Others*, 1st edn (Baden-Baden, Nomos, 2012) 52; see also M Bungenberg and C Titi, 'Developments in International Investment Law' [2014] *EYIEL* 425, 425f.

[51] Bronckers, 'Is Investor–State Dispute Settlement (ISDS) Superior to Litigation Before Domestic Courts?' (n 13) 672.

[52] L Ankersmit, 'The Compatibility of Investment Arbitration in EU Trade Agreements with the EU Judicial System' (2016) 13 *Journal for European Environmental & Planning Law* 46, 59ff.

[53] ibid 61.

[54] S2B, 'ISDS: Courting foreign investors: Analysis by the Seattle to Brussels Network' (29 September 2015) 5 www.s2bnetwork.org/wp-content/uploads/2015/10/S2B_ISDS.pdf.

# 12

# *Responsibility of Union and Member States for Breaches of Mixed Investment Agreements*

WHO IS LIABLE vis-à-vis the investor in the case of an infringement of the investment agreement: the Union, the Member State, or both?[1] The answer depends on against whom the judgment of the tribunal has been handed down. This, in turn, depends on the responsibility under international law. In principle, every subject of international law can be held responsible under international law. This extends to EU Member States as subjects of international law possessing unlimited legal capacity, as well as the EU. Since the responsibility of the EU results from a violation of an agreement between the Union and a third country, it does not matter whether the EU's subjectivity of international law results from Article 47 TEU (stipulating the EU's legal personality), or from the explicit recognition by the third country.[2] The basis for EU's responsibility is stated in the 'Draft Articles on the Responsibility of International Organisations' (DARIO) of the International Law Commission.[3] Every measure of an international organisation in violation with international law leads to responsibility under international law.[4] A measure is considered a breach of international law, if the measure can be attributed to the international organisation and if it violates a specific obligation under international law.[5] Generally, the DARIO also applies to

[1] Chaisse, 'Foreign Investment' (ch 11, fn 3) 78; F Hoffmeister, 'Litigating against the European Union and its Member States: Who Responds Under The ILC's Draft Articles on International Responsibility of International Organizations?' (2010) 21 EJIL 723, 723; see also PJ Kuijper and E Paasivirta, 'EU international responsibility and its attribution: From the inside looking out' in MD Evans and P Koutrakos (eds), The International Responsibility of the European Union: European and International Perspectives (Oxford, Hart Publishing, 2013) 48–67.

[2] K Ginther, 'International Organizations, Responsibility' in R Bernhardt (ed), Encyclopedia of Public International Law, vol 3 (Amsterdam, 1997, North-Holland) 1336.

[3] M Hartwig, 'International Organizations or Institutions, Responsibility and Liability' in R Wolfrum (ed), Max Planck Encyclopedia of Public International Law, vol 6 (Oxford, Oxford University Press, 2012) para 14.

[4] Art 3 DARIO; more generally on international law sources governing international responsibility to international organizations C Tomuschat, 'Attribution of international responsibility: Direction and control' in MD Evans and P Koutrakos (eds), *The International Responsibility of the European Union: European and International Perspectives* (Oxford, Hart Publishing, 2013).

[5] Art 4 DARIO.

the EU as an international organisation, but the principles of the DARIO must be applied in light of the particularities of the EU. Normally, the conduct of Member States cannot be attributed to an international organisation, because its members are sovereign states possessing an autonomous legal personality and subjectivity under international law. In that regard, the EU is a special organisation—it can adopt legal acts binding for its Member States. During the negotiations of the DARIO under the mandate of the International Law Commission, the European Commission supported the idea that the conduct of EU Member States would be attributed to the EU, if such conduct would be the consequence of a binding act under EU law.[6]

From an international law perspective, both EU and Member States are bound equally by a mixed agreement—different consideration apply only if the mixed agreement explicitly limits the scope of bindingness to certain parts of the agreement.[7] EU and Member States would have to unambiguously state which part of the agreement falls in the respective scope of competence.[8] This is not without risk to the autonomy of the EU legal order: if there is unclarity on the delineation of the competences between the EU and Member States, despite an explicit reference in the agreement, the investor–state tribunal might be inclined to interpret the Union's distribution of competences—a task that is genuinely reserved for the CJEU. It is, therefore, advisable not to include explicit reference to the delineation of competences between the EU and its Member States in the international agreement.[9] Both the EU and its Member States are, thus, bound by all parts of the agreement. This allows the Union to leave the question of competence unanswered and decide on a case-by-case basis.[10] However, even if the agreement does not foresee a provision clarifying the distribution of competences, this does not necessarily prevent international tribunals from dealing with the question of the appropriate respondent of the dispute. On several occasions, WTO panels have

[6] PJ Kuijper and E Paasivirta, 'Further Exploring International Responsibility: The European Community and the ILC's Project on Responsibility of International Organizations' (2004) 1 *International Organizations Law Review* 111, 127; S Talmon, 'Responsibility of International Organizations: Does the European Community Require Special Treatment?' in M Ragazzi (ed), *International Responsibility Today: Essays in Memory of Oscar Schachter* (Leiden, Martinus Nijhoff, 2005) 412ff.

[7] From an international law perspective see also *Vienna Convention on the Law of Treaties between States and International Organizations or between International Organizations (adopted 20 March 1986, not yet entered into force)* [1986] 25 ILM 543, Art 26. Cf *Interpretation of the Agreement of 25 March 1951 between the WHO and Egypt, Advisory Opinion* [20 December 1980] ICJ Reports 1980, 73, 89–90, para 37: 'International organizations are subjects of international law and, as such, are bound by any obligations incumbent upon them … under international agreements to which they are parties.'

[8] See only Bischoff, 'Just a Little BIT of 'Mixity'?' (ch 11, fn 19) 1565; E Neframi, 'Quelques Réflexions sur la Réforme de la Politique Commerciale par le Traité d'Amsterdam: Le Maintien du Statu Quo et l'Unité de la Représentation Internationale de la Communauté' [1998] *CDE* 137, 147.

[9] Ahner, *Investor-Staat-Schiedsverfahren* (2015) (ch 11, fn 32) 281f.

[10] M Burgstaller, 'The Energy Charter Treaty as a Mixed Agreement: A Model for Future European Investment Treaties?' in G Coop (ed), *Energy Dispute Resolution: Investment Protection, Transit and the Energy Charter Treaty* (Huntington, Juris, 2011) 142ff; see also Chaisse, 'Foreign Investment' (ch 11, fn 3) 79.

dealt with the questions of competence in proceedings involving the EU, even though the WTO Agreement does not contain any competence clause.[11]

Being bound to the same obligation is a necessary but not sufficient condition in order for joint and several responsibility of the EU and Member States to materialise. Breach of an obligation has to be supplemented by attribution. If both the Union and Member States are bound to all obligations under a mixed agreement, the question arises, under what conditions a certain conduct can be attributed with the effect of establishing responsibility under international law. Difficulties pertaining to attributability may result from the practice that the Union's institutions largely act through legislative acts, and to lesser extent on administrative basis (for example, in the area of competition law). It is mainly the EU Member States who will be acting vis-à-vis the investors when implementing Union law.

## I. ATTRIBUTING RESPONSIBILITY TO THE UNION

As a matter of principle, the Union, as an international organisation, is only liable for the conduct of its own organs.[12] But under what conditions is the Union also liable for the conduct of its Member States? While federal states are typically liable for the conduct of their territorial subdivisions, international organisations are liable for their Member States under specific conditions only. More specifically, according to Art 4 para 1 Draft Articles on State Responsibility, the conduct of territorial sub-units of a State is attributable to the State itself. For international organisations, there is no corresponding provision.

Three situations of attribution of Member States' conduct to the Union can be distinguished: first, a Member State can implement binding legal acts, which, as such, violate investment agreements. Second, Member States can implement an international agreement, which is in line with the investment agreement, in a manner inconsistent with the investment agreement. Third, a Member State can adopt just national law infringing the agreement.[13]

The question is, on the basis of which legal norm the Member States' conduct can be attributed to the EU.[14] Article 6 DARIO stipulating that a conduct of an

[11] WTO: European Communities—Customs Classification of Certain Computer Equipment (EC-LAN)—*Report of the Panel* (5 February 1998), WT/DS62/R, WT/DS67/R, WT/DS68/R, para 8.15ff; WTO: EC—Selected Customs Matters (EC-Customs)—*Report of the Panel* (16 June 2006), WT/DS315/R, para 2.22.

[12] Bischoff, 'Just a Little BIT of 'Mixity'?' (ch 11, fn 19) 1565; Dimopoulos, EU Foreign Investment Law (2011) (ch 11, fn 21) 259f.

[13] E Steinberger, 'The WTO Treaty as a Mixed Agreement' (2006) 17 *EJIL* 837, 850; Ahner, *Investor-Staat-Schiedsverfahren* (2015) (ch 11, fn 32) 284f; Dimopoulos, *EU Foreign Investment Law* (2011) (ch 11, fn 21) 260.

[14] There is a remarkable difference to the EU liability regime as discussed above and the rules under international law. In the Articles on State Responsibility (and the corresponding norms in the DARIO), a wrongful act presumes attribution of the conduct in question to the wrongdoing state. By contrast, under EU liability rules it is the damage that is to be attributed, not the conduct. On the consequences

organ of the organisation can be considered an act of that organisation is not possible, as the Member States are not *de jure* organs of the EU. Member States are autonomous and hold legal personality. According to Article 17 para 1 sent 3 TFEU, the Commission oversees the application of Union law under the control of the CJEU. However, this task is limited to a general supervisory task regarding the lawfulness of Member States' conduct. This provision does not establish a standing as an organ and the Member States are not mentioned as the Union's institutions in Article 13 para 1 sent 2 TEU.

Another potential link would be Article 7 DARIO, requiring that an organ be placed at the disposal of another international organisation. In that sense, one could consider that Member States organs would constitute 'de facto' organs of the Union, which the Member States have put at the disposal of the Union and over which the Union exercises effective control within the meaning of Article 7 DARIO.[15] Article 7 DARIO is silent on the definition of 'effective control'. One requisite is the actual control of an international organisation over the Member States' conduct.[16] According to the ILC Commentary, these principles apply in relation to 'seconding states' and 'receiving organisations'. Attributability of a conduct to the receiving organisation is possible, if the organ is 'under its exclusive direction and control, rather than on instructions from the sending State'. The term 'effective control' has further been specified by ICJ jurisprudence in *Military and Paramilitary Activities in and against Nicaragua*[17] and in *Application of the Genocide Convention.*[18] However, in these cases the ICJ dealt with attribution of conduct of individual persons and not of organs. Further references can be made to adjudication of WTO dispute settlement organs. On a number of occasions, WTO panels accepted EU Member State organs implementing EU law as '[...] de facto organs of the Community, for which the Community would be responsible under WTO law and international law in general'.[19] This jurisprudence stands in

of this difference see A Nollkaemper, 'Joint Responsibility between the EU and Member States for Non-Performance of Obligations under Multilateral Environmental Agreements' [2011] *SHARES Research Paper* 5, ACIL 2011-14, 23ff.

[15] Draft articles on the responsibility of international organizations, with commentaries 2011, Art 7, para 6ff.

[16] Draft articles on the responsibility of international organizations, with commentaries 2011, Art 7, para 4.

[17] *Nicaragua v United States of America (MERITS)* [27 June 1986] ICJ Reports 1986, 14ff para 109.

[18] *Bosnia and Herzegovina v Serbia and Montenegro* [26 February 2007] ICJ Reports 2007, 43ff, para 392.

[19] WTO: *European Communities—Protection of Trademarks and Geographical Indications for Agricultural Products and Foodstuffs—Report of the Panel* (15 March 2005) WT/DS174/R, para 7.725; see also WTO: European Communities—Measures Concerning Meat and Meat Products (Hormones)—*Report of the Panel* (18 August 1997) WT/DS26/R, WT/DS48/AB/R, and WTO: *European Communities—EC Measures Concerning Meat and Meat Products (Hormones)—AB-1997-4—Report of the Appellate Body* (16 January 1998) WT/DS26/AB/R, WT/DS48/AB/R; WTO: *European Communities—Customs Classification of Certain Computer Equipment—Report of the Panel* (22 June 1998) WT/DS62/R, WT/DS67/R, WT/DS68/R; WTO: *European Communities—Measures Affecting Asbestos and Asbestos-Containing Products*—Settlement Body, Report of the Panel (2000)

contrast to the practice of the European Court of Human Rights (ECHR). The ECHR has regarded Member States' conduct as autonomous and independent, and did not consider them as factual organs of the EU.[20] The ECHR rulings, however, give little guidance on whether Member States' organs could be considered as factual organs of the EU, as the Union was no member of the ECHR.[21] It seems appropriate that for 'effective control' within the meaning of Article 7 DARIO, one requires at least an exclusive right to give directives over the organs of the Member State.[22] The nature of the obligations under EU law, however, do not meet this standard. Member States are obliged to implement and apply EU law. This obligation exists only under EU law, and does not alter the status of Member States as subject of international law—as such, Member States remain generally free in implementing EU law. The distinction between EU regulations and EU directives illustrates the remaining freedoms of Member States. An EU regulation is directly effective and does not require implementation at the Member State level—it can clearly be attributed to the EU as the originator of this legal act. By contrast, an EU directive is mandatory for Member States as to the attainment of its objective, but it does not impair the freedom to choose the choice of measure and how to reach the objective. Member States' organs always remain under the effective control of the Member States.[23] However, the conduct of Member States can exceptionally be considered as an act of the EU, if the latter recognises the conduct as its own, even though it is not attributable.

Apart from the 'effective control' mechanism of attributability under Article 7 DARIO, there are other ways of attribution, where the Union has determined Member States' conduct otherwise and which are laid down in Articles 14–17 DARIO. Article 16 DARIO does not offer legal ground, because the EU has not ordered an act contrary to its international obligations to be committed. Further, the Union can be considered liable, if it aids or assists a State or another

WT/DS135/R; WTO: *European Communities—Measures Affecting the Approval and Marketing of Biotech Products—Report of the Panel* (2006) WT/DS291/R; WTO: EC-Biotech—*Report of the Panel* (29 September 2006) WT/DS292/R, WT/DS293/R, para 7.101; see also Hoffmeister, 'Litigating' (n 1) 731ff; Dimopoulos, *EU Foreign Investment Law* (2011) (ch 11, fn 21) 261.

[20] *Bosphorus Hava Yollari Turizm ve Ticaret Anonim Sirketi v Irland (GC)* ECHR 2005-VI, para 151ff; see also Case C-402/05 P and C-415/05 P *Kadi v Council and Commission* [2008] ECR I-6351, I-6351ff, para 301ff. In this judgment the Court found that a regulation implementing a binding decision of the Security Council could not be considered as act of the United Nations.

[21] Ahner, *Investor-Staat-Schiedsverfahren* (2015) (ch 11, fn 32) 288f; Kuijper and Paasivirta, 'International Responsibility' (n 6) 210ff.

[22] Ahner, *Investor-Staat-Schiedsverfahren* (2015) (ch 11, fn 32) 289 arguing that the interpretation of Article 6 DARIO should also be extended to Article 7. On the notion of 'normative control' as a criterion for determining EU international responsibility see A Delgado Casteleiro, *The International Responsibility of the European Union* (PhD thesis, EUI, 2011).

[23] "ILC: *Special Rapporteur Gaja, third Report on Responsibility of International Organisations* (13 May 2005) UN Doc A/CN.4/553, para 12; Bischoff, 'Just a Little BIT of "Mixity"?' (ch 11, fn 19) 1565; for a different view see Steinberger, 'WTO Treaty' (n 13) 851; J Karl, 'The competence for foreign direct investment' *JWIT* 414, 432.

international organisation in the commission of an internationally wrongful act (Article 14 DARIO), or if it directs and controls a State (Article 15 DARIO).[24] One might consider the EU to direct or control a Member State by imposing binding legal acts on it—this would require that the terms 'directs' and 'controls' within the meaning of Article 15 DARIO would be interpreted differently from Article 7 DARIO. According to the International Law Commission, for Article 15 DARIO it is only decisive whether an international organisation adopts a decision binding on a Member State.[25] This would apply to the scenario mentioned above, in which the Union would adopt legal acts binding on Member States without leaving any scope to manoeuvre in the implementation.[26] Different considerations apply in cases in which Member States implement an EU legal act, while enjoying discretion and violating international law. This case would not be encompassed by Article 15 DARIO, which is limited to situations where Member States would have no scope for an autonomous decision and would be under the control of the international organisation.[27] Similarly, under Article 17 DARIO, an international organisation incurs international responsibility if it circumvents one of its international obligations, by adopting a decision binding Member States or international organisations. For the purpose of interpreting this rule, the ILC refers to the *Bosphorus* decision of the ECHR.[28] In this case, the ECHR decided that a binding decision cannot release the Member States from their responsibility under international law, and that they could be held liable jointly with the international organisation. If the decision of the international organisation leaves sufficient scope for the Member State to manoeuvre, so that the Member State can implement the Union's legal act without necessarily having to violate the agreement, the decision can only be attributed to the Member State. Hence, Article 17 DARIO is limited to cases in which the Member State has no scope for implementation.

Finally, attributability of Member States' conduct to the EU can be established on the basis of Article 64 DARIO.[29] Accordingly, the DARIO does not apply where the conditions for the existence of an internationally wrongful act are governed by special rules of international law. More specifically, this *lex specialis* could follow the rules of an international organisation, which are applicable to the relations

[24] Ahner, *Investor-Staat-Schiedsverfahren* (2015) (ch 11, fn 32) 290.

[25] Draft articles on the responsibility of international organisations, with commentaries 2011, Art 15, para 4 f.

[26] Ahner, *Investor-Staat-Schiedsverfahren* (2015) (ch 11, fn 32) 290; Kuijper and Paasivirta, 'International Responsibility' (n 6) 136.

[27] Draft articles on the responsibility of international organizations, with commentaries 2011, Art 15, para 4; Steinberger, 'WTO Treaty' (n 13) 851ff; see also M Hirsch, *The Responsibility of International Organizations Toward Third Parties* (Dordrecht, Martinus Nijhoff, 1995), 65; J Crawford and S Olleson, 'The Nature and Forms of International Responsibility' in MD Evans (ed), *International Law*, 3rd edn (Oxford, Oxford University Press, 2010) 457.

[28] ILC: *Report of the 61st Session* (2009) UN Doc A/64/10, Art 16 para 7; see Ahner, *Investor-Staat-Schiedsverfahren* (2015) (ch 11, fn 32) 291.

[29] ibid 292f; with doubts regarding the application of Art 64 DARIO Dimopoulos, 'Investor-state dispute settlement' (ch 11, fn 18) 1685.

between an international organisation and its members. This *lex specialis* rule allows members of an international organisation to internally regulate the consequences of the external responsibility under international law. In other words, Member States cannot alter their international law responsibility, but they can regulate within the organisation as to how to internally deal with the responsibility.[30] The ILC explicitly refers to the case of the EU and its Member States, and considers the attribution to the EU of the conduct of Member States of the Union when they implement binding acts of the Union.[31] Hence, the basis for this special norm of attributability is Article 216 para 2 TFEU, which has been discussed above at length in the context of liability of WTO breaches.[32] This provision requires both the EU institutions and Member States to comply with obligations under international agreements[33]—by virtue of EU law, Member States are thus obliged to abide by the international agreement. This has led to the perception that only the EU should be held responsible under international law, if the EU has adopted a binding measure.[34]

On balance, based on Articles 14 and 17 DARIO, the Union must be held liable for the conduct of Member States, if the Member States implement a binding legal act without leaving them discretionary manoeuvre in the implementation. By contrast, if there is scope for manoeuvre in the implementation on the part of the Member States, the Union can only be held liable if such liability is the results of a *lex specialis* rule enshrined in EU law pursuant to Article 64 DARIO.[35] Moreover, if the BIT provides for an explicit delimitation clause setting out the internal competences, liability is limited to the entity enjoying the competence. The absence of such a delimitation clause would indicate joint and several liability of the EU and the Member States. Finally, the Union can be subject to liability, if it recognises the conduct of Member States as its own, in line with Article 9 DARIO.

## II. ATTRIBUTING RESPONSIBILITY TO THE MEMBER STATE

Under what conditions can the conduct of an organ of a Member State or the EU establish the international responsibility of the Member State for the violation of an investment agreement? Such a situation may be particularly relevant, if responsibility of the EU is at stake in a BIT concluded by Member States without

[30] Dimopoulos, *EU Foreign Investment Law* (2011) (ch 11, fn 21) 265.

[31] Draft articles on the responsibility of international organisations, with commentaries 2011, Art 64 para 2.

[32] Above chapter 3 II.

[33] Hoffmeister, 'Litigating' (n 1) 746; Ahner, *Investor-Staat-Schiedsverfahren* (2015) (ch 11, fn 32) 292f; Dimopoulos, *EU Foreign Investment Law* (2011) (ch 11, fn 21) 265.

[34] Ahner, *Investor-Staat-Schiedsverfahren* (2015) (ch 11, fn 32) 293; Hoffmeister, 'Litigating' (n 1) 746.

[35] Bischoff, 'Just a Little BIT of "Mixity"?' (ch 11, fn 19) 1565; Hoffmeister, 'Litigating' (n 1) 727.

the EU. As the EU cannot be a party to ISDS in these cases, the question arises whether Member States can be held internationally responsible for violations of BIT provisions emanating from EU conduct or a Member State conduct required under EU law.

In principle, Member States can be held liable for the conduct of their organs. A certain conduct can also be attributed to both the Member State and the EU, as can be inferred from Article 19 DARIO.[36] By contrast, acts of international organisations cannot generally be attributed to a Member State—organs of the international organisation are not organs of the Member States, nor are they controlled by Member States. This is not altered by the fact that Member States typically influence the secondary legal acts of international organisations (eg, by voting in the DSB of the WTO). Also, in the EU, Member States collectively determine EU legislation through voting in the Council. However, the role that a Member State performs within the organs of the EU regarding the adoption of EU secondary law, does not justify attribution of the EU legal act to the State. This would imply denying the separate legal personality of the EU.[37]

Liability can particularly be established on basis of Articles 61 and 62 DARIO, if the Member State takes advantage of the fact that the organisation has competence in relation to the subject matter, thereby circumventing that obligation to the end that the organisation commits an act, which, if committed by the State, would have constituted a breach of the obligation. More broadly, under these norms, the Member State takes advantage of the legal personality of the international organisation in order to circumvent its own obligations.[38] However, in light of legislative practice, it will hardly be able to demonstrate such circumvention conduct.[39] The decision-making process in the EU is highly differentiated and involves various stages and different institutions acting autonomously, without leaving considerable scope of circumvention. In practice, the only way the EU organs' conduct could be considered as an act of a Member State is based on Article 62 para 1(a) DARIO—if the Member State accepts responsibility for that act towards the injured party.

[36] Ahner, *Investor-Staat-Schiedsverfahren* (2015) (ch 11, fn 32) 294.

[37] '[T]he role that a member State may have within the organs of an international organization would not justify attribution of responsibility to the State for the conduct of the organization: this would be tantamount to denying the separate legal personality of the organization', see ILC: *Special Rapporteur Gaja, Fourth Report on Responsibility of International Organizations* (12 April 2006) UN Doc A CN.4/564/Add. 1 para 67.

[38] See also N Blokker, 'Abuse of the Members, Questions concerning Draft Article 16 of the Draft Articles on Responsibility of International Organizations' (2010) 7 *International Organizations Law Review* 35, 35; J d'Aspremont, 'Abuse of the Legal Personality of International Organizations and the Responsibility of Member States' [2007] *International Organizations Law Review* 91, 91.

[39] In the area of human rights, Member State international responsibility for measures adopted by EU organs has been occasionally been found, as Member States were held responsible for EU acts infringing human rights obligations, eg *Matthews v United Kingdom* (*GC*) Appl No. 24833/94, ECtHR 1999-I, paras 26–35.

## III. JOINT AND SEVERAL LIABILITY OF EU AND MEMBER STATES?

We have assumed that investment agreements are going to be concluded as mixed agreements—hence, both EU and Member States are generally responsible under international law. The question then is whether EU and Member States are jointly liable[40] or whether they are liable only to a certain share.[41] The question is relevant from an investor's perspective: whether the investor can claim full damages or just a part of the damage claim from one of the two parties. Public international law does not foresee a clear solution to this question.[42] On the one hand, joint and several liability intends to protect the injured party. On the other hand, joint and several liability is in conflict with the general principle of sovereignty under public international law, because an obligation to pay damages could eventually be established for a conduct, which was not caused by the respective state, thus amounting to an intrusion into the sovereignty principle.[43] If the two injuring parties contribute to the damage by way of two independent actions undertaken by the EU and the Member States respectively, one possible avenue would be to implement liability based on the respective damage contributions.[44]

In the literature, there is a predominant view supporting a comprehensive binding effect for both parties.[45] Also, the jurisprudence of the Court seems to support the concept of joint and several liability: in *Demirel*, the Court considered itself competent to interpret the ACP agreement at stake, without entering into

[40] In Case C-316/91, *Parliament v Council*, Advocate General Jacobs argued that 'Under a mixed agreement the Community and the Member States are jointly liable unless the provisions of the agreement point to the opposite conclusion'; Case C-316/91 *Parliament v Council* [1990] ECR I-625, Opinion of Advocat General Jacobs I-625, para 69. Similarly, A Rosas, 'Mixed Union—Mixed Agreements' in M Koskenniemi (ed), *International Law Aspects of the European Union* (The Hague, Kluwer Law International, 1998) 142; Bischoff, 'Just a Little BIT of "Mixity"?' (ch 11, fn 19) 1564; Burgstaller, 'The Energy Charter Treaty' (n 10) 124ff; see also G Lysen, 'Three Questions on the Non-contractual Liability of the EEC' (1985) 2 *LIEI* 86, 104; also see P Oliver, 'Joint Liability of the Community and the Member States' in HG Schermers, T Heukels and P Mead (eds), *Non-Contractual Liability of the European Communities* (Dordrecht, Martinus Nijhoff, 1988).

[41] MacLeod, Hendry and Hyett, *External Relations* (1996) (ch 3, fn 45) 159; Neframi, 'Mixed Agreements' (ch 11, fn 22) 197.

[42] JE Noyes and BD Smith, 'State Responsibility and the Principle of Joint and Several Liability' (1988) 13 *YJIL* 225, 226; Draft articles on the responsibility of international organizations, with commentaries 2001, Art 47, para 6; ILC: *Special Rapporteur Gaja, Second Report on Responsibility of International Organisations* (3 May–4 June and 2004) UN Doc A/CN.4/541, para 8; Chaisse, 'Foreign Investment' (ch 11, fn 3) 79; see also RP Alford, 'Apportioning Responsibility among Joint Tortfeasors for International Law Violations' (2001) 38 *Pepperdine Law Review* 233, 233.

[43] Noyes and Smith, 'State Responsibility' (n 42) 259.

[44] Ahner, *Investor-Staat-Schiedsverfahren* (2015) (ch 11, fn 32) 299.

[45] Castillo de la Torre, 'The Status of GATT' (ch 1, fn 7) 67f; Cremona, 'The Doctrine of Exclusivity' (ch 3, fn 151) 426f; A Peters, 'The Position of International Law within the European Community Legal Order' [1977] *GYIL* 9, 32; NA Neuwahl, 'Joint Participation in International Treaties and the Exercise of Power by the EEC and its Member States: Mixed Agreements' (1991) 28 *CML Rev* 717, 733ff; G Nolte, 'Case 12/86, Meryem Demirel v. Stadt Schwäbisch Gmünd, Judgment of 30 September 1987' (1988) 25 *CML Rev* 403, 408f; Burgstaller, 'The Energy Charter Treaty' (n 10) 144ff; Dimopoulos, *EU Foreign Investment Law* (2011) (ch 11, fn 21) 252.

the questions of internal competences between the Union and Member States, because the Union would be responsible for proper implementation of the agreement under international law.[46] The Court observed a joint and several liability of the Union and Member States vis-à-vis ACP countries.[47] Similarly, AG *Tesauro* argued in relation to the WTO agreements that, given the common responsibility of Union and Member States under international law, there was an indication of joint and several liability.[48] Other views in literature argue that joint and several liability would be contradictory to the nature of mixed agreements, which rest on the notion of limited competences of Member States and EU.[49]

Similar rules prevail in the domain of public international law. The internal relations between some contracting parties have no relevance, unless so provided by the contracting parties. This is underscored by Article 5 para 1 of Annex IX of the United Nations Convention on the Law of the Sea (UNCLOS), which requires international organisations acceding to UNCLOS to specify the matters for which competence has been transferred to the organisation by its Member States. Consequently, Article 6 para 1 of Annex IX of UNCLOS stipulates that the contracting party competent according to the declaration, is liable for a breach of the obligations under UNCLOS by either the contracting state or organisation. If the contracting parties fail to provide unambiguous information on the allocation of competences within a reasonable time, they incur joint and several liability according to Article 6 para 2 of Annex IX of UNCLOS. There is, thus, the general assumption of joint and several liability, unless the parties have clearly specified the allocation of competences.[50]

In any case, joint and several liability is unproblematic, if the internal relationship between the parties jointly held liable foresees specific rules dealing with the financial responsibility internally—this is precisely the objective of Regulation No 912/2014 establishing a framework for managing financial responsibility linked to ISDS tribunals.[51] Moreover, joint and several liability is not alien to EU law.[52] Article 27 para 2 EAEC foresaw the joint liability of several Member States for collectively caused damages.[53]

[46] *Demirel v Stadt Schwäbisch Gmünd* (ch 11, fn 21) 3751, para 11.

[47] *Parliament v Council* (n 40) I-625ff, para 29: 'The Convention was concluded, according to its preamble and Article 1, by the Community and its Member States of the one part and the ACP States of the other part. It established an essentially bilateral ACP-EEC cooperation. In those circumstances, in the absence of derogations expressly laid down in the Convention, the Community and its Member States as partners of the ACP States are jointly liable to those latter States for the fulfilment of every obligation arising from the commitments undertaken, including those relating to financial assistance.'

[48] Case C-53/96 *Hermès v FHT Marketing Choice BV* [1998] ECR I-3603, Opinion of AG Terauro, I-3603ff, para 14.

[49] Cremona, 'External Relations' (ch 11, fn 22) 25. See also Kuijper and Paasivirta, 'International Responsibility' (n 6) 120.

[50] Bischoff, 'Just a Little BIT of "Mixity"?' (ch 11, fn 19) 1563.

[51] See below chapter 13 II.

[52] See also Dimopoulos, 'Investor-state dispute settlement' (ch 11, fn 18) 1692.

[53] Ahner, *Investor-Staat-Schiedsverfahren* (2015) (ch 11, fn 32) 300f.

# 13

# *Internal Allocation of Financial Responsibility within the EU*

A DISTINCTION MUST be made between responsibilities on the level of international law, on the one hand, and the internal allocation of liability between the EU and Member States, on the other. We will shed light on the issue of internal allocation of liability within the context of a mixed agreement—this finding will allow us also to make a statement on which party should act as a respondent before the investor tribunal, and whether (and how) claims regarding financial responsibility within the EU can be enforced.

As discussed above, both Union and Member States are responsible under international law for breaches of a mixed agreement, unless this agreement contains a competence clause clearly and unambiguously delineating the respective allocation of competences between the EU and Member States. The investor can hold both EU and Member States jointly liable. Regarding the internal allocation of financial responsibility, joint debtors are typically liable due to their individual contributions to the damage.[1] The respective responsibility for the unlawful treatment afforded is, thus, decisive for determining internal financial responsibility.

Four types of internal liability can be distinguished: first, organs of the EU may adopt a legal act and implement it in violation of the investment agreement, without further involvement of Member States. Second, a Member State may implement a secondary EU legal act, where the latter infringes the agreement. Third, Member States may implement a secondary EU legal act, where the latter does not violate the agreement, in a way inconsistent with the agreement. Fourth, a Member State can adopt purely national measures violating the agreement without further incitement by the EU.[2]

[1] See generally W Friedmann, 'The Growth of State Control Over the Individual and its Effect Upon the Rules of International State Responsibility' (1938) 19 *Brit YB Int'l L* 118, 118; G Handl, 'State Liability for Accidental Transnational Environmental Damage by Private Persons' (1980) 74 *AJIL* 525, 531; on the internal liability when several subjects of international law are involved, Noyes and Smith, 'State Responsibility' (ch 12, fn 42) 261f.

[2] Steinberger, 'WTO Treaty' (ch 12, n 13) 850; Ahner, *Investor-Staat-Schiedsverfahren* (2015) (ch 11, fn 32) 314; Dimopoulos, *EU Foreign Investment Law* (2011) (ch 11, fn 21) 260.

## I. DIFFICULTIES IN ATTRIBUTION

The internal allocation of contributions to damages is not alien to EU law. A clear delineation of the conduct causing damages underlies the differentiation between EU liabilities pursuant to Article 340 para 2 TFEU, on the one hand, and Member States liability, on the other—for the individual seeking redress it is crucial to know who will be the respondent to the dispute. As has been discussed above (ch 6 II) in the context of WTO law violations, there must be causality between the damage and the unlawful conduct of an organ of the EU, in order to establish EU liability.[3] The Court has developed a restrictive concept of causality, largely determined by considerations related to the foreseeability of the course of action.[4] In this vein, the Court has required a 'sufficiently direct consequence'[5] of the damage resulting from an unlawful act. In situations where both the EU and Member States have contributed to the damage, the 'sufficiently direct consequence' requirement allows for a normative limitation or extension of liability, in order to delineate the respective spheres of responsibility between the EU and Member States. Attribution is limited to those damages, which have been the foreseeable consequence of a typical course of action induced by the unlawful conduct.[6] The adequacy of the causal relationship is put into question, if several causality factors coincide and impede clear attribution.[7]

## II. APPORTIONMENT OF FINANCIAL RESPONSIBILITY

How can financial responsibility be regulated internally between the EU and Member States? One approach would be to refer to the last treatment in the course of action leading to the damage as the decisive link of attribution. However, this approach would disregard that Member States' organs must implement unlawful EU law, because they are obliged to do so. Only the CJEU can declare a provision binding Member States as invalid. Since Member States have no right to disregard EU law, it appears inappropriate to burden Member States with financial responsibility, where they have no choice to act lawfully. In turn, referring to the first action, setting in motion the unlawful measures leading to the breach of the agreement, does not offer a satisfactory solution either. This would lead to reasonable results only if the implementing measure of the Member State would be a

[3] *Cato v Commission* (ch 6, fn 34) I-2533, para 18.

[4] Berg (ch 1, fn 47) Art 340 TFEU, para 62; Reinisch, 'Opfer des Hormon- und Bananenstreites' (Introduction, fn 7) 50f.

[5] Joined Cases 64/76, 113/76, 167/78, 239/78, 27/79, 28/79 and 45/79 *Dumortier and Others v Council* [1979] ECR 3091, 3091, para 21; Case T-452/05 *Belgian Sewing Thread v Commission* [2010] ECR II-1373, II-1373ff, para 166.

[6] Ossenbühl, 'Haftung' (ch 6, fn 8) para 57.

[7] Smith and Woods, 'Causation in Francovich' (ch 6, fn 39) 938ff; Toth, 'Damage and Causality' (ch 6, fn 22) 193ff.

'sufficiently direct consequence' of the EU measure. Convincingly, a distinction should be made: if the Member State has no discretionary scope to manoeuvre when implementing the Unions' measures, its decision is a 'sufficiently direct consequence' of the EU act. But if the Member State's measure is only one among several (including lawful) measures implementing EU law, it does not constitute a 'sufficiently direct consequence' and, thus, should be attributed to the Member State. This approach takes account of the economic function of liability as discussed above.[8] Liability should be imposed on a party, only if the incentives set by liability may lead the party to avoid the unlawful measure in the future.

One achieves a similarly differentiated solution, if the freedom of scope for legislative measures is at the centre of the analysis. A measure violating the agreement can be attributed to the entity, which is in the position to alter the legal position of the injured party.[9] When Member States implement Union law, it is decisive whether or not the Member State's organs enjoy a margin to manoeuvre, within which they could act either lawfully or unlawfully. If the Member States can only act in violation within the agreement, in order to comply with EU law, the measure cannot be considered as a Member State's act.

Regulation No 912/2014, governing the financial responsibility in the EU, seems to follow this approach.[10] For the EU legislator, it is decisive who is the author of the violation of the measure.[11] More specifically, 'the Union shall bear the financial responsibility arising from treatment afforded by a Member State where such treatment was required by Union law'.[12] The term 'required' should be interpreted in line with the above differentiation. If the Member State's action was required in a way that no lawful alternative of implementation would be in line with the EU legal act, the financial obligation should be allocated to the EU. The definition provided in Article 2 para 1 of Regulation No 912/2014 stipulates accordingly that the Member State must not have any discretion or margin of appreciation. By contrast, if the Member State was 'required' to implement an EU legal act while maintaining the scope to manoeuvre, including measures compatible with the investment agreement, the Member States should remain financially liable. Thus, the current legal regime governing the apportionment of financial responsibility allows for a differentiation accounting of the individual responsibility in infringement of the investment agreement.

[8] Above ch 8 I.

[9] Ahner, *Investor-Staat-Schiedsverfahren* (2015) (ch 11, fn 32) 318.

[10] See also Dimopoulos, 'Investor-state dispute settlement' (ch 11, fn 18) 1703.

[11] (EU) No 912/2014 of the European Parliament and of the Council of 23 July 2014 establishing a framework for managing financial responsibility linked to investor-to-state dispute settlement tribunals established by international agreements to which the European Union is party (Introduction, fn 5), Art 3 para 1.

[12] ibid, Art 3 para 1(c).

## III. WHO SHOULD BE A PARTY TO THE DISPUTE?

Having clarified the principles of allocating financial responsibility internally leads to the follow-up question: who should be the respondent in an investor–state dispute. Given the above principles, there should be some flexibility depending on the authorship of the violating measure, allowing EU and Member States to determine the respondent on a case-by-case basis. In fact, Regulation No 912/2014 determines the conduct of disputes. In principle, the Union acts as the respondent, where the dispute concerns treatment afforded by the institutions, bodies, offices or agencies of the Union.[13] In turn, Member States will assume respondent status in cases where the treatment was afforded by a Member State, unless exceptions apply.[14] According to this rule, the party affording the contested treatment acts as the respondent. This is generally in the interests of both sides: the author of the measure is likely to be the one bearing financial responsibility within the EU, and the investor seeks to sue the entity which could modify the contested measure.

There are exceptions to this general rule, and these exceptions can be seen as the attempt to harmonise the standing in the dispute with the above principles on allocating financial responsibility. More specifically, there may be cases where the Union rather than Member States should be the respondent party. The Union can become the respondent in cases where it would bear all or at least part of the potential financial responsibility arising from the dispute,[15] or where the dispute also concerns treatment afforded by the institutions.[16] There is obvious discretion in applying these exceptions. Also, they require an initial assessment of which party has to bear the financial responsibility, which is a question that is not necessarily easy to answer. The Commission is in a strong position, because it ultimately decides on who is going to be the respondent—the practical application of the exceptions will show how Article 9 para 2 of Regulation No 912/2014 will be interpreted. In particular, the term 'treatment afforded by the institutions' could be interpreted to the effect that every Member State measure adopted to implement EU law, could justify the Commission to act as a respondent to the dispute. There is thus scope for the Commission to apply these exceptions widely and act as a respondent in most cases—the hurdles to do so are not very high, since the Commission's decision only needs to be 'based on a full and balanced factual analysis and legal reasoning provided to the Member States'.

As a further exception, the Commission can become the respondent in the proceedings where a 'similar treatment is being challenged in a related claim against the Union in the WTO, where a panel has been established and the claim concerns the same specific legal issue, and where it is necessary to ensure a consistent argumentation in the WTO case'.[17] This exception aims at ensuring legal coherence

[13] ibid, Art 4 para 1.
[14] ibid, Arts 5 and 9 para 1.
[15] ibid, Art 9 para 2(a).
[16] ibid, Art 9 para 2(b).
[17] ibid, Art 9 para 3.

between the WTO dispute settlement mechanism and the ISDS. In particular, streamlining representation before the WTO and investor–state tribunals ensures the principles of *lis alibi pendens and res iudicata.*[18] It should be noted that the Commission had initially envisaged wider-reaching ambitions, regarding its standing in investor–state disputes. The Commission sought to be the respondent where 'it is likely that similar claims will be brought under the same agreement against treatment afforded by other Member States and the Commission is best placed to ensure an effective and consistent defence'.[19] Moreover, the Commission was going to act as a respondent when 'the dispute raises unsettled issues of law which may recur in other disputes under the same or other Union agreements'.[20] Needless to say that on this basis, there would have been practically no limitations for the Commission to decide to act as a respondent. The argument of legal coherence could have been raised in virtually all disputes, especially given that the EU is only beginning to act as a party in the investments dispute arena. Under these circumstances, controversies between the Commission and Member States on the status as a respondent could have given raise to long-lasting suits against the Commission's decision before the CJEU.[21] Not surprisingly, as the outcome of long discussions, Member States ultimately did not approve their replacement as respondent by the Commission.[22] The final version of the regulation limits the coherence argument to disputes brought before the WTO, with the well-founded purpose to ensure the consistency of jurisprudence under investment treaties and WTO provisions. Also, from a strategic point of view, uniform representation of the EU before the WTO and investor-state tribunals ensures consistence in defending the EU's interest.

In any case, determination of the respondent must ultimately be subject to the ruling of the CJEU, and cannot be decided by a judicial body outside the EU institutional setting. This has been made abundantly clear by the Court in Opinion 2/13:

> The question of the apportionment of responsibility must be resolved solely in accordance with the relevant rules of EU law and be subject to review, if necessary, by the Court of Justice, which has exclusive jurisdiction to ensure that any agreement between co-respondent [that is, the European Union] and respondent [that is, the Member State] respects those rules. To permit the ECtHR to confirm any agreement that may exist

[18] A Reinisch, 'The Use and Limits of Res Judicata and Lis Pendens as Procedural Tools to Avoid Dispute Settlement Outcomes' (2004) 3 *L&P* 37, 61ff.

[19] European Commission, 'Proposal for a Regulation of the European Parliament and of the Council establishing a framework for managing financial responsibility linked to investor-state dispute settlement tribunals established by international agreements to which the European Union is party' (Communication) COM (2012) 335 final, Art 8 para 2(c).

[20] ibid, Art 8 para 2(d).

[21] RA Lorz, 'Trying to change the rules for responding to arbitration unilaterally: The proposed new framework for investor-state dispute settlement for the EU' [2013] *Columbia FDI Perspectives* No 87.

[22] See also C Tietje, E Sipiorski and G Töpfer, 'Responsibility in Investor-State-Arbitration in the EU: Managing Financial Responsibility Linked to Investor-State Dispute Settlement Tribunals Established by EU's International Investment Agreements' (2013) 10 *TDM*, 24f.

> between the EU and its Member States on the sharing of responsibility would be tantamount to allowing it to take the place of the Court of Justice in order to settle a question that falls within the latter's exclusive jurisdiction.[23]

That is, any uncertainty concerning the delineation of competences can only be clarified by the CJEU. More generally, this may put in question whether in agreements concluded by the EU, ISDS impairs the autonomy of the EU legal order by subjecting the interpretation of EU law to the judgement of a non-EU court. However, any awards rendered under EU investment agreements may apply EU law, as long as they cannot offer an authoritative interpretation of EU law rules. More specifically, the investment dispute tribunals may take recourse to EU law as the standard for assessing the legality of a measure, as long as their ruling does not offer a binding interpretation of EU law.[24]

## IV. COOPERATION IN PROCEEDINGS

Irrespective of who is the respondent before the tribunal, both Union and Member States are under the obligation to sincere cooperation (or loyalty) pursuant to Article 4 para 3 TEU when conducting dispute settlement proceedings. This obligation encompasses the obligation to inform each other and to cooperate in good faith.[25] This duty is of particular relevance in investor–state proceedings: Union and Member States inform and notify each other about investors' requests for consultation,[26] and give each other notice of claimants' intention to initiate arbitration proceedings.[27] Particularly in cases in which the Commission has assumed the respondent status based on Article 9 para 2, the Commission must 'consult the Member State concerned on any pleading or observation prior to the finalisation and submission thereof'.[28] Conversely, in cases where a Member State acts as the respondent, it must provide the Commission in a timely manner with relevant documents relating to the proceeding,[29] inform the Commission in a timely manner of all significant procedural steps[30] and permit representatives of the Commission as part of the delegation representing the Member State.[31]

[23] Opinion 2/13 *Accession to the ECHR* [2014] ECLI:EU:C:2014:2454, para 234.

[24] Dimopoulos, 'Investor-state dispute settlement' (ch 11, fn 18) 1699.

[25] Instructively, Dimopoulos, 'Investor-state dispute settlement' (ch 11, fn 18) 1681.

[26] (EU) No 912/2014 of the European Parliament and of the Council of 23 July 2014 establishing a framework for managing financial responsibility linked to investor-to-state dispute settlement tribunals established by international agreements to which the European Union is party (Introduction, fn 5), Art 7.

[27] ibid, Art 8.

[28] ibid, Art 9, para 6.

[29] ibid, Art 10, para 1(a).

[30] ibid, Art 10, para 1(b).

[31] ibid, Art 10, para 1(c).

Procedurally, the obligations to cooperate can be the subject of an infringement procedure under Article 258 TFEU and the follow-up proceedings under Article 260 para 2 TFEU.

Particular cooperation requirements apply where the Union acts as the respondent in any disputes, in which a Member State would be liable to bear financial responsibility. In these cases, the Commission shall, among others, take all necessary measures to defend and protect the interests of the Member State concerned[32] and the Commission and the Member State concerned shall prepare the defence in close cooperation with each other;[33] also, the Union's delegation to the proceedings shall comprise the Commission and representatives of the Member State concerned.[34]

Finally, regarding the potential settlement of disputes, the financial consequences should be decisive. The party bearing the internal financial responsibility in the relation between EU and Member States should generally be entitled to decide about potential settlement of the dispute. Hence, the Commission should be allowed to settle a case involving the financial responsibility of the Union, where this would be in the interests of the Union.[35] By contrast, the Member State should remain free to settle the case at all times, provided that it accepts full financial responsibility and that any such settlement is consistent with Union law.[36] Where the case is conducted by the Union, but also concerns treatment afforded by a Member State, the Union would only be able to settle a dispute if the settlement would not have any financial implications for the Member State. In such cases, it is appropriate that there should be close cooperation and consultations between the Commission and the Member State concerned.[37]

Overall, Regulation No 912/2014 is the outcome of careful balancing between EU's and Member States interests, where the latter are particularly sensitive because they are giving up their autonomy in conducting investment policy. Hence, cooperation obligations are a predominant requirement in taking account of national interests and the regulation has established a set of mutual cooperation obligations. They also reflect the common responsibility under international law, as a consequence of investment agreements being designed as mixed agreements. Also, since judgments of tribunals contain obligations to pay monetary damages, the financial implications naturally have a sensitive character. The regulation seeks to streamline internal financial responsibility, representation as a respondent and cooperation principles. However, only the practice under EU investment agreements will highlight how smoothly this principle works in reality.

[32] ibid, Art 11, para 1(a).
[33] ibid, Art 11, para 1(d).
[34] ibid, Art 11, para 1(e).
[35] ibid, Art 14, para 5.
[36] ibid, Art 14, para 3.
[37] ibid, Preamble, para 18.

## V. LIABILITY CLAIMS BETWEEN UNION AND MEMBER STATES

Problems may arise if, despite the regulation's attempt to harmonise the standing as a respondent (and thus the obligation to pay damages) and the allocation of financial responsibility, external and internal obligations diverge. In other words, it may happen that the party obliged under international law does not coincide with the party financially responsible under EU law. For example, if the Union is a respondent for a treatment afforded exclusively (and without being bound by EU law) by Member States' organs, there is a discrepancy between international law and EU law obligations. Similarly, divergence between international law and EU law may arise, if the EU acts as a respondent for a violation which occurred due to a joint violation of both Union organs and Member States. This case may prove practically very relevant, because it encompasses cases where the EU adopted a directive and Member States chose the measures to attain the directive's objective. One example might be the Tobacco Products Directive, where both the plain-packaging obligation by Member States and the mandatory health warnings on the pack of cigarettes required by EU law have been considered to be infringing investment protection norms.[38]

### A. Compensation or claim for damages?

In a situation of divergence between international law and EU law obligation, the question is: on what basis can EU or Member States claim damages against each other, respectively, and how it could be enforceable before a court? A Union or Member State conduct violating a provision of a mixed investment agreement vis-à-vis the third party also constitutes an infringement of EU law. If the Member States have assumed international responsibility for the violation of the mixed agreement, based on an EU act establishing internal financial responsibility of the Union under EU law, the Member State could hold a damage claim against the Union based on Article 340 para 2 TFEU. Conversely, the Union can launch an action for damages against the Member States before national courts, if the latter is financially responsible under EU law.

The requirements for an action for damages under EU law have been extensively discussed above.[39] There must be a violation of a binding norm—in the present context, the mixed agreement is concluded by the EU and Member States and a violation of this agreement constitutes a breach of EU law. In *Haegeman*, the Court explored the validity of a mixed agreement in the legal order and found the agreement to be an integrated part of the EU legal order[40]—similar findings

[38] Ahner, *Investor-Staat-Schiedsverfahren* (2015) (ch 11, fn 32) 328.
[39] See above chapters 1–7.
[40] *R & V Haegeman v Belgian State* (ch 1, fn 4) 449, para 2 and 6.

were then reiterated in *Bresciani*,[41] *Razantsimba*[42] and *Greece v Commission*.[43] Since mixed agreements become an integrated part of the EU legal order, they can generally serve as standard for a legality review based on Article 216 para 2 TFEU.

However, the suitability of the action for damages as an instrument to regulate internal regulation between the joint debtors could generally be questionable.[44] There is no indication in case law suggesting that an action for damages would be the appropriate mechanism for settling issues, in which the Union and Member States cooperate. In fact, general considerations applying to the purpose and objective of compensation claims and damage claims militate against taking recourse to an action for damages. In principle, the objective of the damage suits is to compensate damages suffered and to protect individual interests.

By contrast, an internal compensation claim could be derived directly from the duty of sincere cooperation and the loyalty principle. Article 4 para 3 TEU constitutes a fundamental principle of EU law and has been applied in the various cooperation modes foreseen in Regulation 912/2014, in order to balance the EU and Member States' interests. The loyalty principle has already become particularly visible in the Court's Opinion 1/94. On that occasion, the Court stressed the duty to cooperate between EU and Member States in areas of shared competences. The Court elaborated that close cooperation is essential to comply with the obligations assumed under the agreement.[45] Even if the Court primarily referred to the obligations of EU and Member States vis-à-vis an external partner, the duty to cooperate is particularly manifest in the internal relationship, in order to avoid the negative effect of non-uniform application of agreements. If the Union or a Member State has individually paid damages, even though there is joint and several liability, and if one of the joint debtors refuses to compensate the other joint debtor internally, this leads to tension incompatible with the duty to cooperate. Refusal to regulate the damage between the joint debtors through compensatory payments, is thus tantamount to a violation of Article 4 para 3 TEU. Unlike under the action for damages, the compensatory payments required under the duty to cooperate serves to regulate the risks involved with the activities in which the joint debtors are exposed under international law.

## B. Enforceability

How can the Union enforce its compensation claim against a Member State, and vice versa, in a scenario described above, in which there is internal joint and several liability due to the common external international responsibility?

[41] Case 87/75 *Bresciani v Amministrazione italiana delle finanze* [1976] ECR 129, 129, para 17.

[42] Case 65/77 *Razanatsimba* [1977] ECR 2229, 2229.

[43] Case 30/88 *Greece v Commission* [1989] ECR 3711, 3711, para 12.

[44] Ahner, *Investor-Staat-Schiedsverfahren* (2015) (ch 11, fn 32) 331.

[45] Opinion 1/94 *WTO* [1994] ECR I-5267, I-5276, para 108; likewise in Case C-25/94 *Commission v Council (FAO Case)* [1996] ECR I-1469, I-1469, para 48.

### *i. Union versus Member State*

Regulation 912/2014 only foresees a mechanism for the enforcement of the compensatory claim of the Union against Member States. By contrast, there is no mechanism according to which a Member State can submit a compensatory claim against the Union. If the Union acts in an investor–state dispute as a respondent and there is controversy between the Union and the Member State regarding the internal financial responsibility, the Commission can simply decide which amount the Member States owes to the Commission.[46] The Member States can object to the decisions, but the Commission can adopt another decision requiring the Member State concerned to reimburse the amount.[47] Article 263 TFEU is available to a Member State that deems the decision as falling short of the criteria set out in the regulation governing the apportionment of financial responsibility.[48]

If a Member State accepts any potential financial responsibility arising from the arbitration in which the Union acts as the respondent, the Member State concerned and the Commission may enter into arrangements dealing with mechanisms for periodic payment of costs arising from the arbitration.[49] Further, the Commission may adopt a decision requiring the Member State concerned to advance financial contributions to the budget of the Union, in respect of foreseeable or incurred costs arising from the arbitration.[50]

Hence, the Union has been equipped by EU secondary law with strong tools to enforce the financial claims it may hold against Member States due to their financial responsibility. There is no need for the Union to initiate a procedure of infringement according to Article 258 para 2 TFEU against the jointly liable Member State.[51] Taking recourse to this proceeding would also raise the question of the direct effect of investment agreements.[52] The substantial provisions that grant rights to individuals are sufficiently precise and unconditional to be considered as directly effective. Moreover, institutionalisation of the investor–state dispute settlement mechanism underscores the objective of investment agreements to grant individual rights.[53] However, the Commission is not dependent from direct effect of investment agreements because it gained the necessary channels to enforce its

[46] (EU) No 912/2014 of the European Parliament and of the Council of 23 July 2014 establishing a framework for managing financial responsibility linked to investor-to-state dispute settlement tribunals established by international agreements to which the European Union is party (Introduction, fn 5), Art 19 para 3.

[47] ibid, Art 19 para 5.

[48] ibid, para 20. See also Dimopoulos, 'Investor-state dispute settlement' (ch 11, fn 18) 1707.

[49] (EU) No 912/2014 of the European Parliament and of the Council of 23 July 2014 establishing a framework for managing financial responsibility linked to investor-to-state dispute settlement tribunals established by international agreements to which the European Union is party (Introduction, fn 5), Art 12.

[50] ibid, Art 20.

[51] On the relevance of infringement proceedings in this context Dimopoulos, 'Investor-state dispute settlement' (ch 11, fn 18) 1676.

[52] ibid 1700.

[53] See Haghighi (2007) (ch 11, fn 31) 217ff; Dimopoulos, *EU Foreign Investment Law* (2011) (ch 11, fn 21) 301f.

claims under the rules governing financial responsibility, through its decision-making power enshrined in Regulation No 914/2014.

### *ii. Member State versus Union*

The reverse relation is more difficult, notably if a Member State was found responsible for a breach of the investment agreement and seeks to hold the EU internally liable as a joint debtor. Unlike in the above case, the Member State has no legal basis in Regulation 912/2014 in order to enforce its claim—it can rely only on an action for annulment and a suit for damages against the EU. Pursuing an action for annulment based on Article 263 TFEU, the Member State must seek a finding that the EU's violation of the agreement constitutes a breach of superior EU law. Irrespective of whether the violation concerns parts of the agreement falling into Member State or EU competence, the Union infringes the duty of loyalty under Article 4 para 3 TEU. The Court can combine a finding of unlawfulness with the order to make a compensatory payment to the Member State.

In such proceedings, the issue of direct effect of the investment agreement becomes relevant, as the Member State is invoking the agreement as a standard of legality. The preceding question is whether and to what extent the CJEU may assume the competence to interpret the mixed agreement. A limitation of the Court's competence to interpretation along the lines of competences of Member States and EU would mean that national courts would gain the right to interpret parts of the agreement. An argument in favour of the Court's comprehensive interpretation regarding both parts falling into Member State and EU's competence, is to ensure uniform interpretation and application of the agreement.[54] On this basis, the Court would have to assess the respective contributions to the violation afforded by the Union and Member State. This highlights the asymmetry in the enforcement of compensatory claims: while the EU has very comfortable tools at hand under Regulation 912/2014 to enforce its claims by simple decisions, Member States would have to rely on the cumbersome mechanisms provided under EU primary law and go through legal actions before the CJEU. In practice, it seems likely that Member States would enforce their compensatory claims by offsetting them against the payments of contributions due by the Member State to the EU.

## VI. CONCLUSIONS

The EU does not possess comprehensive competence for an agreement establishing the ISDS mechanism. In particular, the EU's competence does not extend to

[54] *Hermès v FHT Marketing Choice BV* (ch 12, fn 48) Opinion of AG Tesauro, I-3603, para 19ff; regarding the systematic connection of the different parts of the agreement Castillo de la Torre, 'The Status of GATT' (ch 1, fn 7) 67f.

the scope of the current Member States' BITs. The conclusion of comprehensive investment agreements, thus, requires joint commitment by Member States and the EU to craft a mixed agreement. From the perspective of international law, the mixed agreement is in its entirety binding on both, unless a competence clause would unambiguously implement a delineation of competences into the agreement. For the attribution of acts of infringements of the agreement, in principle this implies the following for the EU: a measure is considered a breach of international law, if the measure can be attributed to the international organisation—the DARIO offers a useful tool to assess attributability in light of the respective treatments afforded at the EU and Member State level. Besides the obvious responsibility for breaches of its own organs, the Union must be held liable for the conduct of Member States, if the Member States implement a binding legal act without leaving them discretionary room to manoeuvre in the implementation. By contrast, if there is scope to manoeuvre in the implementation on the part of the Member States, the Union can be held liable only if such liability is the result of a *lex specialis* rule enshrined in EU law pursuant to Article 64 DARIO—under EU rules, such liability may arise from a violation of the obligations under Article 216 para 2 TFEU and Article 4 para 3 TEU. By contrast, the only way the EU organs' conduct could be considered as an act of a Member State is by explicitly accepting responsibility for that act towards the injured party.

Internally, liability within the EU can deviate from international responsibility. A decisive element of attribution is the margin to manoeuvre for Member States' organs to act lawfully or unlawfully when implementing EU law. Only if the Member States' margin is limited to the effect that it must act in violation with the agreement, in order to comply with EU law, the measure cannot be considered as a Member State's act. In that regard, Regulation 912/2014 seeks to streamline internal financial responsibility, and representation as a respondent before the investor–state tribunal. Frictions are to be avoided by comprehensive cooperation obligations applying to both the EU and Member States. More broadly, these cooperation duties reflect both the sensitivity of this issue falling into genuine Member States' domain, and the common responsibility under international law as a consequence of investment agreements being designed as mixed agreements. In incidents where financial balancing claims exist due to the joint debtor position, there is considerable asymmetry in the enforcement of compensatory claims, because the EU enjoys a convenient basis in Regulation 912/2014 to enforce its claims vis-à-vis the Member States, while the latter must undertake cumbersome recourse to the CJEU for enforcement of their claims.

# *Summary*

1 EU liability regimes relating to international economic law vary, depending on the issue concerned. In international trade law, the individual holds a weak position, being deprived of both legal remedies to seek annulment and damages. This is due to the traditionally subordinate role of the individual in this area of law, which to a large degree is determined by reciprocal rights and obligations on the inter-state level. This not only led to the constant refusal of the direct effect of international trade rules on the domestic level, but also to an underdeveloped system of legal protection for individuals. By contrast, international investment law has been designed in an 'individualistic' manner from the outset—states agree reciprocally to grant certain procedural and substantial individual rights, which they invoke to claim damages before international tribunals rather than domestic courts. There is no issue of direct effect as a prerequisite for liability, as the enforcement regime has been established outside the domestic legal order.

2 The divergent role of the individual in the respective area of international economic law leads to a different set of research questions related to liability. In international trade law, the doctrinal exercise of decoupling the notion of direct effect from liability is at the core of establishing liability. In international investment law, liability is connected to a number of issues emerging from the recent transfer of competence pertaining to investment issues from Member States to the EU and the nature of investment agreements as mixed agreements. The ensuing questions concern both the external level (who can be held liable on the level of international law?) and internal level (who bears financial responsibility internally?)

3 Rulings of the WTO Dispute Settlement Body (DSB) are binding and valid within the EU legal order, but they do not enjoy any direct effect. For the purpose of assessing DSB rulings as grounds for liability, a distinction should be drawn between 'whether' the losing party has to comply and 'how or when' it must comply. Regarding the 'whether', the DSB ruling is unconditional and clear, not leaving an alternative to compliance. By contrast, there is significant leeway and flexibility as to how the losing party complies with the DSB decision. Consequently, the decision cannot have any direct effect, but the unconditionality regarding the obligation to comply (at all) may serve as the basis to justify the DSB ruling as grounds for an action for damages. The distinction can be employed to account for the different objectives of actions for annulment and damages. Refusing legal redress regarding the former is sound, in order not to compromise the scope to manoeuvre for EU legislation—the freedoms related to the 'how or when' of compliance with the DSB ruling would be impaired. By contrast, this reasoning cannot be applied to the action for damages—given the unconditionality of the 'whether' to

comply, liability can be recognised without interfering with the EU's freedoms to decide on the 'how and when' to comply.

4 The Court has transferred the junctim between direct effect and an action for annulment into the context of liability. According to the Court, liability requires the WTO agreements to be directly effective. This junctim can be overcome by employing the *Francovich* doctrine for the present context. Transferring *Francovich* into the WTO context requires a parallel application of the three fundamental pillars bearing the *Francovich* approach, notably the principle of *effet utile*, the notion of legal redress accruing from the rule of law and the loyalty principle laid down in Article 4 para 3 TEU.

5 The *effet utile* principle can be applied to the primary law obligation enshrined in Article 216 para 2 TFEU, stipulating the binding character of international treaties for EU secondary law. Article 216 para 2 TFEU corresponds to the function of Article 288 TFEU in *Francovich*—the former provision implies the obligation of the EU to implement the DSB ruling. Similar to the Court's approach in *Francovich*, the *effet utile* principle can be applied to Article 216 para 2 TFEU to allow liability even without direct effect of the act required to be implemented (ie, the DSB ruling in the WTO context and the EU directive in the *Francovich* context). The individual can be instrumentalised towards making the order of Article 216 para 2 TFEU more effective. Even though a comparison of Article 216 para 2 TFEU and Article 288 TFEU is impeded by the different quality of integration purposes regarding the WTO and the EU, there are good reasons to accept the application of *effet utile* to Article 216 TFEU pertaining to the implementation of DSB rulings.

6 The principle of legal redress (as referred to in *Francovich*) requires a legal ground providing an individual right—in the present context, there is an 'objective' duty of implementation under Article 216 para 2 TFEU and a 'subjective' protection of individual interests in the DSB ruling. Moreover, the loyalty principle stipulated in Article 4 para 3 TEU requires a careful account of Member States' interest and can also justify an obligation of the EU to pay damages for WTO violations.

7 The principle of *parallelisme necessaire* between EU and Member State liability implies a wide understanding of the necessary protection of individual rights. It suffices if individual interests are protected only indirectly or secondarily. Even if the WTO system is not designed to grant individuals explicit and enforceable rights, the intention of WTO rules aims at expanding and ensuring individual rights at least indirectly (as a 'reflex'). The primary purpose of WTO rules is to regulate inter-state trade affairs, but private actors are at the core of the freedoms and concessions agreed under the WTO agreements.

8 There must be specificity of individual rights in order be a valid ground for an action for damages. The DSB ruling must provide a 'normative minimum' in the sense that the rights accorded by the DSB ruling must be discernible at a minimum level, and the scope of persons to which the rights is afforded must be sufficiently determinable. For the victims of retaliation (case group C), the Court would be

in the position to recognise the absence of retaliation measures as a normative minimum right accorded by the WTO rules, and to identify the companies concerned. Also, in the bananas and hormones case, the companies otherwise affected by the EU import regimes (case group B) do meet these conditions. However, this does not apply in general—for the individual right from the DSB decision to be sufficiently discernible, there must be some kind of indication enshrined in the DSB ruling, as to which measures the losing party is expected to adopt in order to implement the DSB decision.

9 The 'sufficiently serious breach' threshold restricts EU liability and shields the EU legislator's margin to manoeuvre against judicial intrusion. The *gravity* and the *effects* have been identified as indicative factors for this requirement. They must be applied and decided on an individual case-by-case basis. At least for the long-standing bananas case, the EU's persistent refusal, and the evident discrepancy between the required and actual conduct, underscore the seriousness of the breach. Further, in the hormones dispute, over a period of five years the EU did not undertake any attempt to bring its import regime into compliance with the DSB decision. Given the clarity of the DSB ruling, there are good reasons to apply the strict liability standard developed for the transposition of EU directives into the context of liability for non-implementation of DSB decisions—continuous inactivity of the EU gives an indication of the seriousness of the breach. Also, *delimitability* of the group concerned is not an issue for the victims of retaliation. By contrast, the *delimitability* of the companies is likely to be hardly possible for case group B, because the disadvantages would practically extend to all companies somehow involved in trading with bananas, even if only indirectly. The disadvantages incurring to case group B must be considered to lie typically within the bounds of what constitute the inherent market risks of importing activities.

10 Violation of fundamental rights, because of breaches of WTO law, has led the Court to undertake a judicial review limited to evident breaches and an assessment of arbitrariness. This impedes the review of proportionality as a cornerstone of the legality review in order to balance both individual rights and common interests. There is scope for undertaking the proportionality assessment in a WTO-consistent way. Taking the DSB decision into account does not necessarily lead to reducing the weight of public interests, especially not in a case where the intrusion of individual freedoms to pursue business opportunities can be justified on grounds pertaining to public health and the protection of life. However, careful balancing of the rights concerned also requires that the economic freedoms of the market participants involved in external trade must only stand back if public interests are sufficiently substantiated.

11 The Court's refusal to recognise liability for WTO breaches can be explored from an economic perspective. There is extensive literature on the economic analysis of civil liability, which can (at least to some extent) offer some insight for the present analysis. Also, given the nature of EU liability as connected to political

decision-making and incomplete information, the insight produced by institutional economics is fruitful for the purpose of the present analysis. In principle, recognition of liability forces the EU legislator to internalise the costs for companies, which the legislator is currently able to externalise. These costs translate into political costs and become a factor in the cost–benefit rationale of the policymaker. At the same time, the legislator faces a deficit of information, because he does not have *ex ante* certainty on whether his legislative activities will be found WTO-incompatible and whether (and under what condition) this may give rise to liability. This lack of information is problematic in combination with the risk of overcompensation of the claimant, because as a consequence private damages exceed social welfare losses. The discrepancy between private and social losses (in combination with the lack of information) will lead to an over-deterrence effect and paralysis of the legislator. Thus, both no-liability and liability may lead to inefficiencies. However, the 'sufficiently serious breach' requirement developed by the Court for liability claims turns out to have a corrective function from an efficiency perspective, by reducing the over-deterrence effect. In sum, from an economic point of view, liability is desirable (confirming the arguments of the legal analysis) within the limitations recognised under the *Schöppenstedt*-jurisprudence.

12 Despite new competences granted to the EU under the Lisbon Treaty, the EU does not have comprehensive competence for all relevant issues pertaining to current practice under investment agreements. Future EU investment agreements are likely to be concluded as mixed agreements. Both the EU and Member States are bound by mixed agreements in their entirety, unless a competence clause explicitly regulates otherwise. Union acts as well as Member States' acts can be attributed to the Union. If a Member State's act violates the agreement, both the Union and the Member States are held jointly liable. Liability within the EU (and the financial responsibility tied to it) does not necessarily correspond with responsibility under international law. Rather, internal liability depends on the scope to manoeuvre that Member States have in determining the lawfulness of the act implementing EU law. Regulation 912/2014 is the first legislative act providing a regime for future EU agreements, which set principles and rules for allocating financial responsibility between the EU and Member States. A comprehensive system of duties to cooperate for both the EU and Member States has been established on the basis of Article 4 para 3 TEU. There remains asymmetry between the EU and Member States and their respective possibilities to claim financial compensation from the other jointly liable party.

13 There remains a lack of coherence in the enforcement of individual rights across the area of international economic law, due to fundamental differences in the design of dispute resolution. The state-to-state design prevalent in international trade law favours political negotiations and diplomatic flexibility over rigid legality and individual rights enforcement. Refusal of the direct effect of international trade law hinders the alternative avenues of enforcement of rights before

domestic courts weakening the position of the individuals' liability claims, both at the international and domestic level. However, the individual-to-state enforcement design of ISDS under investment agreements goes the contrary way—it allows liability claims and promotes the alignment of national (policy) measures with international agreements through a well-defined enforcement mechanism, which is not subject to political willingness to enforce, and which may impact a government's policy manoeuvre.

# *References*

Aalto, P, *Public Liability in EU Law: Brasserie, Bergaderm and Beyond*, 1st edn (Oxford, Hart Publishing, 2011).

Adams, M, *Ökonomische Analyse der Gefährdungs-und Verschuldenshaftung* (Heidelberg, v Decker, 1985).

Ahner, J, *Investor-Staat-Schiedsverfahren nach Europäischem Unionsrecht: Zulässigkeit und Ausgestaltung in Investitionsabkommen der Europäischen Union*, 1st edn (Tübingen, Mohr Siebeck, 2015).

Albers, C, *Die Haftung der Bundesrepublik Deutschland für die Nichtumsetzung von EG-Richtlinien* (Baden-Baden, Nomos, 1995).

Alemanno, A, 'Private Parties and WTO Dispute Settlement System' (2004) *Cornell Law School Inter-University Graduate Student Conference Papers* Paper 1.

Alford, RP, 'Apportioning Responsibility among Joint Tortfeasors for International Law Violations' (2001) 38 *Pepperdine Law Review* 233.

Anderson, K, 'Pecularities of Retaliation in WTO Dispute Settlement' (2002) *CIES Discussion Paper* no 0207.

Ankersmit, L, 'The Compatibility of Investment Arbitration in EU Trade Agreements with the EU Judicial System' (2016) 13 *Journal for European Environmental & Planning Law* 46.

Appleyard, DR, Field, AJ and Cobb, SL, *International Economics*, 7th edn (New York, McGraw-Hill, 2010).

Arndt, H-W, Knemeyer, FL, Kugelmann, D, Meng, W and Schweitzer, M, (eds), *Völkerrecht und deutsches Recht: Festschrift für Walter Rudolf zum 70. Geburtstag* (München, CH Beck, 2001).

Arnold, R and Meindl, E, 'Außenhandelsrecht—Grundregeln' in MA Dauses (ed), *Handbuch des EU-Wirtschaftsrechts*, 38th edn (München, CH Beck, 2015).

Arnull, A, 'Liability for Legislative Acts under Article 215(2) EC' in T Heukels and A McDonnell (eds), *The Action For Damages In Community Law* (The Hague, Kluwer Law International, 1997).

Backes, P, 'Die neuen Streitbeilegungsregeln der Welthandelsorganisation (WTO)' (1995) *RIW* 916.

Bagwell, K and Staiger, RW, 'An Economic Theory of GATT' (1997) *NBER Working Paper* No 6049.

Bahlmann, K, 'Haftung der Mitgliedstaaten bei fehlerhafter Umsetzung von EG-Richtlinien' (1992) *DWiR* 61.

Baird, DG, Gertner, RH and Picker, RC, *Game Theory and the Law* (Cambridge, Harvard University Press, 1994).

Balassa, B, *The Theory of Economic Integration* (Abingdon, Routledge, 2011).

Bartelt, S, 'Die Haftung der Gemeinschaft bei Nichtumsetzung von Entscheidungen des WTO-Streitbeilegungsgremiums' (2003) *EuR* 1077.

Bebr, G, 'Joined Cases C-6/90 and 9/90, Francovich v. Italy, Bonifaci v. Italy Judgment of the Court of Justice of 19 November 1991' (1992) 29 *CML Rev* 557.

Becker, T, *Das WTO-Subventionsübereinkommen: Einfluss auf die Rechtsschutzmöglichkeiten Dritter gegen Beihilfen im Rahmen des EG-Rechts* (Frankfurt am Main, P Lang, 2001).

Becker-Celik, A, 'Ist die Ablehnung der unmittelbaren Anwendbarkeit der GATT-Vorschriften durch den EuGH heute noch gerechtfertigt?' (1997) *EWS* 12.

Beghin, J, Disdier, AC, Marette, S, Van Tongeren, F, 'Welfare Costs and Benefits of Non-tariff Measures in Trade: A Conceptual Framework and Application' (2012) 11 *World Trade Review* 356.

Behrens, P, 'Integrationstheorie' (1981) 45 *RabelsZ* 8.

—— 'Die private Durchsetzung von WTO-Recht' in C Nowak and W Cremer (eds), *Individualrechtsschutz in der EG und der WTO: Der zentrale und dezentrale Rechtsschutz natürlicher und juristischer Personen in der Europäischen Gemeinschaft und der Welthandelsorganisation*, 1st edn (Baden-Baden, Nomos, 2002).

Bell, A, 'Enforcing Community Law Rights Before National Courts—Some Developments' (1994) 21 *LIEI* 111.

Bello, JH, 'The WTO Dispute Settlement Understanding: Less is More' (1996) 90 *AJIL* 416.

Beneyto, JM, 'The EU and WTO: Direct Effect of the New Dispute Settlement System' (1996) *EuZW* 295.

Berg, W, 'Opfer von Handelsstreitigkeiten können auf Ersatz hoffen. Unternehmen können sich leichter auf WTO-Vorschriften berufen' (15 October 2003) *Frankfurter Allgemeine Zeitung*.

Berg, W and Beck, J, 'Zur jüngsten Rechtsprechung der Gemeinschaftsgerichte zur unmittelbaren Anwendung von WTO-Recht im Gemeinschaftsrecht' (2005) *RIW* 401.

Berkey, J, 'The European Court of Justice and Direct Effect of GATT. A Question Worth Revisiting' (1998) 9 *EJIL* 626.

Bernstein, J and Skully, D, 'Calculating Trade Damages in the Context of the World Trade Organization's Dispute Settlement Process' (2003) 25 *Review of Agricultural Economics* 385.

Berrisch, G, 'Zum "Bananen"–Urteil des EuGH vom 05.10.1994' (1994) *EuR* 461.

Berrisch, G and Kamann, HG, 'WTO Recht im Gemeinschaftsrecht—(k)eine Kehrtwende des EuGH' (2000) *EWS* 89.

Besse, D, 'Die Bananenmarktordnung im Lichte deutscher Grundrechte und das Kooperationsverhältnis zwischen BVerfG und EuGH' (1996) *JuS* 396.

Betlem, G and Rood, E, 'Francovich-aansprakelijkheid' (1992) *NJB* 250.

Bhagwati, JN, 'Directly Unproductive, Profit-Seeking (DUP) Activities' (1982) 90 *JPE* 988.

Bischoff, JA, 'Just a Little BIT of "Mixity"? The EU's Role in the Field of International Investment Protection Law' (2011) 48 *CML Rev* 1527.

Bishop, RD, Crawford, J and Reisman, WM, *Foreign Investment Disputes: Cases Materials and Commentary*, 2nd edn (The Hague, Kluwer Law International, 2014).

Bishop, W, 'Economic Loss in Tort' (1982) 2 *Oxford Journal of Legal Studies* 1.

Bleckmann, A, *Begriff und Kriterien der innerstaatlichen Anwendbarkeit völkerrechtlicher Verträge* (Berlin, Duncker & Humblot, 1970).

—— 'Die Position des Völkerrechts im inneren Rechtsraum der EG—Monismus oder Dualismus der Rechtsordnungen?' (1975) *JIR* 300.

'Der gemischte Vertrag im Europarecht' (1976) *EuR* 301.

—— 'Mixity in Public International Law' in D O'Keeffe and HG Schermers (eds), *Mixed Agreements* (Deventer, Kluwer Law and Taxation Publishers, 2009).

Blokker, N, 'Abuse of the Members, Questions Concerning Draft Article 16 of the Draft Articles on Responsibility of International Organizations' (2010) 7 *International Organizations Law Review* 35.

Bogdandy, Av, 'Europa 1992—Die außervertragliche Haftung der Europäischen Gemeinschaften' (1990) *JuS* 872.

—— 'Rechtsgleichheit, Rechtssicherheit und Subsidiarität im transnationalen Wirtschaftsrecht' (2001) *EuZW* 357.

—— 'Legal Effects of World Trade Organization Decisions Within European Union Law: A Contribution to the Theory of the Legal Acts of International Organizations and the Action for Damages Under Article 288(2) EC' (2005) *JWT* 45.

—— 'Pluralism, Direct Effect, and the Ultimate Say: On the Relationship between International and Domestic Constitutional Law' (2008) *Int'l J Const L* 397.

Borchert, M, *Aussenwirtschaftslehre: Theorie und Politik*, 7th edn (Wiesbaden. Gabler-Lehrbuch, Gabler, 2001).

Bown, CP and Pauwelyn, J (eds), *The Law, Economics and Politics of Retaliation in WTO Dispute Settlement* (Cambridge, Cambridge University Press, 2010).

Bown, CP and Ruta, M, 'The Economics of Permissible WTO Retaliation' in CP Bown and J Pauwelyn (eds), *The Law, Economics and Politics of Retaliation in WTO Dispute Settlement* (Cambridge, Cambridge University Press, 2010).

Breuss, F, 'WTO Dispute Settlement in Action: An Economic Analysis of Four EU–US Mini Trade Wars' (EcoMod2003) *Paper presented at the International Conference on Policy Modeling*.

—— 'WTO Dispute Settlement in Practice: An Economic Assesssment' in F Breuss, S Griller and E Vranes (eds), *The Banana Dispute: An Economic and Legal Analysis* (New York, Springer, 2003).

—— 'WTO Dispute Settlement: An Economic Analysis of Four EU–US Mini Trade Wars—A Survey' (2004) *Journal of Industry, Competition and Trade* 275.

Brimeyer, BL, 'Bananas, Beef and Compliance in the World Trade Organization: The Inability of the WTO Dispute Settlement Process to Achieve Compliance from Superpower Nations' (2001) 10 *Minn J Global Trade* 133.

Bronckers, M, 'Is Investor–State Dispute Settlement (ISDS) Superior to Litigation Before Domestic Courts? An EU View on Bilateral Trade Agreements' (2015) 18 *JIEL* 655.

Brown, JP, 'Toward an Economic Theory of Liability' (1973) 2 *J Legal Stud* 323.

Buchanan, JM, 'From Private Preferences to Public Philosophy: The Development of Public Choice' in JM Buchanan (ed), *Constitutional Economics* (Cambridge, Blackwell, 1991).

Bungenberg, M, 'Going Global? The EU Common Commercial Policy After Lisbon' (2010) 1 *EYIEL* 123.

Bungenberg, M and Titi, C, 'Developments in International Investment Law' (2014) *EYIEL* 425.

Burgstaller, M, 'The Energy Charter Treaty as a Mixed Agreement: a Model for Future European Investment Treaties?' in G Coop (ed), *Energy Dispute Resolution: Investment Protection, Transit and the Energy Charter Treaty* (Huntington, Juris, 2011).

Butler, JK, *Die Beteiligung von Privatpersonen am WTO-Streitbeilegungsverfahren: Bestandsaufnahme und Entwicklungsperspektiven* (Frankfurt am Main, P Lang, 2002).

Calabresi, G, *The Costs of Accidents: A Legal and Economic Analysis* (New Haven, Yale University Press, 1970).

Cascante, C, *Rechtsschutz von Privatrechtssubjekten gegen WTO-widrige Maßnahmen in den USA und in der EG* (Berlin, Duncker & Humblot, 2003).
Cascante, JC and Sander, GG, *Der Streit um die EG-Bananenmarktordnung: The EC Banana Organization Dispute* (Berlin, Duncker & Humblot, 1999).
Castillo de la Torre, F, 'The Status of GATT in EC Law, Revisited' (1995) 29 *JWT* 53.
Ceyssens, J, 'Towards a Common Foreign Investment Policy? Foreign Investment in the European Union' (2005) 32 *LIEI* 259.
Chacholiades, M, *International Economics* (New York, McGraw-Hill, 1990).
Chaisse, J, 'Promises and Pitfalls of the European Union Policy on Foreign Investment: How will the New EU Competence on FDI affect the Emerging Global Regime?' (2012) 15 *JIEL* 51.
Clapham, A, 'The Role of the Individual in International Law' (2010) 21 *EJIL* 25.
Coase, R, 'The Problem of Social Cost' (1960) 3 *J L Econ* 1.
Coleman, J, Hershovitz, S and Mendlow, G, 'Theories of the Common Law of Torts' in EN Zalta (ed), *The Stanford Encyclopedia of Philosophy* (Stanford, Stanford University, 2014).
Coleman, JL, 'The Economic Structure of Tort Law' (1988) 97 *Yale L J* 1233.
Cooper, AF and Skogstad, GD, 'Introduction: Domestic Pressures, International Tensions, and the MTN' in GD Skogstad and AF Cooper (eds), *Agricultural Trade: Domestic Pressures and International Tensions: Papers presented at a conference held at the University of Toronto in January 1989* (Halifax, Institute for Research on Public Policy, 1990).
Cooter, R and Ulen, T, *Law and Economics*, 6th edn (London, Pearson, 2012).
Coppel, J and O'Neill, A, 'The European Court of Justice: Taking Rights Seriously?' (1992) 29 *CML Rev* 669.
Cornils, M, *Der gemeinschaftsrechtliche Staatshaftungsanspruch: Rechtsnatur und Legitimität eines richterrechtlichen Haftungsinstituts*, 1st edn (Baden-Baden, Nomos, 1995).
Corporate Europe Observatory, 'The right to say no: EU-Canada trade agreement threatens fracking bans' (6 May 2013) www.corporateeurope.org/climate-and-energy/2013/05/right-say-no-eu-canada-trade-agreement-threatens-fracking-bans.
Cottier, T, 'Dispute Settlement in the World Trade Organization: Characteristics and Structural Implications for the European Union' (1998) 35 *CML Rev* 325.
—— 'Das Streitschlichtungsverfahren in der Welthandelsorganisation: Wesenszüge und Herausforderungen' in P-C Müller-Graff (ed), *Die Europäische Gemeinschaft in der Welthandelsorganisation: Globalisierung und Weltmarktrecht als Herausforderung für Europa*, 1st edn (Baden-Baden, Nomos, 1999/2000).
—— 'A Theory of Direct Effect in Global Law' in AV Bogdandy, PC Mavroidis and Y Mény (eds), *European Integration and International Coordination: Studies in Transnational Economic Law in Honour of Claus-Dieter Ehlermann* (The Hague, Kluwer Law International, 2002).
Cottier, T and Nadakavukaren Schefer, K, 'The Relationship between World Trade Organization Law, National and Regional Law' (1998) 1 *JIEL* 83.
Craig, P and Búrca, G de, *EU Law: Text, Cases, and Materials*, 6th edn (Oxford, Oxford University Press, 2015).
Craswell, R and Calfee, J, 'Some Effects of Uncertainty in Compliance with Legal Standards' (1984) 70 *Va L Rev* 965.
—— 'Deterrence and Uncertain Legal Standards' (1986) *JLEO* 279.
Crawford, J and Olleson, S, 'The Nature and Forms of International Responsibility' in MD Evans (ed), *International law*, 3rd edn (Oxford, Oxford University Press, 2010).

Cremona, M, 'External Relations of the EU and the Member States: Competence, Mixed Agreements, International Responsibility, and Effects of International Law' *EUI Working Paper* LAW No 2006/22.

—— 'The Doctrine of Exclusivity and the Position of Mixed Agreements in the External Relations of the European Community' (1982) *OJLS* 393.

Curtin, D, 'Directives: The Effectiveness of Judicial Protection of Individual Rights' (1990) 27 *CML Rev* 709.

—— 'State Liability under Community Law: A New Remedy for Private Parties' (1992) *ILJ* 74.

Czaja, A, *Die außervertragliche Haftung der EG für ihre Organe*, 1st edn (Baden-Baden, Nomos, 1996).

Dahm, G, Delbrück, J and Wolfrum, R, *Völkerrecht: Die Grundlagen. Die Völkerrechtssubjekte*, vol I/1, 2nd edn (Berlin, De Gruyter, 1989).

Danwitz, T v, 'Die gemeinschaftliche Staatshaftung der Mitgliedstaaten' (1997) *DVBl* 1.

d'Aspremont, J, 'Abuse of the Legal Personality of International Organizations and the Responsibility of Member States' (2007) *International Organizations Law Review* 91.

Davies, A, 'Bananas, Private Challenges, the Courts and the Legislature' (2002) 21 *YEL* 299.

Deardoff, AV, 'Why do goverments prefer nontariff barriers?' *University of Michigan Research Seminar in International Economics Seminar* Discussion Paper no 186.

Deckert, M, 'Zur Haftung des Mitgliedstaates bei Verstößen seiner Organe gegen europäisches Gemeinschaftsrecht' (1997) *EuR* 203.

Delgado Casteleiro, A, *The International Responsibility of the European Union: From Competence to Normative Control* (PhD thesis, EUI 2011).

Dendrinos, A, *Rechtsprobleme der Direktwirkung der EWG-Richtlinien: unter besonderer Berücksichtigung der Rechtslage in Griechenland* (Frankfurt am Main, P Lang, 1989).

Desmedt, A, 'European Court of Justice on the Effect of WTO Agreements in the EC Legal Order' (2000) 27 *LIEI* 93.

Detterbeck, S, 'Staatshaftung für die Mißachtung von EG-Recht' (1994) 85 *VerwArch* 159.

Diehr, U, *Der Staatshaftungsanspruch des Bürgers wegen Verletzung des Gemeinschaftsrechts durch die deutsche öffentliche Gewalt* (Frankfurt am Main, P Lang, 1997).

Dimopoulos, A, *EU Foreign Investment Law* (Oxford, Oxford University Press, 2011).

—— 'The Involvement of the EU in Investor-State Dispute Settlement: A Question of Responsibilities' (2014) *CML Rev* 1671.

Dolzer, R and Schreuer, C, *Principles of International Investment Law*, 2nd edn (Oxford, Oxford University Press, 2012).

Dolzer, R and Stevens, M, *Bilateral Investment Treaties* (The Hague, Kluwer Law International, 1995).

Douglas, Z, *The International Law of Investment Claims* (Cambridge, Cambridge University Press, 2009).

Drexl, J, *Entwicklungsmöglichkeiten des Urheberrechts im Rahmen des GATT: Inländerbehandlung, Meistbegünstigung, Maximalschutz: eine prinzipienorientierte Betrachtung im Lichte bestehender Konventionen* (München, CH Beck, 1990).

—— 'Unmittelbare Anwendbarkeit des WTO-Rechts in der globalen Privatrechtsordnung' in B Grossfeld (ed), *Festschrift für Wolfgang Fikentscher zum 70. Geburtstag* (Tübingen, Mohr Siebeck, 1998).

Due, O, *Der Grundsatz der Gemeinschaftstreue in der Europäischen Gemeinschaft nach der neueren Rechtsprechung des Gerichtshofs* (Bonn, Rheinische Friedrich-Wilhelms-Universität Bonn 1992).

Dumon, F, 'La responsabilité extracontractuelle des Communautés Européennes et de leurs agents' (1969) *CDE* 3.

Dunker, J, *Regionale Integration im System des liberalisierten Welthandels: EG und NAFTA im Vergleich* (Frankfurt am Main, P Lang, 2002).

Eeckhout, P, 'The Domestic Legal Status of the WTO Agreement: Interconnecting Legal Systems' (1997) 34 *CML Rev* 11.

—— 'Judicial Enforcement of WTO Law in the European Union—Some further Reflections' (2002) *JIEL* 91.

—— 'Remedies and Compliance' in DL Bethlehem and others (eds), *The Oxford Handbook of International Trade Law* (Oxford, Oxford University Press, 2009).

—— *EU External Relations Law*, 2nd edn (Oxford EU Law Library, Oxford University Press, 2011).

Eggers, B, 'Die Entscheidung des WTO Appellate Body im Hormonfall' (1998) *EuZW* 147.

Ehlermann, C-D, 'Mixed Agreements: A List of Problems' in D O'Keeffe and HG Schermers (eds), *Mixed Agreements* (Deventer, Kluwer Law and Taxation Publishers, 2009).

Eilmansberger, T, *Rechtsfolgen und subjektives Recht im Gemeinschaftsrecht: Zugleich ein Beitrag zur Dogmatik der Staatshaftungsdoktrin des EuGH*, 1st edn (Baden-Baden, Nomos, 1997).

—— 'Bilateral Investment Treaties and EU Law' (2009) *CML Rev* 383.

El-Agraa, AM, 'What is Economic Integration?' in AM El-Agraa (ed), *The European Union: Economics and Policies*, 9th edn (Cambridge, Cambridge University Press, 2011).

Emmert, F, *Europarecht* (München, CH Beck, 1996).

Endres, A, 'Allokationswirkungen des Haftungsrechts' (1989) 40 *Jahrbuch für Sozialwissenschaft* 115.

Englard, I, 'Victor Mataja's Liability for Damages from an Economic Viewpoint: A Centennial to an Ignored Economic Analysis of Tort' (1990) 10 *IRLE* 173.

Epiney, A, 'Gemeinschaftsrecht und Föderalismus: "Landes-Blindheit" und Pflicht zur Berücksichtigung innerstaatlicher Verfassungsstrukturen' (1994) *EuR* 301.

—— 'Zur Stellung des Völkerrechts in der EU' (1999) *EuZW* 5.

Epping, V, *Die Außenwirtschaftsfreiheit* (Tübingen, Mohr Siebeck, 1998).

Erlei, M, Sauerland, D and Leschke, M, *Neue Institutionenökonomik*, 2nd edn (Stuttgart, Schäffer-Poeschel, 2007).

Errico, J, 'The WTO in the EU: Unwinding the Knot' (2011) 44 *Cornell Int'l L J* 179.

Everling, U, 'Will Europe Slip on Bananas? The Bananas Judgment of the Court of Justice and National Courts' (1996) 33 *CML Rev* 401.

Fetzer, R, *Die Haftung des Staates für legislatives Unrecht* (Berlin, Duncker & Humblot, 1994).

Fikentscher, W, 'Was Bedeutet "Self executing"?' in JF Baur, KJ Hopt and KP Mailänder (eds), *Festschrift für Ernst Steindorff* (Berlin, De Gruyter, 1990).

Financial Times, 'Germans seek lawsuits over Greek debt swap' (12 March 2012) www.ft.com/cms/s/0/79ed422c-6c67-11e1-bd0c-00144feab49a.html.

Fischer, H-G, 'Staatshaftung nach Gemeinschaftsrecht' (1992) *EuZW* 41.

Flemisch, CA, *Umfang der Berechtigungen und Verpflichtungen aus völkerrechtlichen Verträgen: Die Frage der unmittelbaren Anwendbarkeit, dargestellt am Beispiel des WTO-Übereinkommens* (Frankfurt am Main, P Lang, 2002).

Footer, M, 'The EU and the WTO Global Trading System' in P-H Laurent and M Maresceau (eds), *The State of the European Union: Deepening and Widening* (Boulder, Lynne Rienner Publishers, 1998).

Frey, B, 'The Public Choice View of International Political Economy' (1984) 38 *International Organization* 199.

Friedmann, W, 'The Growth of State Control Over the Individual and its Effect Upon the Rules of International State Responsibility' (1938) 19 *Brit YB Int'l L* 118.

Friese, C, *Kompensation von Embargoschäden bei Embargomassnahmen der Europäischen Union* (Köln, Heymanns, 2000).

Furrer, A and Epiney, A, 'Staatliche Haftung für quantifizierbare Wettbewerbsnachteile aus nicht umgesetzten Richtlinien' (1995) *JZ* 1025.

Furubotn, EG and Richter, R, *Institutions and Economic Theory: The Contribution of the New Institutional Economics*, 2nd edn (Ann Arbor, University of Michigan Press, 2005).

Fuß, E-W, 'Zur Rechtsprechung des Europäischen Gerichtshofs über die Gemeinschaftshaftung für rechtswidrige Verordnungen' in H Kipp, F Mayer and A Steinkamm (eds), *Um Recht und Freiheit: Festschrift für von der Heydte* (Berlin, Duncker & Humblot, 1977).

Gabler, T, *Das Streitbeilegungssystem der WTO und seine Auswirkungen auf das Antidumping-Recht der Europäischen Gemeinschaft* (Frankfurt am Main, P Lang, 1997).

Gaja, G, 'The European Community's Rights and Obligations under Mixed Agreements' in D O'Keeffe and HG Schermers (eds), *Mixed Agreements* (Deventer, Kluwer Law and Taxation Publishers, 2009).

Garcia Bercero, I, 'Dispute Settlement in European Union Free Trade Agreements: Lessons Learned?' in L Bartels and F Ortino (eds), *Regional Trade Agreements and the WTO Legal System* (Oxford, Oxford University Press, 2006).

Gasparon, P, 'The Transposition of the Principle of Member States Liability into the Context of External Relations' (1999) 10 *EJIL* 605.

Gattinara, G, 'Consistent Interpretation of WTO Rulings in the EU Legal Order?' in E Cannizzaro, P Palchetti and RA Wessel (eds), *International Law as Law of the European Union* (Boston, Martinus Nijhoff Publishers, 2011).

Geiger, J, 'Die Entwicklung eines europäischen Staatshaftungsanspruchsrechts' (1993) *DVBl* 465.

Geistfeld, MA, 'Compensation as a Tort Norm' in J Oberdiek (ed), *Philosophical Foundations of the Law of Torts*, 1st edn (Oxford, Oxford University Press, 2014).

Gerken, A, *Rechtsschutzmöglichkeiten europäischer Wirtschaftsteilnehmer gegen GATT-widrige Wirtschaftshemmnisse* (Frankfurt am Main, P Lang, 2004).

Gilead, I, 'Tort Law and Internalization: The Gap between Private Loss and Social Cost' (1997) 17 *IRLE* 589.

Ginther, K, 'International Organizations, Responsibility' in R Bernhardt (ed), *Encyclopedia of Public International Law vol 3* (Amsterdam, North-Holland Publishing Co, 1997).

Glismann, HH et al, *Weltwirtschaftslehre: Eine problemorientierte Einführung* (München, dtv wissenschaft, 1980).

Godt, C, 'Der Bericht des Appellate Body der WTO zum EG-Einfuhrverbot von Hormonfleisch: Risikoregulierung im Weltmarkt' (1998) *EWS* 202.

Goldberg, VP, 'Accountable Accountants: Is Third-Party Liability Necessary?' (1994) 23 *J Legal Stud* 1.

Görgens, S, *Die außervertragliche Haftung der Europäischen Gemeinschaft für Verletzungen des WTO-Rechts durch ihre Organe: Die Haftung bei Nichtumsetzung von Entscheidungen des Streitbeilegungsgremiums der WTO*, 1st edn (Berlin, Duncker & Humblot, 2006).

Grabitz, E, 'Zur Haftung der Europäischen Gemeinschaften für normatives Unrecht' in WG Grewe, H Rupp and H Schneider (eds), *Europäische Gerichtsbarkeit und nationale Verfassungsgerichtsbarkeit: Festschrift zum 70. Geburtstag von Hans Kutscher* (Baden-Baden, Nomos, 1981).

Grady, MF, 'A New Positive Economic Theory of Negligence' (1983) 92 *Yale L J* 799.

Griller, S, 'Judicial Enforceability of WTO Law in the European Union. Annotation to case C-149/96, Portugal vs. Council' (2000) 3 *JIEL* 441.

—— 'Enforcement and Implementation of WTO Law in the European Union' in F Breuss, S Griller and E Vranes (eds), *The Banana Dispute: An Economic and Legal Analysis* (New York, Springer, 2003).

Haack, SA, *Die ausservertragliche Haftung der Europäischen Gemeinschaften für rechtmässiges Verhalten ihrer Organe* (Frankfurt am Main, P Lang, 1995).

Haghighi, SS, *Energy Security: The External Legal Relations of the European Union with Major Oil and Gas Supplying Countries*, 1st edn (Oxford, Hart Publishing, 2007).

Hailbronner, K, 'Staatshaftung bei säumiger Umsetzung von EG-Richtlinien' (1992) *JZ* 284.

Handl, G, 'State Liability for Accidental Transnational Environmental Damage by Private Persons' (1980) 74 *AJIL* 525.

Harten, G van, *Investment Treaty Arbitration and Public Law* (Oxford, Oxford University Press, 2007).

Hartley, TC, *The Foundations of European Union Law: An Introduction to the Constitutional and Administrative Law of the European Union*, 8th edn (Oxford, Oxford University Press, 2014).

Hartwig, M, 'International Organizations or Institutions, Responsability and Liability' in R Wolfrum (ed), *Max Planck Encyclopedia of Public International Law vol* 6 (Oxford, Oxford University Press, 2012).

Hatje, A, *Loyalität als Rechtsprinzip in der Europäischen Union* (Baden-Baden, Nomos, 2001).

Hauser, H, 'Domestic Policy Foundation and Domestic Policy Function of International Trade Rules' (1986) 41 *Aussenwirtschaft* 171.

Hauser, H et al, 'Der Beitrag von Jan Tumfir zur Entwicklung einer ökonomischen Verfassungstheorie internationaler Handelsregeln' (1988) 39 *ORDO* 219.

Hauwe van den, L, 'Public Choice, Constitutional Political Economy and Law and Economics' in Gd Geest and B Bouckaert (eds), *Encyclopedia of Law and Economics I: The History and Methodology of Law and Economics* (Cheltenham, Edward Elgar Publishing, 2000).

Heliskoski, J, *Mixed Agreements As a Technique for Organizing the International Relations of the European Community and Its Member States* (The Hague, Kluwer Law International, 2001).

Henrichs, C, *Haftung der EG-Mitgliedstaaten für Verletzung von Gemeinschaftsrecht: Die Auswirkungen des Francovich-Urteils des Europäischen Gerichtshofs in den Rechtsordnungen der Gemeinschaft und der Mitgliedstaaten*, 1st edn (Baden-Baden, Nomos, 1995).

Herdegen, M, *Die Haftung der Europäischen Wirtschaftsgemeinschaft für fehlerhafte Rechtsetzungsakte* (Berlin, Duncker & Humblot, 1983).

—— *Principles of International Economic Law*, 1st edn (Oxford, Oxford University Press, 2013).

—— *Europarecht*, 17th edn (München, CH Beck, 2015).
Herdegen, M and Rensmann, T, 'Die neue Konturen der Gemeinschaftlichen Staatshaftung' (1997) 161 *ZHR* 522.
Hermes, CJ, *TRIPS im Gemeinschaftsrecht: Zu den innergemeinschaftlichen Wirkungen von WTO-Übereinkünften* (Berlin, Duncker & Humblot, 2002).
Herrmann, C, *Richtlinienumsetzung durch die Rechtsprechung*, 1st edn (Berlin, Duncker & Humblot, 2003).
Herten, G van, *Investment Treaty Arbitration and Public Law* (Oxford, Oxford University Press, 2007).
Hilf, M, 'The Role of National Courts in International Trade Relations' (1997) *MJIL* 321.
—— 'Grundfragen der Beteiligung der EG an der WTO' in P-C Müller-Graff (ed), *Die Europäische Gemeinschaft in der Welthandelsorganisation: Globalisierung und Weltmarktrecht als Herausforderung für Europa*, 1st edn (Baden-Baden, Nomos, 1999/2000).
Hindelang, S and Maydell, N, 'Die Gemeinsame Europäische Investitionspolitik: Alter Wein in neuen Schläuchen?' in M Bungenberg, J Griebel and S Hindelang (eds), *Internationaler Investitionsschutz und Europarecht vol* 2, 1st edn (Baden-Baden, Nomos, 2010).
Hinderer, HA, *Rechtsschutz von Unternehmen in der WTO*, 1st edn (Berlin, Berliner Wissenschafts-Verlag, 2004).
Hirsch, G, 'Die Rechtsprechung des Europäischen Gerichtshofs zu Assoziierungsabkommen' (1997) *BayVBl* 449.
Hirsch, M, *The Responsibility of International Organizations Toward Third Parties: Some Basic Principles* (Dordrecht, Martinus Nijhoff, 1995).
Hix, J-P, 'Indirect Effect of International Agreements' (2013) *Jean Monnet Working Paper* 03/13.
Hoekman, BM and Mavroidis, PC, 'Bite the Bullet: Trade Retaliation, EU Jurisprudence and the Law and Economics of "Taking One for the Team"' (2014) 20 *European Law Journal* 317.
Hoffmeister, F, 'Litigating against the European Union and its Member States: Who Responds Under The ILC's Draft Articles on International Responsibility of International Organizations?' (2010) 21 *EJIL* 723.
Höher, K, *Die Haftung der Europäischen Gemeinschaft für Verstöße gegen das WTO-Recht: Eine Untersuchung am Beispiel des WTO-Bananenstreitverfahrens*, 1st edn (Baden-Baden, Nomos, 2006).
Hörmann, S and Göttsche, G, 'Die Haftung der EG für WTO-Rechtsverletzungen—Neue Tendenzen in der EuGH-Rechtsprechung?' (2003) *RIW* 689.
Hsiung, B, 'Economic Analysis of Law: An Inquiry of its Underlying Logic' (2006) 2 *ELER* 1.
International Arbitration Law, 'The Cypriot Debt Crisis and Recourse to Internatoinal Arbitration' (1 May 2013) www.internationalarbitrationlaw.com/the-cypriot-debt-crisis-and-recourse-to-international-arbitration.
Ipsen, HP, *Europäisches Gemeinschaftsrecht* (Tübingen, Mohr Siebeck, 1972).
Isaac, G and Blanquet, M, *Droit communautaire général*, 10th edn (Paris, Armand Colin, 2012).
Jackson, JH, *The World Trading System: Law and Policy of International Economic Relations*, 2nd edn (Cambridge, MIT Press, 1997).
—— 'The WTO Dispute Settlement Understanding—Misunderstandings on the Nature of Legal Obligations' (1997) *AJIL* 60.

—— 'Designing and Implementing Effective Dispute Settlement Procedures: WTO Dispute Settlement, Appraisal and Prospects' in A Krueger (ed), *The WTO as an International Organization* (Chicago, University of Chicago Press, 1998).

—— 'Direct Effect of Treaties in the US and the EU, the Case of the WTO: Some Perceptions and Proposals' in A Arnull, P Eeckhout and T Tridimas (eds), *Continuity and Change in EU Law: Essays in Honour of Sir Francis Jacobs* (Oxford, Oxford University Press, 2008).

Jackson, JH and Grane, P, 'The Saga Continues: An Update on the Banana Dispute and Its Procedural Offspring' (2001) 4 *JIEL* 581.

Jacob, M, 'Faith Betrayed: International Investment Law and Human Rights' in R Hofmann and CJ Tams (eds), *International Investment Law and Its Others*, 1st edn (Baden-Baden, Nomos, 2012).

Jacobs, M, 'Smart Threats and Success in WTO Dispute Settlement: The Bush Steel Tariffs' (24 March 2016) www.e-ir.info/2016/03/24/smart-threats-and-success-in-wto-dispute-settlement-the-bush-steel-tariffs.

Jarass, HD, 'Voraussetzungen der innerstaatlichen Wirkung von EG-Richtlinien' (1990) *NJW* 2420.

—— 'Haftung für die Verletzung von EU-Recht durch nationale Organe und Amtsträger' (1994) *NJW* 881.

—— 'Die Kompetenzverteilung zwischen der Europäischen Gemeinschaft und den Mitgliedstaaten' (1996) *AöR* 173.

Jiménez de Aréchaga, E, 'Self-executing Provisions of International Law' in K Hailbronner, G Ress and T Stein (eds), *Staat und Völkerrechtsordnung: Festschrift für Karl Doehring* (Berlin, Springer, 1989).

Johnson, HG, 'Optimum Tariffs and Retaliation' (1953–54) 21 *Review of Economic Studies* 142.

Jost, P, *Effektivität von Recht aus ökonomischer Sicht* (Berlin, Duncker & Humblot, 1998).

Jovanović, MN, *The Economics of European Integration*, 2nd edn (Cheltenham, Edward Elgar Publishing, 2014).

Jürgensen, T, 'WTO-Konformität der reformierten Gemeinsamen Marktorganisation für Bananen' (1999) *RIW* 241.

Karl, J, 'The Competence for Foreign Direct Investment' (2006) *JWT&I* 413.

Kelman, M, *A Guide to Critical Legal Studies* (Cambridge, Harvard University Press, 1987).

Kelsen, H, *Principles of International Law* (Clark, The Lawbook Exchange Ltd, 2012).

Kennan, J and Riezman, R, 'Do Big Countries Win Tariff Wars?' (1998) 29 *IER* 81.

Kennedy, D, 'Cost-Benefit Analysis of Entitlement Problems: A Critique' (1981) 33 *Stanford Law Review* 387.

Klamert, M and Maydell, N, 'Lost in Exclusivity: Implied Non-Exclusive External Competences in Community Law' (2008) 13 *EFA Rev* 493.

Kleinheisterkamp, J, 'Financial Responsibility in European International Investment Policy' (2014) 63 *ICLQ* 449.

Klinke, U, 'Europäisches Unternehmensrecht und EuGH in den Jahren 1991–1992' (1993) *ZGR* 1.

Kokott, J, 'Die Grundrechte des europäischen Gemeinschaftsrechts' (1996) 121 *AöR* 599.

Koller, A, *Die unmittelbare Anwendbarkeit völkerrechtlicher Verträge und des EWG-Vertrages im innerstaatlichen Bereich* (Bern, Stämpfli, 1971).

Kolstad, CD, Ulen, T and Johnson, GV, 'Ex post Liability for Harm vs. ex ante Safety Regulation: Substitutes or Complements?' (1990) 80 *AER* 888.

Komuro, N, 'The EC Banana Regime and Judicial Control' (2000) 34 *JWT* 1.

Kopp, S, 'Staatshaftung wegen Verletzung von Gemeinschaftsrecht' [1994] *DÖV* 201.

Koutrakos, P, *EU International Relations Law*, 2nd edn (Oxford, Hart Publishing, 2015).

Kovar, R, 'La participation des Communautés Européennes aux conventions multilatérales' [1975] *AFDI* 903.

Krajewski, M, *Verfassungsperspektiven und Legitimation des Rechts der Welthandelsorganisation (WTO)* (Berlin, Duncker & Humblot, 2001).

—— 'External Trade Law and the Constitution Treaty: Towards a Federal and More Democratic Common Commercial Policy?' (2005) *CML Rev* 91.

Kriesi, H (ed), *Vollzugsprobleme. Schweizerisches Jahrbuch für Politische Wissenschaften* (Bern, Haupt, 1993).

Krück, H, *Völkerrechtliche Verträge im Recht der Europäischen Gemeinschaften* (Berlin, Springer, 2011).

Krugman, PR, Obstfeld, M and Melitz, M, *International Economics: Theory and Policy*, 10th edn (Boston, Pearson, 2015).

Kuijper, PJ, 'Study on Investment Protection Agreements as Instruments of International Economic Law' in European Parliament (ed), *Investor-State Dispute Settlement (ISDS) Provisions in the EU's International Investment Agreements vol* 2 (2014).

Kuijper, PJ and Paasivirta, E, 'Further Exploring International Responsibility: The European Community and the ILC's Project on Responsibility of International Organizations' (2004) 1 *International Organizations Law Review* 111.

—— 'EU International Responsibility and its Attribution: From the Inside Looking Out' in MD Evans and P Koutrakos (eds), *The International Responsibility of the European Union: European and International Perspectives* (Oxford, Hart Publishing, 2013).

Kuilwijk, KJ, *The European Court of Justice and the GATT Dilemma: Public Interest versus Individual Rights?* (Beuningen, Nexed Editions, 1996).

Kuschel, H-D, 'Die EG-Bananenmarktordnung vor deutschen Gerichten' (1995) *EuZW* 689.

—— 'Wie geht es weiter mit der Bananenmarktordnung?' (1996) *EuZW* 645.

—— 'Bananenstreit—und kein Ende?' (1998) *RIW* 122.

—— 'Auch die revidierte Bananenmarktordnung ist nicht WTO-konform' (1999) *EuZW* 74.

Lambert Abdelgawad, E, 'The Execution of the Judgments of the European Court of Human Rights: Towards a Non-coercive and Participatory Model of Accountability' (2009) 69 *ZaöRV* 471.

Landes, WM and Posner, RA, *The Economic Structure of Tort Law* (Cambridge, Harvard University Press, 1986).

Lavranos, N, 'Die Rechtswirkung von WTO Panel Reports im Europäischen Gemeinschaftsrecht und Deutschen Verfassungsrecht' (1999) *EuR* 289.

—— 'Die EG darf WTO-Recht weiter ignorieren' (2004) *EWS* 293.

—— 'In Defence of Member States' BITs Gold Standard: The Regulation 1219/2012 Establishing a Transitional Regime for Existing Extra-EU BITs A Member State's Perspective' (2013) *TDM*.

Lee, P and Kennedy, B, 'Potential Direct Effect of GATT 1994 in European Community Law' (1996) 30 *JWT* 67.

Lehr, S, *Einstweiliger Rechtsschutz und Europäische Union: Nationaler einstweiliger Verwaltungsrechtsschutz im Widerstreit von Gemeinschaftsrecht und nationalem Verfassungsrecht* (Berlin, Springer, 2012).

Lorz, RA, 'Trying to change the rules for responding to arbitration unilaterally: The proposed new framework for investor-state dispute settlement for the EU' (2013) *Columbia FDI Perspectives*, No 87.

Lück, M, *Die Gemeinschaftstreue als allgemeines Rechtsprinzip im Recht der Europäischen Gemeinschaft: Ein Vergleich zur Bundestreue im Verfassungsrecht der Bundesrepublik Deutschland*, 1st edn (Baden-Baden, Nomos, 1992).

Lysen, G, 'Three Questions on the Non-contractual Liability of the EEC' (1985) 2 *LIEI* 86.

Machlup, F, *A History of Thought on Economic Integration* (New York, Columbia University Press, 1977).

Mackenzie, R and Sands, P, 'International Courts and Tribunals and the Independence of the International Judge' (2003) 44 *Harv Int'l L J* 271.

MacLeod, I, Hendry, ID and Hyett, S, *The External Relations of the European Communities: A Manual of Law and Practice* (Oxford, Oxford University Press, 1996).

Magiera, S, 'Die Durchsetzung des Gemeinschaftsrechts im europäischen Integrationsprozess' (1998) *DÖV* 173.

Makatsch, T, *Gesundheitsschutz im Recht der Welthandelsorganisation (WTO): Die WTO und das SPS-Übereinkommen im Lichte von Wissenschaftlichkeit, Verrechtlichung und Harmonisierung* (Berlin, Duncker & Humblot, 2004).

Malloy, RP and Braun, CK (eds), *Law and Economics: New and Critical Perspectives* (New York, P Lang, 1995).

Manin, P, 'A propos de l'accord sur les marchés publics: la question de l'invocabilité des accords internationaux conclus par la Communauté européenne' (1997) *RTDeur* 399.

Marboe, I, 'Compensation and Damages in International Law' (2006) 7 *JWIT* 723.

Martines, F, 'Direct Effect of International Agreements of the European Union' (2014) 25 *EJIL* 129.

Masing, J, *Die Mobilisierung des Bürgers für die Durchsetzung des Rechts: Europäische Impulse für eine Revision der Lehre vom subjektiv-öffentlichen Recht* (Berlin, Duncker & Humblot, 1997).

Matsushita, M and others, *The World Trade Organization: Law, Practice, and Policy*, 3rd edn (Oxford, Oxford University Press, 2015).

Meier, G, 'Bananas IV: Der Bericht des WTO-Panels vom 12.4.1999' (1999) *EuZW* 428.

Mendez, M, *The Legal Effects of EU Agreements: Maximalist Treaty Enforcement and Judicial Avoidance Techniques*, 1st edn (Oxford, Oxford University Press, 2013).

Meng, W, 'Verfahrensrechtliche Rechtsstellung der Individuen in Bezug auf das WTO-Recht' in H-W Arndt and others (eds), *Völkerrecht und deutsches Recht: Festschrift für Walter Rudolf zum 70. Geburtstag* (München, CH Beck, 2001).

—— 'Gedanken zur Frage unmittelbarer Anwendung von WTO-Recht in der EG' in U Beyerlin and others (eds), *Recht zwischen Umbruch und Bewahrung: Völkerrecht Europarecht Staatsrecht. Festschrift für Rudolf Bernhardt* (Berlin, Springer, 2014).

Mercuro, N, 'Toward a Comparative Institutional Approach to the Study of Law and Economics' in N Mercuro (ed), *Law and Economics* (Dordrecht, Springer Netherlands, 1989).

Meyer-Cording, U, 'Fortschritte der Europapolitik nur mit wirklich integrierenden Maßnahmen möglich!' in E-J Mestmäcker, H Möller and H-P Schwarz (eds), *Eine Ordnungspolitik für Europa: Festschrift für Hans von der Groeben zu seinem 80. Geburtstag* (Baden-Baden, Nomos, 1987).

Miceli, TJ, *Economics of the Law: Torts, Contracts, Property, and Litigation* (New York, Oxford University Press, 1997).
Mitchell, W and Munger, MC, 'Economic Models of Interest Groups: An Introductory Survey' (1991) 35 *AJPS* 512.
Mola, L, 'Which Role for the EU in the Development of International Investment Law?' *SIEL Working Paper* No 26/2008.
Montanà I Mora, M, 'Equilibrium: A Rediscovered Basis for the Court of Justice of the European Communities to Refuse Direct Effect to the Uruguay Round Agreements?' (1996) 30 *JWT* 43.
Mosiek, M, *Effet utile und Rechtsgemeinschaft: Zugleich ein Beitrag zur Kompetenzordnung der Europäischen Gemeinschaft* (Münster, LIT, 2003).
Mueller, DC, *Public Choice III* (Cambridge, Cambridge University Press, 2003).
Mueller-Langer, F and Schäfer, H-B, 'Strict Liabilty versus Negligence' in M Faure (ed), *Tort Law and Economics* (Cheltenham, Edward Elgar Publishing, 2009).
Musil, A, 'Richtliniensetzung und Normerlassanspruch' (1998) *EuR* 705.
Neframi, E, 'Quelques Réflexions sur la Réforme de la Politique Commerciale par le Traité d'Amsterdam: Le Maintien du Statu Quo et l'Unité de la Représentation Internationale de la Communauté' (1998) *CDE* 137.
—— 'International Responsibility and Mixed Agreements' in E Cannizzaro (ed), *The European Union as an Actor in International Relations* (The Hague, Kluwer Law International, 2002).
Nettesheim, M, 'Grundrechtliche Prüfdichte durch den EuGH' (1995) *EuZW* 106.
Neuwahl, NA, 'Joint Participation in International Treaties and the Exercise of Power by the EEC and its Member States: Mixed Agreements' (1991) 28 *CML Rev* 717.
Nicolaysen, G, 'Der Gerichtshof—Funktion und Bewährung der Judikative' (1972) *EuR* 375.
Noll, P, 'Die Berücksichtigung der Effektivität der Gesetze bei ihrer Schaffung' in T Öhlinger (ed), *Methodik der Gesetzgebung: Legistische Richtlinien in Theorie und Praxis* (Wien, Springer, 1982).
Nollkaemper, A, 'Joint Responsibility between the EU and Member States for Non-Performance of Obligations under Multilateral Environmental Agreements' (2011) *SHARES Research Paper* 5, ACIL 2011–14.
Nolte, G, 'Case 12/86, Meryem Demirel v. Stadt Schwäbisch Gmünd, Judgment of 30 September 1987' (1988) 25 *CML Rev* 403.
Nørgaard, CA, *The Position of the Individual in International Law* (Kopenhagen, Munksgaard, 1962).
North, DC, 'Structure and Performance: The Task of Economic History' (1978) 16 *J Econ Lit* 963.
Nowak, C, 'Subventionen' in S Oeter and M Hilf (eds), *WTO-Recht: Rechtsordnung des Welthandels*, 2nd edn (Baden-Baden, Nomos, 2010).
Noyes, JE and Smith, BD, 'State Responsibility and the Principle of Joint and Several Liability' (1988) 13 *YJIL* 225.
Oehmichen, A, *Die unmittelbare Anwendbarkeit der völkerrechtlichen Verträge der EG: Die EG-Freihandels- und Assoziierungsverträge* (Frankfurt am Main, P Lang, 1992).
Oeter, S, 'Gibt es ein Rechtsschutzdefizit im WTO-Streitbeilegungsverfahren' in C Nowak and W Cremer (eds), *Individualrechtsschutz in der EG und der WTO: Der zentrale und dezentrale Rechtsschutz natürlicher und juristischer Personen in der Europäischen Gemeinschaft und der Welthandelsorganisation*, 1st edn (Baden-Baden, Nomos, 2002).

——'Welthandelsordnung im Spannungsfeld von Wirtschaft, Recht und Politik' in S Oeter and M Hilf (eds), *WTO-Recht: Rechtsordnung des Welthandels*, 2nd edn (Baden-Baden, Nomos, 2010).

Öhlinger, T, *Der völkerrechtliche Vertrag im staatlichen Recht: Eine theoretische, dogmatische und vergleichende Untersuchung am Beispiel Österreichs* (Wien, Springer, 1973).

—— 'Planung der Gesetzgebung und Wissenschaft' in T Öhlinger (ed), *Methodik der Gesetzgebung: Legistische Richtlinien in Theorie und Praxis* (Wien, Springer, 1982).

Oldag, A, 'Zölle wider alle Vernunft' (12 November 2003) *Süddeutsche Zeitung*.

Oliver, P, 'Joint Liability of the Community and the Member States' in HG Schermers, T Heukels and P Mead (eds), *Non-Contractual Liability of the European Communities* (Dordrecht, Martinus Nijhoff, 1988).

Oppermann, T, 'Die Europäische Gemeinschaft und Union in der Welthandelsorganisation (WTO)' (1995) *RIW* 919.

Ossenbühl, F, 'Der gemeinschaftsrechtliche Staatshaftungsanspruch' (1992) *DVBl* 993.

—— 'Die außervertragliche Haftung der Europäischen Gemeinschaft' in H-W Rengeling (ed), *Handbuch zum europäischen und deutschen Umweltrecht: Eine systematische Darstellung des europäischen Umweltrechts mit seinen Auswirkungen auf das deutsche Recht und mit rechtspolitischen Perspektiven*, 2nd edn (Köln, C Heymanns, 2003).

Ossenbühl, F and Cornils, M, *Staatshaftungsrecht*, 6th edn (München, CH Beck, 2013).

Ott, A, *GATT und WTO im Gemeinschaftsrecht: Die Integration des Völkervertragsrechts in die Europäische Gemeinschaftsrechtsordnung am Bsp. des GATT-Vertrags und der WTO-Übereinkünfte* (Köln, Heymanns, 1997).

——'Der EuGH und das WTO-Recht: Die Entdeckung der politischen Gegenseitigkeit—altes Phänomen oder neuer Ansatz?' (2003) *EuR* 504.

Pauwelyn, J, 'Calculation and Design of Trade Retaliation' in CP Bown and J Pauwelyn (eds), *The Law, Economics and Politics of Retaliation in WTO Dispute Settlement* (Cambridge, Cambridge University Press, 2010).

Peers, S, 'Banana Split: WTO Law and Preferential Agreements in the EC Legal Order' (1999) 4 *EFA Rev* 195.

—— 'WTO Dispute Settlement and Community Law' (2001) *EL Rev* 605.

Pernice, I, 'L'accès á la justice dans l'Union Européenne: Le recours en indemnité' (1995) *CDE*.

Perrin, J-F, 'Was versteht man unter der Effektivität einer Rechtsnorm?' in M Rehbinder (ed), *Schweizerische Beiträge zur Rechtssoziologie* (Berlin, Duncker & Humblot, 1984).

Pescatore, P, 'Die Rechtsprechung des Europäischen Gerichtshofs zur innergemeinschaftlichen Wirkung völkerrechtlicher Abkommen' in R Bernard and others (eds), *Völkerrecht als Rechtsordnung Internationale Gerichtsbarkeit Menschenrechte: Festschrift für Hermann Mosler* (Berlin, Springer, 1983).

—— 'The Doctrine of "Direct Effect": An Infant Disease of Community Law' (1983) *EL Rev* 155.

Peters, A, 'The Position of International Law within the European Community Legal Order' (1977) *GYIL* 9.

Petersmann, E-U, 'Application of GATT by the Court of Justice of the European Communities' (1983) 20 *CML Rev* 397.

—— 'Wie kann Handelspolitik konstitutionalisiert werden?' (1989) *EA* 55.

—— *Constitutional Functions and Constitutional Problems of International Economic Law: International and Domestic Foreign Trade Law and Foreign Trade Policy in the United*

*States, the European Community and Switzerland* (Fribourg, Switzerland, University Press, 1991).
—— 'Darf die EG das Völkerrecht ignorieren?' (1997) *EuZW* 325.
—— 'GATT/WTO-Recht: Dublik' (1997) *EuZW* 651.
—— *The GATT/WTO Dispute Settlement System: International Law, International Organizations and Dispute Settlement* (London, Kluwer Law International, 1997).
—— 'Darf die EG das Völkerrecht ignorieren? Zu den verfassungs- und völkerrechtlichen Grundlagen des Europäischen Wirtschaftsrechts' in B Grossfeld (ed), *Festschrift für Wolfgang Fikentscher zum 70. Geburtstag* (Tübingen, Mohr Siebeck, 1998).
—— 'Grundfragen der Beteiligung der Europäischen Gemeinschaft an der Welthandelsorganisation' in P-C Müller-Graff (ed), *Die Europäische Gemeinschaft in der Welthandelsorganisation: Globalisierung und Weltmarktrecht als Herausforderung für Europa*, 1st edn (Baden-Baden, Nomos, 1999/2000).
Pieper, SU, 'Mitgliedstaatliche Haftung für die Nichtbeachtung von Gemeinschaftsrecht' (1992) *NJW* 2454.
Pierros, PX and Maciejewski, M, 'Specific Performance or Compensation and Countermeasures: Are These Alternative Means of Compliance under the WTO Dispute Settlement System' (2001) 6 *ITLR* 167.
Pinder, J, 'Problems of European Integration' in GR Denton (ed), *Economic Integration in Europe* (London, Weidenfeld & Nicolson, 1969).
Pitschas, C, 'EuGH: Kein Schadensersatz wegen Importverbots für Hormonfleisch' (2003) *EuZW* 758.
Polinsky, AM, *An Introduction to Law and Economics*, 4th edn (New York, Wolters Kluwer Law & Business, 2011).
Posner, RA, *The Problems of Jurisprudence* (Cambridge, Harvard University Press, 1990).
—— *Economic Analysis of Law*, 9th edn (New York, Wolters Kluwer Law & Business, 2014).
Prat, JW and Zeckhauser, RJ (eds), *Principals and Agents: The Structure of Business* (Boston, Harvard Business School Press, 1985).
Prechal, S, *Directives in EC Law*, 2nd edn (Oxford, Oxford University Press, 2005).
Prieß, H-J, 'Die Haftung der EG-Mitglieder bei Verstößen gegen das Gemeinschaftsrecht' (1993) *NVwZ* 118.
Prieß, H-J and Berrisch, G, *WTO-Handbuch* (München, CH Beck, 2003).
Rabe, H-J, 'Ausgerechnet Bananen' (1996) *NJW* 1320.
Rehbinder, M and Schelsky, H, *Zur Effektivität des Rechts. Jahrbuch für Rechtssoziologie und Rechtstheorie*, vol III (Düsseldorf, Bertelsmann, 1972).
Reiff, T and Florestal, M, 'Revenge of the Push-me, Pull-You: The Implementation Process under the WTO Dispute Settlement Understanding' (1998) 32 *International Lawyer* 755.
Reinisch, A, 'Entschädigung für die Opfer des Hormon- und Bananenstreites nach Art 288 II EG?' (2000) *EuZW* 42.
—— 'The Use and Limits of Res Judicata and Lis Pendens as Procedural Tools to Avoid Dispute Settlement Outcomes' (2004) *L&P* 37.
—— 'The EU on the Investment Path—QuoVadis Europe? The Future of EU BITs and other Investment Agreements' [2014] *Santa Clara Journal of International Law* 111.
Rengeling, H-W, 'Deutsches und europäisches Verwaltungsrecht—wechselseitige Einwirkungen' (1994) 53 *VVDStRL* 202.

Rengeling, H-W, Middeke, A and Gellermann, M, *Rechtsschutz in der Europäischen Union. Durchsetzung von Gemeinschaftsrecht vor europäischen und deutschen Gerichten* (München, CH Beck, 1994).

Rosas, A, 'Mixed Union—Mixed Agreements' in M Koskenniemi (ed), *International Law Aspects of the European Union* (The Hague, Kluwer Law International, 1998).

—— 'Case C-149/96, Portugal v. Council. Judgment of the Full Court of 23 November 1999, nyr' (2000) 37 *CML Rev* 797.

—— 'The European Union and Mixed Agreements' in A Dashwood and C Hillion (eds), *The General Law of E.C. External Relations* (London, Sweet & Maxwell, 2000).

Rose, K and Sauernheimer, K, *Theorie der Außenwirtschaft*, 14th edn (München. Vahlens Handbücher der Wirtschafts- und Sozialwissenschaften, Vahlen, 2006).

Ross, M, 'Beyond Francovich' (1993) 56 *MLR* 55.

Royla, P, 'WTO-Recht—EG-Recht: Kollision, Justiziabilität, Implementation' (2001) *EuR* 495.

Ruffert, M, *Subjektive Rechte im Umweltrecht der Europäischen Gemeinschaft: Unter besonderer Berücksichtigung ihrer prozessualen Durchsetzung* (Heidelberg, v Decker, 1996).

—— 'Dogmatik und Praxis des subjektiv-öffentlichen Rechts unter dem Einfluss des Gemeinschaftsrechts' (1998) *DVBl* 69.

Ruiz Fabri, H, 'Is There a Case—Legally and Politically—for Direct Effect of WTO Obligations?' (2014) 25 *EJIL* 151.

Russo Spena, F, 'La Corte di giustizia ridefinisce la responsabilità degli Stati membri per violazione del diritto comunitario' (1992) *RIDPC* 163.

Ryffel, H, *Rechtssoziologie: Eine systematische Orientierung* (Neuwied, Luchterhand, 1988).

S2B, 'ISDS: Courting foreign investors: Analysis by the Seattle to Brussels Network' (29 September 2015) www.s2bnetwork.org/wp-content/uploads/2015/10/S2B_ISDS.pdf.

Sack, J, 'Von der Geschlossenheit und den Spannungsfeldern in einer Weltordnung des Rechts' (1997) *EuZW* 650.

Saenger, I, 'Staatshaftung wegen Verletzung europäischen Gemeinschaftsrechts' (1997) *JuS* 865.

Salacuse, JW, *The Law of Investment Treaties*, 2nd edn (Oxford, Oxford University Press, 2015).

Salas, M and Mauricio, JH, 'Procedural Overview of the WTO EC—Banana Dispute' (2000) 3 *JIEL* 145.

Salvatore, D, *International Economics*, 11th edn (Hoboken, Wiley, 2014).

Sander, GG, *Rechtsprobleme der EG-Bananenmarktordnung* (Marburg, Tectum Verlag, 1996).

Sattorova, M, 'Return to the Local Remedies Rule in European BITs? Power (Inequalities), Dispute Settlement, and Change in Investment Treaty Law' (2012) 39 *LIEI* 223.

Schäfer, HB and Schönenberger, A, 'Strict liability versus negligence' in Gd Geest and B Bouckaert (eds), *Encyclopedia of Law and Economics II: Civil Law and Economics* (Cheltenham, Edward Elgar Publishing, 2000).

Schäfer, H-B and Bergh, R van den, 'Member States Liability for Infringement of the Free Movement of Goods in the EC: An Economic Analysis' 2001 *German Working Papers in Law and Economics*.

—— 'State Liability for Infringement of the E.C. Treaty: Economic Arguments in Support of a Rule of "Obvious Negligence"' (1998) *EL Rev* 552.

Schäfer, H-B and Ott C, *Lehrbuch der ökonomischen Analyse des Zivilrechts*, 5th edn (Berlin, Springer, 2012).
Schill, S, *The Multilateralization of International Investment Law* (Cambridge, Cambridge University Press, 2009).
Schimke, M, 'Zur Haftung der Bundesrepublik Deutschland gegenüber Bürgern wegen Nichtumsetzung der EG-Richtlinie über Pauschalreisen' (1993) *EuZW* 698.
Schmid, C, 'Immer wieder Bananen: Der Status des GATT/WTO-Systems im Gemeinschaftsrecht' (1998) *NJW* 190.
Schmidt-Aßmann, E, 'Deutsches und Europäisches Verwaltungsrecht—wechselseitige Einwirkungen' (1993) *DVBl* 924.
—— 'Empfiehlt es sich, das System des Rechtsschutzes und der Gerichtsbarkeit in der Europäischen Gemeinschaft weiterzuentwickeln?' (1994) *JZ* 832.
Schoch, F, 'Die Europäisierung des Allgemeinen Verwaltungsrechts' (1995) *JZ* 109.
Schockweiler, F, Wivenes, G and Godart, JM, 'Le règime de la responsabilité extra-contractuelle du fait d'actes juridiques dans la Communauté européenne' (1990) *RTDeur* 27.
Schoißwohl, B, 'Haftung der Gemeinschaft für WTO-Rechtsverletzungen ihrer Organe: Doktrin der "Nichtverantwortung"?' (2001) *ZEuS* 689.
—— *Staatshaftung wegen Gemeinschaftsrechtsverletzung: Anspruchsgrundlage und materielle Voraussetzungen*, 1st edn (Wien, Verlag Österreich, 2002).
Schroeder, W and Schonard, P, 'Die Effektivität des WTO-Streitbeilegungssystems' (2001) *RIW* 658.
Schuknecht, L, *Trade Protection in the European Community* (Chur, Switzerland, Harwood Academic Publishers, 1992).
Schwab, F, *Der Europäische Gerichtshof und der Verhältnismäßigkeitsgrundsatz* (Frankfurt am Main, P Lang, 2002).
Schwartmann, R, *Private im Wirtschaftsvölkerrecht* (Tübingen, Mohr Siebeck, 2005).
Schwarze, J, 'Rechtsschutz Privater gegenüber normativen Rechtsakten im Recht der EWG' in I von Münch (ed), *Staatsrecht—Völkerrecht—Europarecht: Festschrift für Hans-Jürgen Schlochauer zum 75. Geburtstag am 28. März 1981* (Berlin, De Gruyter, 1981).
Sebastian, T, 'The law of permissible WTO retaliation' in CP Bown and J Pauwelyn (eds), *The Law, Economics and Politics of Retaliation in WTO Dispute Settlement* (Cambridge, Cambridge University Press, 2010).
Selmer, P, *Die Gewährleistung der unabdingbaren Grundrechtsstandards durch den EuGH: Zum "Kooperationsverhältnis" zwischen BVerfG und EuGH am Beispiel des Rechtsschutzes gegen die Bananenmarkt-Verordnung*, 1st edn (Baden-Baden, Nomos, 1998).
Seltenreich, S, *Die Francovich-Entscheidung des EuGH und ihre Auswirkungen auf das deutsche Staatshaftungsrecht* (Konstanz, Hartung-Gorre, 1997).
Semertzi, A, 'The Preclusion of Direct Effect in the Recently Concluded EU Free Trade Agreements' (2014) 51 *CML Rev* 1125.
Shaffer, GC, *Defending Interests: Public-Private Partnerships in WTO Litigation* (Washington, DC, Brookings Institution Press, 2003).
Shan, LW, 'Towards a Common European Community Policy on Investment Issues' (2001) 2 *JWIT* 603.
Shan, W and Zhang, S, 'The Treaty of Lisbon: Half Way toward a Common Investment Policy' (2011) 21 *EJIL* 1049.
Shavell, S, 'Strict Liability versus Negligence' (1980) 9 *J Legal Stud* 1.
—— *Economic Analysis of Accident Law* (Cambridge, Harvard University Press, 1987).

—— *Foundations of Economic Analysis of Law* (Cambridge, Harvard University Press, 2004).
Simon, D, 'Droit communautaire et la responsabilité de la puissance publique: Glissements progressifs ou révolution tranquille' (1993) *AJDA* 235.
Smith, F and Woods, L, 'Causation in Francovich: The Neglected Problem' (1997) 46 *ICLQ* 925.
Snyder, F, 'The Effectiveness of European Community Law: Institutions, Processes, Tools and Techniques' (1993) 56 *MLR* 19.
—— 'The Gatekeepers: The European Courts and WTO Law' (2003) *CML Rev* 313.
Sornarajah, M, *The International Law on Foreign Investment*, 3rd edn (Cambridge, Cambridge University Press, 2010).
Staebe, E, *Europarecht*, 1st edn (Baden-Baden, Nomos, 1998).
Stein, T, '"Bananen-Split"? Entzweien sich BVerfG und EuGH über den Bananenstreit?' (1998) *EuZW* 261.
Steinbach, A, 'Zur Rechtswirkung von WTO-Streitbeilegungsentscheidungen in der Gemeinschaftsrechtsordnung' (2005) *EuZW* 331.
—— *Die Haftung der EG und ihrer Mitgliedsstaaten für WTO-Rechtsverletzungen aus rechtswissenschaftlicher und ökonomischer Perspektive* (Berlin, Duncker & Humblot, 2009).
—— 'Investor-Staat-Schiedsverfahren und Verfassungsrecht' (2016) *RabelsZ* 1.
Steinberger, E, 'The WTO Treaty as a Mixed Agreement' (2006) 17 *EJIL* 837.
Stoll, PT, 'Freihandel und Verfassung. Einzelstaatliche Gewährleistung und die konstitutionelle Funktion der Welthandelsordnung' (1997) 57 *ZaöRV* 83–14.
Streinz, R, 'Staatshaftung für Verletzungen primären Gemeinschaftsrechts durch die Bundesrepublik Deutschland' (1993) *EuZW* 599.
—— 'Der "effet utile" in der Rechtsprechung des Gerichtshofs der Europäischen Gemeinschafts' in O Due, M Lutter and J Schwarze (eds), *Festschrift für Ulrich Everling*, 1st edn (Baden-Baden, Nomos, 1995).
—— 'Primär- und Sekundärrechtsschutz im Öffentlichen Recht' (2002) *VVDStRL* 300.
—— *Europarecht*, 10th edn (Heidelberg, CF Müller, 2016).
Subedi, SP, *International Investment Law: Reconciling Policy and Principle* (Oxford, Hart Publishing, 2008).
Sugarman, S, 'Tort Reform through Damages Law Reform: An American Perspective' (2005) 27 *Sydney Law Review* 507.
Sykes, A, 'The Remedy for Breach of Obligations under the WTO Dispute Settlement Understanding: Damages or Specific Performance' in M Bronckers and R Quick (eds), *New Directions in International Economic Law: Essays in Honour of John H. Jackson* (The Hague, Kluwer Law International, 2000).
Talmon, S, 'Responsibility of International Organizations: Does the European Community Require Special Treatment?' in M Ragazzi (ed), *International Responsibility Today: Essays in Memory of Oscar Schachter* (Leiden, Martinus Nijhoff, 2005).
Tams, CJ, *An Appealing Option? The Debate about and ICSID Appellate Structure* (Halle (Saale), Inst für Wirtschaftsrecht, 2006).
Temple Lang, J, 'New Legal Effects Resulting from the Failure of States to Fulfil Obligations under Community Law; The Francovich Judgment' (1992) 16 *Fordham Int'l L J* 1.
The Economist, 'Free-trade agreements: A better way to arbitrate' (11 October 2014) www.economist.com/news/leaders/21623674-protections-foreign-investors-are-not-horror-critics-claim-they-could-be-improved.

Thies, A, 'Biret and Beyond: The Status of WTO Rulings in EC Law' (2004) 41 *CML Rev* 1661.

—— 'The Impact of General Principles of EC Law on its Liability Regime Towards Retaliation Victims after FIAMM' (2009) *EL Rev* 889.

Thies, A, *International Trade Disputes and EU Liability*, 1st edn (Cambridge, Cambridge University Press, 2013).

Thompson, H, *International Economics: Global Markets and Competition*, 3rd edn (Hackensack, World Scientific Pub, 2011).

Tietje, C, Sipiorski, E and Töpfer, G, 'Responsibility in Investor-State-Arbitration in the EU: Managing Financial Responsibility Linked to Investor-State Dispute Settlement Tribunals Established by EU's International Investment Agreements' (2013) 10 *TDM*.

Tinbergen, J, *International Economic Integration*, 2nd edn (Amsterdam, Elsevier Applied Science, 1965).

Titi, A, *The Right to Regulate in International Investment Law*, 1st edn (Baden-Baden, Nomos, 2014).

Tomuschat, C, 'Zur Rechtswirkung der von der Europäischen Gemeinschaft abgeschlossenen Verträge in der Gemeinschaftsrechtsordnung' in G Lüke and G Ress (eds), *Rechtsvergleichung, Europarecht und Staatenintegration: Gedächtnisschrift für Léontin-Jean Constantinesco* (Köln, Heymanns, 1983).

—— 'Aller guten Dinge sind III? Zur Diskussion um die Solange-Rechtsprechung des BVerfG' (1990) *EuR* 340.

—— 'Liability for Mixed Agreements' in D O'Keeffe and HG Schermers (eds), *Mixed Agreements* (Deventer, Kluwer Law and Taxation Publishers, 2009).

—— 'Attribution of International Responsibility: Direction and Control' in MD Evans and P Koutrakos (eds), *The International Responsibility of the European Union: European and International Perspectives* (Oxford, Hart Publishing, 2013).

Toth, AG, 'The Concepts of Damage and Causality as Elements of Noncontractual Liability' in T Heukels and A McDonnell (eds), *The Action For Damages In Community Law* (The Hague, Kluwer Law International, 1997).

Trachtman, JP, 'Decisions of the Appellate Body of the World Trade Organization' (1999) 10 *EJIL* 655.

Trautmann, B, *Die Konkurrenz von Haftpflicht- und Versicherungsanspruch: Ein Beitrag zur ökonomischen Analyse des Rechts unter Berücksichtigung von Unsicherheit und Verhaltensanomalien* (Frankfurt am Main, P Lang, 2002).

Trebilcock, MJ and Howse, R, *The Regulation of International Trade*, 3rd edn (London, Routledge, 2005).

Triantafyllou, D, 'Haftung der Mitgliedstaaten für Nichtumsetzung von EG-Recht' (1992) *DÖV* 564.

Ulen, T, 'Rational Victims—Rational Injurers: Cognition and the Economic Analysis of Tort Law' in RP Malloy and CK Braun (eds), *Law and Economics: New and Critical Perspectives* (New York, P Lang, 1995).

UNCTAD, 'International Investment Agreement Navigator' (2016) http://investmentpolicyhub.unctad.org/IIA.

Vanberg, V, 'A Constitutional Political Economy Perspective on International Trade' (1992) 43 *ORDO* 375.

Vandall, FJ, *Strict Liability: Legal and Economic Analysis* (New York, Quorum Books, 1989).

Vandevelde, KJ, *Bilateral Investment Treaties: History, Policy, and Interpretation* (Oxford, Oxford University Press, 2010).

Verdross, A and Simma, B, *Universelles Völkerrecht: Theorie und Praxis* (Berlin, Duncker & Humblot, 2010).
Villalta Puig, G and Al-Haddab, B, 'The Common Commercial Policy after Lisbon: An Analysis of the Reforms' (2011) 36 *EL Rev* 289.
Volker, ELM, 'The Direct Effect of International Agreements in the Community's Legal Order' (1983) 10 *LIEI* 131.
Voß, M, *Symbolische Gesetzgebung: Fragen zur Rationalität von Strafgesetzgebungsakten* (Ebelsbach, Gremer, 1989).
Wälde, T, 'The "Umbrella" Clause in Investment Arbitration—A Comment on Original Intentions and Recent Cases' (2005) 6 *JWIT* 183.
Weber, A and Moos, F, 'Rechtswirkungen von WTO-Streitbeilegungsentscheidungen im Gemeinschaftsrecht' [1999] *EuZW* 229.
Weber, C, 'Wirtschaftsabkommen im System der Europäischen Gemeinschaft: Die Rechtsprechung des Europäischen Gerichtshofs' (1997) 35 *AVR* 295.
Weiß, W, 'Zur Haftung der EG für die Verletzung des WTO-Rechts' (2005) *EuR* 277.
—— 'Das Streitbeilegungsverfahren' in C Herrmann, W Weiß and C Ohler (eds), *Welthandelsrecht*, 2nd edn (München, CH Beck, 2007).
Whalley, J, *Trade Liberalization among Major World Trading Areas* (Cambridge, MIT Press, 1985).
Wiers, J, 'One Day, You're Gonna Pay: The European Court of Justice in Biret' (2004) 31 *LIEI* 143.
Williamson, J and Milner, C, *World Economy: A Textbook in International Economics* (New York, New York University Press, 1991).
Williamson, OE, 'Franchise Bidding for Natural Monopolies—in General and with Respect to CATV' [1976] *Bell Journal of Economics* 73.
—— 'The Economics of Organization: The Transaction Cost Approach' (1981) *AJS* 548.
Winkler, RM and Trölitzsch, T, 'Wende in der EuGH-Rechtsprechung zur Haftung der EG für fehlerhafte EG-Rechtsetzungsakte und prozessuale Bewältigung der Prozeßflut' (1992) *EuZW* 663.
Winter, JA, 'Direct Applicability and Direct Effect: Two Distinct and Different Concepts in European Community Law' (1972) 9 *CML Rev* 425.
Wuermeling, J, 'Die Gemeinschaftstreue und die Rechtsakte der Gesamtheit der Mitgliedstaaten der EG' (1987) *EuR* 237.
Wüger, D, 'The Never Ending Story: The Implementation Phase in the Disputes between the EC and the United States on Hormone-Treated Beef' (2002) 33 *L & Policy Intl Bus* 777.
Wünschmann, A, *Geltung und gerichtliche Geltendmachung völkerrechtlicher Verträge im Europäischen Gemeinschaftsrecht* (Berlin, Duncker & Humblot, 2003).
Zonnekeyn, GA, 'The Status of WTO Law in the EC Legal Order—The Final Curtain?' (2000) 34 *JWT* 111.
—— 'EC Liability for non-implementation of Adopted WTO Panel and Appellate Body Reports' in V Kronenberger (ed), *The European Union and the International Legal Order: Discord or Harmony?* (The Hague, Kluwer Law International, 2001).
—— 'The Latest On Indirect Effect of WTO Law in the EC Legal Order. The Nakajima Case Law Misjudged?' (2001) *JIEL* 597.
—— 'The Bed Linen Case and its Aftermath—Some Comments on EC's "WTO Enabling Regulation"' (2002) *JWT* 993.

—— 'EC Liability for Non-implementation of WTO Dispute Settlement Decisions—Are the Dice Cast?' (2004) *JIEL* 483.

Zuleeg, M, 'Die innerstaatliche Anwendbarkeit völkerrechtlicher Verträge am Beispiel des GATT und der Europäischen Sozialcharta' (1975) 35 *ZaöRV* 341.

—— 'Die Rechtswirkung europäischer Richtlinien' (1980) *ZGR* 466.

—— 'Umweltschutz in der Rechtsprechung des Europäischen Gerichtshofs' (1993) *NJW* 31.

—— 'Deutsches und europäisches Verwaltungsrecht—wechselseitige Einwirkungen' (1994) *VVDStRL* 154.

—— 'Die föderativen Grundsätze der Europäischen Union' (2000) *NJW* 2846.

# *Index*